The DOCK
MANUAL

The DOCK MANUAL

- DESIGNING

- BUILDING

- MAINTAINING

Max Burns

Storey Publishing

The mission of Storey Publishing is to serve our customers by publishing practical information that encourages personal independence in harmony with the environment.

Edited by Elizabeth McHale, Janet Lape, and Bob Moran
Cover design by Rob Johnson, Johnson Design
Front cover photograph © Envision, Jane Higgins
Back cover photograph © Index Stock
Text design by Mark Tomasi
Production assistance by Susan B. Bernier
Interior photographs by Muskoka Leisure
except for page 102, top, by Max Burns
Illustrations by Terry Dovaston and Associates
Indexed by Hagerty & Holloway

The information in this book is true and complete to the best of our knowledge. All recommendations are made without guarantee on the part of the author or Storey Publishing. The author and publisher disclaim any liability in connection with the use of this information. For additional information, please contact Storey Publishing, 210 MASS MoCA Way, North Adams, MA 01247.

Storey books are available for special premium and promotional uses and for customized editions. For further information, please call 1-800-793-9396.

Printed in the United States by Versa Press
25 24 23 22 21 20 19 18 17 16 15 14 13 12

Library of Congress Cataloging-in-Publication Data

Burns, Max, 1948-
    The dock manual / by Max Burns.
       p.   cm.
    Includes index.
    ISBN-13: 978-1-58017-098-7 (pbk.);
    ISBN-10: 1-58017-098-6 (pbk.)
    1. Docks—Design and construction—Handbooks, manuals, etc. I. Title.
TC355 .B87 1999
627'.31—dc21
                                                                    47045
                                                                    CIP

table of contents

Section 1: The Path to a Successful Waterfront

Section 2: Dock Types

Section 3: The Art of Dock Building

Section 4: Your Dock Meets Planet Earth

Section 5: Your Dock and Your Watercraft

Section 6: Repairing and Upgrading

Section 7: Plans and Sources

The Path to a Successful Waterfront

Basic residential dock building is not a difficult process — certainly much easier in my experience than constructing, say, a staircase. That's the good news. It's also the bad news. Such simplicity tends to encourage building without the necessary planning. Even the best-looking waterfront structure in the world fails if it suits neither the shoreline nor the dock user's needs. So even when equipped with complete plans for a dandy dock, it's still possible to build a berth of the blues — a beauty to behold but with enough congestion to get a mention on the local radio's traffic report.

If you glean only one thing from this book, make it this: No dock exists as a stand-alone structure. A dock has to work in harmony with the uneasy marriage of land and water we know as shoreline, and with the various uses you and your family envision for that shoreline. No two sites are alike. The combination of your waterfront's assets and your intended use of those assets is unique to you, just as it is to your neighbors. It's your shoreline, your wish list, and your dock. It only makes sense to make it your solution.

Section 1 leads you to that solution, beginning in chapter 1 by analyzing what you have and what you would like to have, and then in chapter 2 by using that information to determine the type of dock best suited to your particular situation.

analyzing your shore-line and situation

Planning for any dock should always begin with a *site evaluation*. What does the waterfront look like? How do you intend to use it? Doing a site evaluation may sound like a daunting task, but it's surprisingly easy. Even if you get professional help for the construction, doing the preliminary evaluation yourself can lead to a better, more personalized result.

A site evaluation should contain two kinds of information: a status report on the existing waterfront and an inventory and activity list of present and proposed uses.

The Existing Water-front: What You See Is What You've Got

The best way to record the status of your existing shoreline is to make a map. I'm admittedly a bit prejudiced here; I happen to love maps, drawing on them and adding features of interest. Maps are just a great way to compile information about an area. But I'm not alone in my love of maps; many jurisdictions insist on seeing a scale map of your shoreline before issuing approvals to build. So do the map now and use it throughout the entire design process.

What you're after is a gull's-eye view of the waterfront, with nearly as much detail as a gull would spot. Draw it at an appropriate scale with everything labeled just in case you forget what the little blob in the upper right-hand corner is.

To keep the process simple, buy a pad of graph paper already divided into ¼-inch squares, then use a scale such as one square equals 4 feet (¹⁄₁₆ inch equals 1 foot) or whatever is needed to squeeze your waterfront onto the paper. If the shoreline is festooned with inlets and rocks and logs and the like, or you need more space to exercise your cartographic creativity, sheets of graph paper can be taped together

Before you can even think about building a dock, you will need to assess your shoreline. Consider how you and your family currently use the water, as well as potential future uses. What will you expect of your dock?

to accommodate a larger scale. You also will need a good measuring tape, preferably at least a 50-footer. (I also find a 100-foot rope handy for lot measurements.) Get plenty of pencils equipped with erasers — the combination allows you to make adjustments rather than mistakes. Colored pencils often make the map more readable and will impress your friends.

What to put on the map? Everything you can measure and make note of and nothing more. So draw in the shoreline, the trees, existing buildings, driveways, the path to the outhouse — the whole works as a gull would see it — but absolutely no speculative docks, walkways, or the like. Remember, this is the "before" plan. A gull's eyesight may be good, but it still can't see into the future.

The past, however, can be remembered, so take full advantage of this mixed blessing. Note when and how much the water level fluctuates, especially if faced with tides. Note wave and ice conditions, and the farthest point of nature's aquatic advance, like the flood of '67. If you're new to the area and unfamiliar with what could be in store for you, ask the neighbors. Longtime residents are always eager, delighted even, to terrorize newcomers with horror stories about nature's previous tantrums. Take notes, deleting the adjectives.

As an aside, tales of huge waves should be tempered by the fact that the height of the water at your shoreline only rises about half the height of the wave, the other half of the height reflecting a similar-sized

Suggested Items for Your Map

- Lot lines. Locate the survey markers if you can; folklore is notoriously inaccurate. This is important if you want to avoid building your neighbor a new dock.

- Lot-line setbacks. These are imaginary lines that establish how close to your lot line your local jurisdiction allows you to build. Note that these often extend out into the water, meaning that you can't start your dock within your setback line and then branch over in front of your neighbor's. With irregularly shaped shorelines or converging lot lines, this can sometimes severely restrict your options. Not all jurisdictions specify what the water-based setback should be, but even without legal constraints, never install a dock right on the lot line. Some jurisdictions suggest 15 feet as the minimum setback. Added to your neighbor's 15-foot setback you'll have at least 30 feet for maneuvering small boats or paddling around in an inner tube.

- A compass rose showing north, south, east, and west to remind us where the sun rises and sets.

- The topography of both uplands and submerged lands, including notes about water depths and heights of land along the shoreline 12, 24, and 36 feet to either side of it. Also the composition — rock, clay, gravel, sand, squish-between-the-toes muck, and so on.

- The location of submerged real and potential navigational hazards. Go for a swim to find them, or if the water's cold get the kids to do the swimming.

- The water-intake line if you draw water from the lake or river.

- Any existing boat-launch area.

- Direction of prevailing winds (a cloud with puffed cheeks blowing in the prevailing direction adds a nice artistic touch).

- The direction of prevailing currents if those currents are notably strong.

- Land-based vegetation, including grass, brush, and trees, noting shaded areas and time of day shaded. A line of maximum shade works well for this.

- Aquatic vegetation, such as cattails, bulrushes, purple loosestrife, and underwater weeds where monsters of the deep might be hiding.

- The best views out over the water from the shoreline, your yard, and your cottage or house, and looking back onto land from the water. Mark these with an eye looking in the appropriate direction if you're feeling creative.

- Any existing environmental concerns, such as nesting sites for waterfowl, fish spawning areas, and ecologically sensitive wetland areas.

- Existing uses, such as the tree that holds the recycled car tire in which the kids swing out over the water, preferred fishing spots, and the horseshoe pits. Any existing docks, even if dilapidated and toppling over, should be shown as well.

Here are a few possible dock uses to consider. Delete any that don't interest you and replace them with your own ideas.

- Waterskiing
- Fishing
- Sailboarding
- Entertaining (Large groups or small?)
- Sunbathing
- Swimming (A designated swim area, without cleats or other toe jammers, is always a dandy idea for kids and adults alike.)
- Mooring of boats, both in the water and on shore, including canoes and sailboards
- Skipping stones
- Watching sunsets in lawn chairs (There should always be space for people to just sit and think about absolutely nothing if they choose.)

"valley" between waves. For instance, a 3-foot-high wave rises about 1½ feet above the theoretical flat, calm surface, and is followed by a 1½-foot trough below that surface. This doesn't diminish the strength of the wave or the potential damage it can do, but it does mean that a dock need not be 3 feet above flat water to avoid 3-foot waves.

Another handy map note, scribbled off to the side, lists any known regulations that might restrict or influence waterfront building and alterations. This could include everything from maximum dock dimensions to choice of color — check with the appropriate authorities.

Take photos to supplement the map, including members of the family in the shots for a sense of scale. Some jurisdictions require photographs of the existing site as part of

the permit process, perhaps to ensure that you didn't make it all up.

Speaking of making things up, let me introduce you to *the Sampel family* — Gord, Joyce, and daughter Bess — all camera shy. The Sampels have graciously allowed us to eavesdrop on their fictitious lives as they go from shoreline to solution, starting with the map of the existing shoreline. Please note how well they've been paying attention.

The Inventory and Activity List: What You Want Is What You Get

This is a list of all the people, activities, and things you want your new dock to accommodate. It includes both present and future needs and desires. For materials, any blank

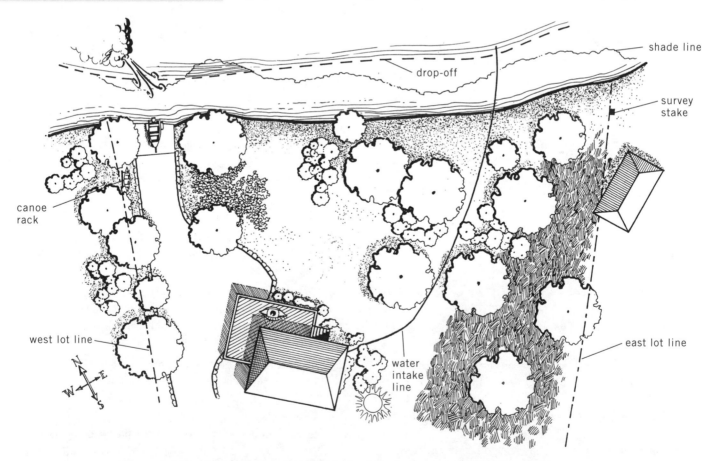

Your map should be drawn to scale, and it should include as much detail as possible. Be sure to mark property boundaries, high and low water marks, wave and ice conditions, and anything else that might affect your selection of dock type and location.

paper and the ubiquitous erasable lead pencil will do. Begin by taking inventory:

▸ How big is the gang — family, friends, and relatives — that will use the dock?
▸ How old is each member?
▸ Are any members elderly, disabled, or hammock confined, requiring special considerations?
▸ Do you need to plan for future expansion to accommodate a gaggle of grand (or not-so-grand) children?
▸ How big is the family flotilla? List types, sizes, and the various mooring requirements of all current boats, plus any floating fantasies that might become realities in the near future.

Once your inventory is complete, begin a list of current and proposed waterfront activities. What do you want to do down at the water, anyway? Don't attempt to answer this question in one sitting. Begin the list, then post it for family members to add to as the idea-bulbs light up over their heads. And no erasing of other family members' ideas without a family consensus. (Budgetary vetoes will come later.)

Also, don't get bogged down with the physical aspects of design. Divorce yourself entirely from structures, such as the size and shape of the proposed dock. Instead, think solely about the activity. For example, if what you want is a shaded sitting area, don't write down "canopy." Instead, write down "shaded sitting area." These concepts should dictate the end result, not some preconceived notion of what a waterfront should be or should look like.

Give some thought to general concepts. For instance, how does the family feel about the property? Is it primarily an investment? Or an established family tradition? A shoreline can have more memories than rocks and spiders. Note the features that conjure up those memories.

Do you lean toward the manicured school of landscape design, perhaps with shrubbery neatly trimmed into the shape of ducks, or does the family prefer a more natural setting, with nesting areas for real ducks?

Then, just as your page of dreams begins to look like a book, start thinking about finances — the nemesis of all wish lists. How much can you afford to spend? A reasonable guess will do, since it's written in erasable pencil. The reason for saving this reality-check for last is to avoid intimidating wishful thinkers. At this point in the planning process, you want to be searching for ideas. And besides, as we shall see, there are often ways to accommodate both dreams and financial reality.

So what have you got so far? In one hand, assuming you've been as diligent as the Sampels, a detailed survey of the existing waterfront — there it is, your waterfront in living erasable pencil on blue-squared graph paper. In the other hand, a list of waterfront users and activities, present and potential, plus a budget estimate. In other words, your shoreline and your dreams but no dock in any shape or form. What you and the Sampels have done instead is equip yourselves with the information necessary to make dock decisions. Chapter 2 reveals the directions that this information can lead you in.

The Sampel Family's List of Dock Priorities

People inventory
- Gord, age 31
- Joyce, age 27
- Bess, age 2
- Floppy, pound dog, about age 3
- Possible addition to family within the next couple of years
- Bob, friend, age 31
- Linda, friend, age 30

Current boat inventory
- 14-foot cedar-strip runabout (a cherished family heirloom)
- 16-foot fiberglass canoe

Future boat inventory
- A sailboat, ideally a 16-foot wet sail, big enough to hold four friends and moor at the dock (but finances may dictate a 14-foot dry sail to start out with)
- Bob's ski boat (Is this a good thing?)

Activity list
- We want to get into the water and swim without mud squishing up between our toes (except for Bess and Floppy, who both like their swim with mud)
- We want safe, easy docking for boats
- We want to fish off the end of the dock
- We want to sit in the sun and breeze, away from the bugs, with room for deck chairs
- We want to watch the sun set (you can't see it set from shore)

Other considerations
- Limited budget, no borrowing allowed
- We want the cottage to be someplace Bess and any future siblings will look forward to visiting in the summer
- We want a simple, unobtrusive structure, not big and flashy
- We want a safe dock that doesn't tip

from lists to reality

The search for the perfect dock is a search for the perfect compromise. Your activities, the characteristics of your waterfront, your finances, and local legislation all will influence that compromise. We will follow the Sampel family through the compromise process to a solution for their waterfront. We'll also look at several other waterfront scenarios and possible solutions, each illustrating the process of going from site evaluation to solution.

But first, a sad truth: Shoreline solutions are not a simple matter of catering to personal preferences — there's bureaucracy to contend with. While most folks would agree that converting the Atlantic Ocean into a boardwalk is a poor idea, many have trouble understanding what that has to do with building a measly dock. But how many measly docks does it take to build a boardwalk? Yours and a few of your neighbors'? They all add up. The bureaucracy that may at times seem to be there only to impede us is also there to prevent those measly docks from adding up to too much. Basically, it's there to protect the environment.

When working on or near the shoreline, we are dealing with the most biologically productive part of any body of water — it doesn't take much to mess it up. Even small projects can affect aquatic life (see Preserving Aquatic Habitats on page 28). They also can upset the neighbors, and are usually of concern to your local dock police. Therefore, I cannot recommend strongly enough that you find out from the local authorities what is permitted at your waterfront. Do it before investing much time in the planning stages, never mind any construction. After all, it would be a shame to have to tear up the boardwalk after all that work.

Speaking of boardwalks, the common element uniting all residential docks is a deck or platform. Every dock must have a surface to walk on, dive off, or hold stuff like deck chairs, gas for the outboard, and lunch just in case the outboard quits again. Ignoring variations in construction techniques for the moment, the distance that the deck sits above water is what differentiates one dock type from another. This distance is called *freeboard* (see Room and Freeboard). We'll be talking a lot about freeboard in the chapters that follow.

The freeboard of a boat changes when the load in the boat changes, decreasing as you load stuff in the boat and increasing as you unload. One type of dock, the floating dock, behaves in the same way. However, the freeboard of neither boat nor floating dock is affected by changes in water level, either seasonal or tidal. Most other dock types, including pipe, crib, concrete pier, permanent pile, cantilever, suspension, and lift pipe docks, are supported directly by land, either submerged or dry. With these dock types, freeboard is unaffected by varying loads but changes whenever the water level changes.

Although the choices within the various dock types are many (see section 2), the characteristics of each type are consistent enough to allow us to squeeze the principal decision-making information into a handy-dandy dock-type decision chart called Dock-Type Choices on pages 8–9. As you pore over the chart, keep in mind that many waterfront solutions use a combination of dock types, gaining the advantages of each as appropriate. For example, a floating dock attached to a crib, concrete pier, or permanent pile can combine durability under duress with a consistent freeboard.

In the boating world, *freeboard* is usually the distance between the surface of the water and the lowest point of a boat where water might begin to pour over the side. When referring to docks, *freeboard* means the height of the deck above water. Designers of residential docks normally aim for between 12 and 24 inches of freeboard, about 18 inches being the average.

It's wise to consider freeboard and activities together. For instance, if one of your prime uses of the dock will be to moor a boat, then aim for a dock freeboard that will ease loading and unloading the boat. This is especially important when the handicapped or elderly are involved.

Higher dock freeboard helps prevent even a small runabout from riding up onto the deck during docking, a particular concern in high waves. High freeboard also lessens the odds of high waves washing cold water over hot, sunbaked bodies stretched out on the decking. Keep in mind, though, that lower freeboard usually means greater dock stability, easier netting of a fish, a shorter climb up a dock ladder and

onto the deck, and easier launching and landing of sailboards. (The noses of sailboards tend to slip under the framing and decking of higher-freeboard docks.)

So, in common with all other aspects of dock design, the ideal freeboard is likely to be a compromise between the various activities.

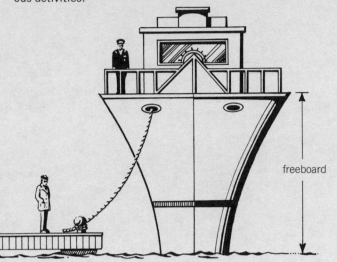

Size and Shape

While the Dock-Type Choices chart is a good place to narrow down the choices of dock type to a few likely suspects, the questions of size and shape still remain. How much room do you need? What was true for Robin Hood and Little John centuries ago is still true today — people need a lane at least 3 feet wide to pass by each other without getting into a shoving match. In fact, experience has taught me that 3 feet is often not enough for young siblings.

The smallest of fold-up lawn chairs occupy an area 3 feet x 3 feet, allowing for the occupant's legs and a safe margin of space between the chair and the dock's edge. Reclining lounge chairs can easily stake out a 3-foot x 7-foot claim to deck space.

Watercraft like canoes and sailboards are serious deck hogs, which

makes storage racks on dry land a must in my book. However, since these craft are often hauled out at the dock and then carted to shore, usually without a great deal of grace, ample room must be allotted to the task. How much room is "ample" depends upon the arc the craft can swing through in a good gust of wind. For instance, if a 16-foot canoe pivots around a centrally located carrier, it can bump into sailboat masts and grandmothers in deck chairs up to 8 feet away. But sailboards are the real space villains. The largest sail I own stretches between a 9-foot boom and a 15-foot mast. That's a lot of area to hold against the wind to keep from clobbering into stuff. It's all dock traffic. So we become waterfront traffic planners, maintaining harmonious relations down at the dock by carefully choosing its shape and size.

Dock-Type Choices

Dock Type	Best Feature	Freeboard	Suitable Sites Best	Suitable Sites Worst	Winter Hardiness
Floating	Most versatile dock	Only type with consistent freeboard; varies somewhat with load	Deep water; fluctuating water levels	Water less than 3' deep, huge waves, sensitive wetlands	Remove if ice is severe; leave in at owner's risk
Pipe	Most versatile for shallow water	Varies with water level; has some adjustability	Less than 6½' depth at high water, firm bottom, waves, wetlands	Deep mud, deep water, mooring large or heavy boats	Remove if water may freeze
Crib	Best permanent dock for DIY	Varies with water level	Less than 8' of water, firm bottom, stable water levels, waves	Deep water, severe ice, fluctuating levels, sensitive aquatic habitats, solid rock bottom	Resistant to most ice conditions
Concrete pier	Strength	Varies with water level	Less than 8' of water, stable water levels, waves	Deep water, severe ice, fluctuating levels, sensitive aquatic habitats, solid rock bottom	Severe ice conditions can move it, but rare
Permanent pile	Strong yet easy on environment	Varies with water level	Depths to 25', waves, high tides	Fluctuating water levels, depths greater than 25', solid rock bottom	Rising ice can lift piles, requiring resetting
Cantilever & suspension	Potential four-season capability	Varies with water level	Any depth or bottom type, stable levels	Big waves, pack ice, fluctuating levels, sensitive wetlands	Theoretically permanent
Lift	Potential four-season capability	See dock type being lifted	Moderate waves and ice, some suited to fluctuating water levels	When lifted: high winds; otherwise, see deck type	Limited only by pack ice

Size Limits		Environmental Impact	Relative Cost	Building Skills
Small	Large			
6' x 20'	Budget/ legalities	Minimal to moderate	$$$	Basic carpentry
Width not less than water depth; never less than 3' wide	Budget/ legalities	Minimal (best)	$$	Basic carpentry for wood versions
Height equal to width	Budget/ legalities	Extreme (worst)	$–$$$$	Basic carpentry, labor intensive
Budget/ legalities	Budget/ legalities	Extreme	$$$$$$	DIY hostile, a job for pros or masochists
Budget/ legalities	Budget/ legalities	Minimal	$$$$	Basic carpentry for decking, possibly framing
Cantilever: none; suspension: 6' wide	Cantilever: 8' overhang; suspension: 12' x 50'	Minimal to moderate	$$$$$	Advanced, best left to pros
See dock type being lifted	See dock type being lifted	Minimal to extreme	Dock plus lifting mechanism	Advanced, best left to pros

Step Right Up

All this talk of dock size and people falling into the drink reminds me — no dock should be without a ladder. And a good ladder, not just some makeshift, slippery two-step fright even an intruder would decline to use. A well-designed, well-manufactured, ergonomically easy-to-use dock ladder not only enhances the recreational aspects of your waterfront but may also someday be a welcome asset in an emergency (such as when little ones tumble into frigid water). So include a quality dock ladder in your plans and budget.

Keeping in Good Shape

In a house, people usually converge on the kitchen. On a dock, people are naturally drawn to the end, usually the area with the most sunshine, fewest bugs, best view, and best place to water-ski, dive, swim, and fish. This means that the traditional, straight, rectangular dock can get pretty crowded when asked to accommodate the waterfront

activities of busy families. And while increasing the size will add space for these activities, venturing beyond the traditional long and narrow rectangle can define specific areas for incompatible activities. Shapes can subtly direct traffic to appropriate areas, limiting congestion. As a bonus, tacking shapes onto the traditional rectangle will usually increase stability too, acting like training wheels on a child's bicycle.

Local regulations aside, there's nothing to restrict you from breaking out of the rectangular mode entirely, choosing octagons, diamond shapes, or U-name-it shapes. However, because most wood comes in rectangles, choosing the unorthodox will add to the cost of the project, both in materials and in labor. (Angles create more waste and take more time to build.)

The idea is not to build a shape for its own sake, but to work out a blend of shape and size favorable to your activities and shoreline. What works best for your situation? If a simple rectangle is all you require, anything beyond that is superfluous — better to save your money for

---

The Truth about the Small Dock

- Less space for boats and folks.
- Less intrusive on the wallet, the environment, and the eyes.
- Leaves more shoreline exposed.
- Less weight, a real advantage when removing a dock for the winter.
- Less stable and nature resistant.
- Safe mooring only for smaller craft in protected waters. Nasty weather and wind can send a small dock (and any boat attached to it) heading for shore quicker than a weatherperson can warn you of the approaching storm. (See chapter 16 for alternative solutions.)

another boat. Of course, then you might need a bigger dock . . .

The accompanying diagrams illustrate the most popular configurations, along with some suggestions for appropriate activities.

Basic Rectangle

The rectangle is the most economical and easiest shape to build, remove, and install, making it the most popular of all dock configurations. It's well suited to narrow lots. However, it doesn't sort out heavy traffic or activities well, and can seem crowded at times. This can be resolved by adding L or T sections at a later time as the budget permits or need requires. For small families with a limited activity list, the basic rectangle can be an excellent choice.

The long, straight sides make parking easy if waves are not a problem. This shape works well with a marine railway or a boat lift.

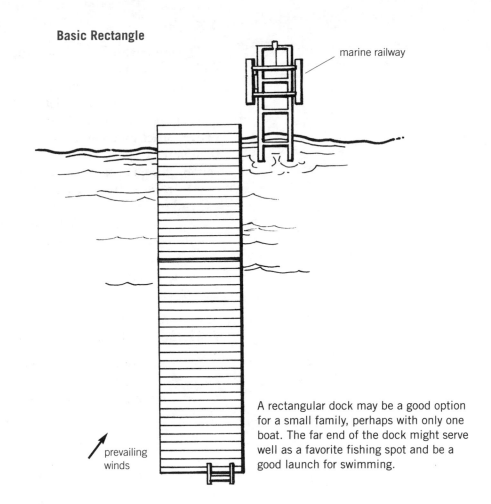

Basic Rectangle

marine railway

prevailing winds

A rectangular dock may be a good option for a small family, perhaps with only one boat. The far end of the dock might serve well as a favorite fishing spot and be a good launch for swimming.

The Truth about the Large Dock

- Provides more space for activities, an asset best appreciated when shoreline space is cramped or not user friendly, such as a beach with sharp, foot-jabbing rocks.
- Usually increases stability, especially for floating docks.
- Holds up better under attacks from nature. This is a particular advantage in areas of open water or severe weather conditions. Extra heft also benefits structures that protect boats or the shoreline.
- Necessary for long-term mooring of big boats.
- More difficult to install and remove.
- Bigger impact on your wallet, the environment, and everybody's eyes.
- Encourages the aggregation of silt and vegetation, particularly along long, open stretches of beach. This accretion disrupts aquatic life and can decrease the water depth near or under the dock, creating problems for boating and shore erosion.

T-Shape

The minimalist T is basically the end section of a rectangular dock turned sideways. This simple change increases stability, defines activity areas, and makes better use of deck space for entertaining. Two semiprotected areas are created, suitable for small craft. Larger boats, however, would have to dock along the end (unless the section perpendicular to shore was made longer). The T doesn't work well with a marine railway, but it's a good choice for an active family with a collection of small watercraft.

L-Shape

For the majority of dock types, an L can be the most cost-effective way to sort out traffic, activities, and boat parking. A protected area is created within the crook of the L, while the long straight side is an ideal spot for a marine railway or boat lift. A lift could also be located along the end or in the protected area (assuming depths are not greater than 6 feet).

However, in the case of a floating dock, that long arm of the L can increase nature's leverage on the rest of the dock. This places a greater load on all connections, especially at the point where the dock meets the shoreline. Therefore, additional anchoring or corner bracing may be required (floating docks anchored to piles are not a problem). Fortunately, a T-shape doesn't suffer this problem to anywhere near the same extent.

T-Shape

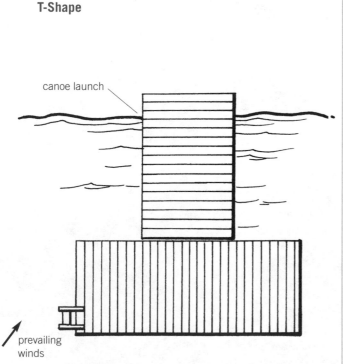

The T creates two semiprotected areas for smaller watercraft or swimming. A larger boat might be docked along the end, parallel to the shore (a good spot for a boat lift).

L-Shape

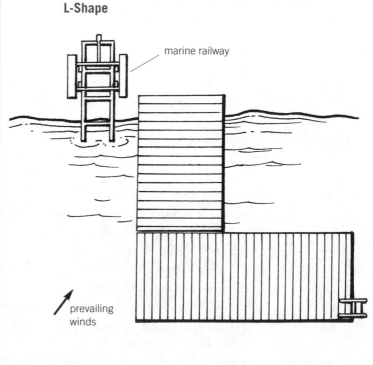

The crook of the L makes a great protected area for mooring, swimming, wading, and launching canoes. And there's still enough room at the end for fishing and entertaining.

U-Shape

High-diddle-diddle, the boat's in the middle, allowing access from both sides. This protected area also could house a boat lift. The optional *corner braces* (dotted lines) add strength and stability to the arms, increasing resistance to wind, waves, and currents. When decked over, these braces also assist traffic flow and permit easier access to the boat's bow from the dock. (L-shaped docks and finger docks also benefit from corner braces.)

Diamond Shape

Okay, so it's not really a true diamond, what with its ends cut off. But "diamond" is what the dock-building industry calls it, and in many ways it's a gem. This shape provides four clearly defined activity areas and mooring zones. Since each angled side offers a different approach from the water, boat parking is easier. The far cutoff end makes an ideal spot to launch a water-skier, go fishing, or maybe diving. At the shore end, the cutoff means that a ramp connects in the same manner as the basic rectangle.

Generally, diamond-shaped docks are large, heavy, and stable — and nifty looking. However, angles are always more labor intensive and costly to build than the conventional rectangle.

U-Shape

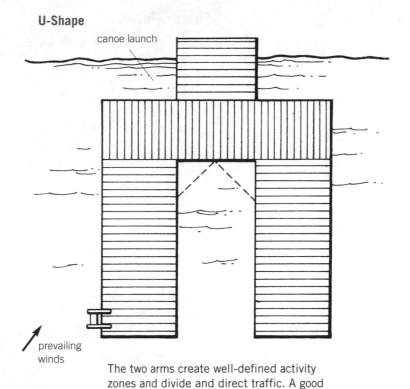

The two arms create well-defined activity zones and divide and direct traffic. A good design for separating incompatible activities.

Diamond Shape

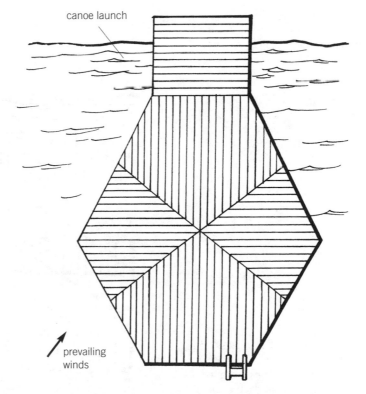

The large central space provides a lounging area safe from splashing swimmers and flying fishing hooks. The diamond shape also provides great stability.

Finger Docks

Finger docks are usually long and skinny and wiggle around, just like fingers. However, in exchange for this loss of stability you get a row of protected boat-docking spaces. These *slips* may provide access to a boat from either side, and if the water is not over 6 feet deep they are dandy spots for a boat lift. When the main section of dock runs perpendicular to the shoreline, the parking of boats can often be made easier by installing the fingers at a 45-degree angle to the main dock (dotted lines). This works particularly well when accommodating more than one powerboat.

Finger Dock (parallel to shore)

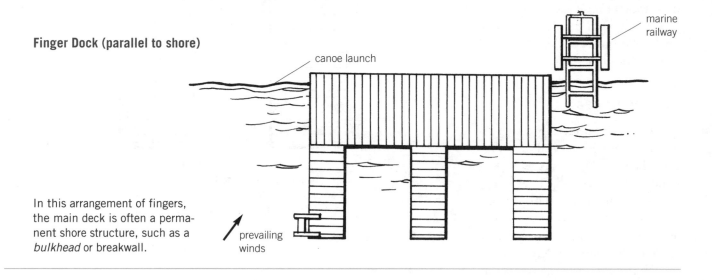

In this arrangement of fingers, the main deck is often a permanent shore structure, such as a *bulkhead* or breakwall.

Finger Dock (perpendicular to shore)

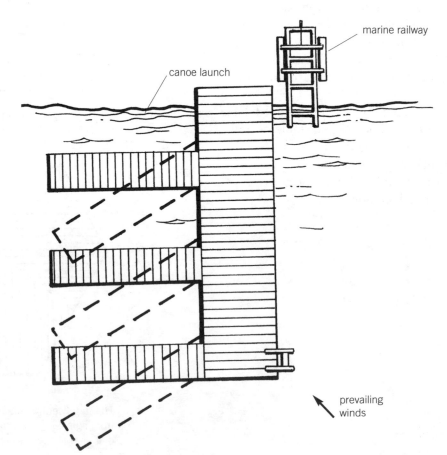

Fingers installed at 30–45° angles to the main dock (dotted lines) may make it easier to park a boat. Fingers installed perpendicular to the main dock provide better protection from waves and wakes.

Location

Dock location is perhaps the most site-dependent aspect of a waterfront plan. Fortunately, you have both a shoreline map and an activity list in front of you. Looking at them, you often will see one or more potential dock locations. While smooth, straight shorelines can ease the angst of the decision, a ragged shoreline sometimes reveals interesting and dramatic siting possibilities or protection from wind and waves. Sometimes running a dock section out at an angle from shore will open up an area that would otherwise be too shallow for mooring a boat. The oblique angle could make it possible to keep the shore end of the boat out of the shallows. Traffic problems too can sometimes be solved by taking advantage of shoreline irregularities, particularly when those irregularities create uniquely suitable areas for specific activities. For example, a protected swim area (or mooring area, depending on your priorities) could be enclosed between a small peninsula and your dock.

Mark promising sites on your shoreline with wooden stakes, or maybe just small piles of stones. Then take each proposed site for a test drive: Walk to the site from the cottage or house, and approach the site in a boat. Go for a swim, too. You may discover a large submerged rock you never knew about, or leeches. Mark their locations on your waterfront survey.

Check that promising sites don't impede the navigation of public waterways, or violate any other regulations. (You've already talked to your local dock police, right?)

Review your activities wish list. Will the proposed sites accommodate your activities? Is the lounging space in the shade or the sun? Did you stick the boating area over a partially submerged rock? Is the swimming space located among the leeches?

Once again we shall peek over the Sampel family's collective shoulder and review their solution for their waterfront, including choosing a dock type, shape (taking into account the potential for future expansion), and location (see pages 4 and 5 for a description of the Sampels' needs). Then, less closely, we will examine five other waterfronts, in each case choosing a dock type and shape for various situations typical to North America's waterways. I also have included alternative solutions and a few "what-if" scenarios for each waterfront. Mix and match, and read them all. While hopefully you will find at least some elements of your shoreline in these waterfronts, the information is presented here more to illustrate the process of arriving at waterfront solutions than as examples of ultimate solutions.

A Solution for the Sampel Waterfront

Although water levels at the Sampels' cottage are relatively stable, deep water a few feet out, muddy submerged lands, mild winds, and minimal winter ice all point to the ever-popular floating dock. A single 6-foot x 20-foot section with a 6-foot x 8-foot ramp would have minimal ecological, visual, and pocketbook impact, yet would offer enough room for the family to sit out on the end and watch the sun go down — away from the bugs, maybe. A dock ladder at the end would allow the adults to swim mud-free.

This size is the minimum for a stable floating dock (as explained in chapter 3). It would provide enough mooring space for the runabout and even Bob's ski boat, at least until the sailboat of Gord's dreams materializes. If the ski boat is already a permanent fixture by then, a second floating section could avoid a potential crisis among friends (assuming it doesn't sink the bank account). An 8- x 16-foot section connected to the leeward side at the end of the 6- x 20-foot section (to make an L-shape) would increase stability, establish a protected mooring site, and provide more room without increasing the distance to the end of the dock.

The Sampel shoreline offers two obvious locations for this dock: the existing boat-launching area and the open area in front of the cottage. The open area moves the dock well away from lot-line setbacks, doesn't compromise space for launching boats, and keeps most of the leeward side of the dock out of the shade (not so at the launch site). Since the leeward shoreline recedes from the lake rather than juts out into it (as it would at the launch site), there's more room for activities, such as swimming and maneuvering boats. This location also provides a good view of the dock from the cottage, making it easier to keep an eye on mischievous offspring.

Because the canoe can now be launched from the dock (eliminating the dreaded mucky-feet-in-the-boat syndrome), the canoe rack should be moved closer to the dock site for easier access.

The lake's moderate ice conditions allow the dock to remain in the water all year.

 A Few What-Ifs

If the Sampels built the L-shaped design and then bought a keel boat rather than a centerboarder, they would have to moor it on the exposed, north side of the L. However, if instead they connected a new 6- x 20-foot section to the end of the initial rectangular section, moving the arm of the L out into deeper water, the resulting harbor would enclose a greater area of deep water, providing safer mooring for the keel boat.

If the Sampels' finances weren't quite as restrictive, a permanent pile dock also would work well here. A floating section attached to the structure could still provide constant freeboard.

If waves or wakes were a problem, or if Bob owned a personal watercraft instead of a ski boat, a small roller ramp next to the dock's ramp would be an economical way to park.

A Solution for the Sampels

A simple rectangular floating dock accommodates the Sampels' needs (see pages 4 and 5), and it is cheap and easy to build. If the Sampels acquire a large boat, an L added to the end of the dock would provide extra room and increased stability.

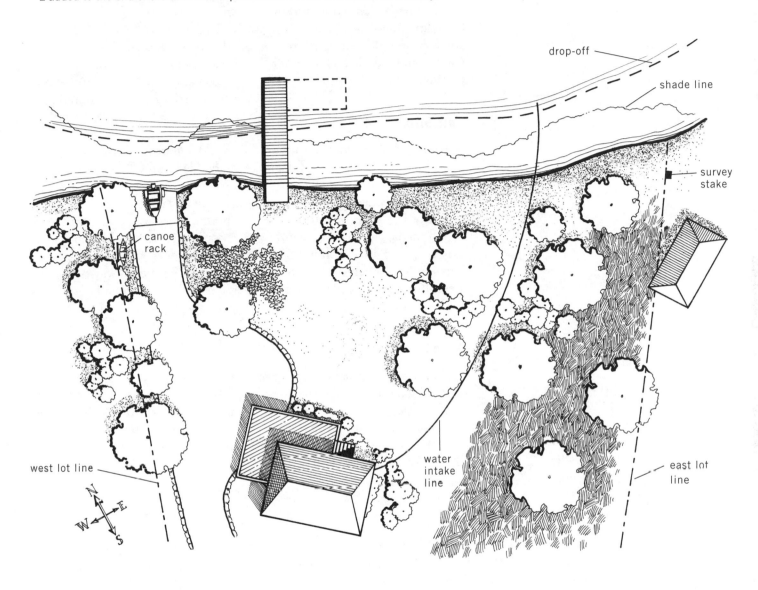

Alternative Solutions

If the Sampels' carpentry skills are as limited as their finances, a dock kit with precut lumber would be a good alternative to building it themselves — same floater, same basic design, but all the pieces come in one nice bundle, ready to assemble. However, the plans in chapter 18 make the task of building this dock from scratch pretty darn simple.

Waterfront #2

This waterfront is home to a family of five. With three kids, ages 3 to 15, they have plenty of water toys, including inflatables, sailboards, and a 20-foot ski boat. Both the parents and kids do a lot of entertaining.

The Shoreline

A long, shallow entry into the water provides only 3 feet of depth 25 feet out from shore. The submerged land consists of 6 to 8 inches of sand over limestone. When the lake blows up, steep, closely spaced waves roll in from 3 to 4 miles of open lake. Water levels fluctuate only moderately from year to year.

A Solution

This is a good situation for a pipe dock. A long rectangular run — such as three 6- x 12-foot sections — would reach out to water deep enough to allow the kids to go diving. Two similarly sized sections attached to the end, forming either a T- or L-shape, would provide room for all the water toys and plenty of space for entertaining while enclosing areas for swimming or launching sailboards. If money is a big issue, the sections could be added as finances permit.

Because of the waves and exposure, the dock sections should be anchored. Cables equipped with turnbuckles for adjustment joining the dock frame to long rock pins embedded in the limestone, or to heavy anchors, would anchor the dock well. However, even when anchored, the wave action against a moored ski boat would be too great for a pipe dock to handle during a storm. A marine railway or boat lift is a must here, preferably one designed so that one person could quickly get the boat out of the water when necessary.

If the water is subject to freezing, the entire pipe dock and shoreline railway sections (or boat lift) would have to be removed for the winter. Fortunately, a winch-equipped marine railway takes most of the labor out of removing dock sections.

Alternative Solutions

Local trades and technology permitting, a permanent pile dock would also work well here. Piles can be pounded directly into limestone without any need to predrill holes, and the strength of the dock would eliminate the need for a marine railway or boat lift. Floating sections at the end of the permanent pile dock forming an L- or T-shape would provide added room and a constant freeboard. The floating sections would also break the waves, creating a protected area for mooring or swimming. Because of the severe ice, floating sections would have to be removed.

A crib dock or concrete pier with floating sections would be a poor choice, since both permanent structures risk problems with shoreline and submerged land erosion and accretion due to littoral drift.

A Solution for Waterfront #2

The pipe dock extends out to the deep water, allowing the kids to go diving. Anchors hold the dock in place, while the marine railway is available to haul the boat if a storm threatens.

marine railway

anchors

 A Few What-Ifs

Problems resulting from littoral drift over that shallow layer of sand over rock could rule out a floating dock unless shoreline depths exceeded about 10 feet.

If the bottom consisted of a thin layer of soft silt and mud instead of sand over limestone, a permanent pile dock would definitely be the preferable choice. If this waterfront faced an ocean instead of a lake, a permanent pile dock would again be just the ticket, this time to cope with the abuses of wind, waves, and a much larger boat suited to ocean travel.

Waterfront #3

At this island waterfront, the family consists of two adults and two kids (ages 5 and 8), but guests often pop in from nearby islands. The family owns a 24-foot powerboat, an aluminum fishing boat, and a sailboard. They're keen swimmers and sailboarders and would like to be able to water-ski from the dock.

The Shoreline

Situated on the point of a rocky, rugged island, the waterfront has close neighbors, limiting its water access. It faces west, with 10 miles of open water. Wind and waves are a problem, and the spring ice conditions are severe. The ice has been known to push up onto the upper shoreline as high as 6 feet during breakup. The shoreline has a gradual 5-foot drop to the water, which is 3 feet deep at the shoreline, dropping to about 5 feet deep 50 to 60 feet out. Submerged lands consist of sand over hard, solid rock. Water levels fluctuate from year to year rather than over the course of the season.

A Solution

The severe wave and ice conditions mean we're butting heads with nature, so any attempt at permanence demands a sturdy structure. Add to that the close proximity of neighbors and it's essential to establish lot lines before building. Having to move a pipe dock installed in the wrong spot is one thing, but having to move a few ton of rocks is quite another. Again, this illustrates the importance of making a detailed map of your shoreline.

The bedrock beneath the sand makes a permanent pile dock impractical in this case. However, with a sand bottom, and provided littoral drift will not cause erosion or accretion to either side of the property, the dock police will normally allow a good-sized, breakwall-style dock. An L-shape would provide excellent protection and safe dockage with three 10- x 16-foot cribs bolted together to form the rectangle and two similarly sized cribs bolted together to form the L at the end, all topped off with the deck. The end will serve as a good launch for water activities.

If freeboard is a concern, a floating finger or two inside of the L, protected by the outer crib section, would create additional safe dockage. A ramp would run from the crib to the floater, hinged at the crib, with ramp wheels resting on the floater to save room (remember, it's a narrow lot). Any floating sections would have to be removed for the winter.

Alternative Solutions

A concrete pier may work instead of cribs, but if littoral drift is a concern, a better solution would be a heavy-duty, steel-tube floating dock consisting of 2-ton, 12- x 20-foot sections. These sections would have to be held in place against wave action with either cables secured back to shore under tension or piles. Sometime before winter arrives, the dock sections would have to be disconnected from shore and moved to a protected bay (or anchored away from land).

A less expensive solution could be a medium-weight floating dock, such as the wood-and-Styrofoam dock in chapter 18, in conjunction with a heavy-duty boat lift. The difficulty here would be removing the lift for the winter. A marine railway also would work instead of the lift, but the steep shore and narrow lot might make installation tricky. A hauled-out boat could also destroy the view.

A Solution for Waterfront #3

Wind, waves, and ice necessitate a strong, sturdy dock. Several cribs bolted together in an L shape provide stability while creating a protected harbor. The attached floating dock makes docking possible even as the water level fluctuates.

floating dock

cribs

? **A Few What-Ifs**

If the lot were wider, the marine railway would be the way to go, perhaps with a boathouse on land to provide safe, year-round storage and an unobstructed view. The railway could also haul the "less expensive" floating dock sections out of the water.

If pack ice were not a problem, any lift dock in conjunction with either a boat lift or railway would work well.

Waterfront #4

This waterfront hosts a lively family including teenagers, one of each gender. They are keen on toys — a 26-foot ski boat, a small sailboat, two sailboards, and two personal watercraft. They like to sunbathe, water-ski, and jump waves on the sailboards and personal watercraft.

The Shoreline

Fluctuating water levels are the number one problem with this waterfront, an oceanfront property. The shoreline and entry into the water are both rough and rocky, but not solid bedrock. The average daily tide is about 5 feet, exposing a 45-degree slope into the water. The property is open to prevailing winds from the west, so wave action can get nasty at times. The area is not subject to ice problems.

A Solution

The fluctuating water levels and harsh conditions demand a heavy-duty floating dock. This is an ideal application for concrete floating sections, although a large steel-tube floater also would work well. Piles would provide the best mooring.

The tricky part of this installation is the shore connection. The ramp leading to the floating sections would have to be at least 12 feet long to keep within the 30-degree maximum acceptable ramp angle and allow safe clearance from submerged lands (see chapter 13). This is particularly important for the concrete floats because of their deep draft. Adding a handrail and 1 x 2 cleats to the ramp's deck surface would make the ramp less intimidating as it angles down. A 20-foot-long ramp would be noticeably easier to use. A 36-footer would be the bare minimum if wheelchair access is a concern.

The large number of watercraft make sorting out traffic a priority here. An L-shape, ideally with one or two fingers attached to the protected east side, would spread the activities over a greater area, prevent traffic bottlenecks, and offer protected, dedicated mooring sites. The main floating sections should extend 30 to 40 feet straight out, with the L about 20 feet long. Finger size would be determined by the smaller craft.

The rocky entry rules out dragging the small sailboat onto shore. Personal watercraft are a pain to tie up. The tides and steep slope prevent shore-mounted ramps. So how do we park all this stuff? One option is to haul the boats up onto the dock (using appropriate ramps in the case of the personal watercraft), but this would consume valuable sunbathing space. A better (and more costly) solution would be separate mini hoists, each attached to the side of a floating section (with additional flotation to compensate for the increased load). The lifts would leave plenty of dry room to sunbathe, fish, or generally cavort about the dock.

Alternative Solutions

A permanent pile dock with attached floating sections would work here, the floating sections moored with piles. Either long ramps or ladders (the last-resort option) could provide access to the floaters.

A concrete pier, pegged to the rock below, might anchor floating sections, but the local dock police would probably disapprove — romantically inclined aquatic fauna often favor rocky shorelines.

A Solution for Waterfront #4

Waxing and waning tides, a unique feature of oceanfront property, demand strong floating docks. Concrete floating sections, moored with piles, are ideal in this environment. The ramp makes access possible even when the tide is at its lowest. An L attached to the end creates a protected docking area, as do the two fingers.

L

fingers

ramp

floating concrete section

pile

A Few What-Ifs

If this waterfront faced a lake rather than an ocean, the same 5-foot drop in water level would occur over the season rather than on a daily basis. Such seasonal fluctuation often occurs if a lake is a feeder for a canal system. To the same wind and wave conditions as above, let's add pack ice in the spring.

Again the solution would be a floating dock, but now the dock would have to be removed for the winter to save it from the pack ice. Since the steep shoreline makes it impractical to drag the dock onto dry land, it would have to be towed to a protected bay and left chained to a tree for the winter, or towed to a marina to be lifted out for storage. A medium-weight dock would make the annual move easier. Spring ice conditions also make anchors and chains a better choice than piles, which the ice can lift out. The chains would have to be adjusted to take up the slack as the water recedes.

A long ramp similar to the above oceanfront solution would help solve the problem of access to the dock. Another option would be to lower the shore end of the ramp as the season progresses by installing shore mounting points at two or three different levels on the shore. These could be rock pins in the rock, or pins embedded in a stepped, concrete shore structure. The risk of spring pack ice would likely rule out a lift dock.

If both the uplands and submerged lands were relatively smooth with a gradual slope, a pipe dock on wheels could be rolled out as the water receded, and then rolled back up onto safe uplands for winter storage. If those submerged lands were also sandy, augered spuds could be used to anchor the shore end in place, the spuds being pulled up and reset when the dock was moved.

Waterfront #5

The family that lives on this waterfront built the cottage themselves and are looking forward to building their own dock. Mom, Dad, and two teenage sons own a 16-foot powerboat and like to water-ski, fish, and watch the year's flock of newborn ducks grow under Ma Duck's quacking vigilance.

The Shoreline

This is a river property. The submerged lands consist of loose rock and shale with some mud and weeds. It has a moderate drop-off (from about 4 feet at shore to 8 feet farther out). Ducks usually nest in the bulrushes and cattails along the shoreline. The site is exposed to wakes from heavy river traffic, a constant current, and bad ice floes in the spring.

A Solution

The waves, the family's desire to protect the shore habitat for ducks, and their willingness to build the dock themselves all point to a pipe dock, yet the 8 feet of water is deeper than is recommended for pipe docks. A permanent pile dock might be a good choice except for the spring ice problem, which could lift the piles and the decking. Besides, pounding in piles doesn't appeal to the family.

Normally, a floater large enough to provide stability (6 x 20 feet) would cause serious disruption to the ducks' habitat. However, the disruption could be avoided with a long, narrow ramp (3 x 12 to 20 feet, for instance) connected to a floating dock, perhaps using two sections to form an L (the leg of the L pointing downcurrent). The ramp would need railings and its own flotation at the dock end. (A standard ramp the width of the dock could be substituted if shoreline flora and fauna were not an issue.) The family could build this dock, which would provide protection to both ducks and boat without disrupting the shoreline habitat and also provide dedicated areas for fishing and waterskiing.

The floating sections, and perhaps the dock end of the ramp, would need to be anchored to submerged lands to handle the waves. The dock would have to be removed for the winter to protect it from ice.

Alternative Solutions

A large lift suspension dock with a long section of narrow decking at the beginning would let the sun reach aquatic vegetation through the open framing. Again, railings would be needed at the entrance. Come winter, the dock could be raised above the reach of the ice. This, however, is a job for a professional dock builder experienced in such docks, the only do-it-yourself elements being the decking and railings. And the fishing.

I have seen river scenarios similar to this, where 2-foot-wide ramps were installed on top of a single row of pilings that were reset annually. If all that is required is a gangway leading to a moored boat, this is a solution with minimal environmental and financial impact. Most of the gangways along this river lacked railings, making them a bit of a fright to use, but railings wouldn't have left sufficient elbowroom to lug stuff between shore and boat — one-way traffic only, please. While I can't recommended this solution, it's a popular one along this particular river.

A Solution for Waterfront #5

Large waves and heavy ice floes are common on rivers. A floating dock with an attached L is stable and easy to remove in winter. Heavy anchors keep the dock from drifting, and a ramp allows access to the dock without disrupting the duck nests along the shoreline.

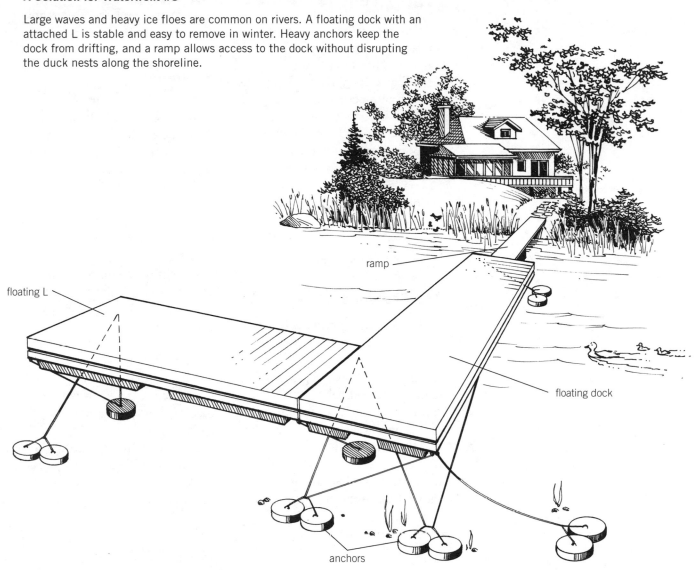

ramp

floating L

floating dock

anchors

? A Few What-Ifs

If river traffic consisted of large commercial vessels, such as cargo ships, the resulting wakes might require pulling the boat out of the water, either on a boat lift or marine railway.

If depths did not exceed 6½ feet, a heavy-duty pipe dock or lift pipe dock would be a good solution. It river traffic were light, a lightweight aluminum-framed pipe dock would simplify seasonal removal. However, such a lightweight would not provide adequate mooring for a larger boat, even in this relatively docile environment. So if larger boats make cameo appearances in your dockside meditations, either go heavy duty from the beginning or purchase a boat lift or marine railway before the new boat arrives.

Waterfront #6

At this waterfront, the cottagers are a retired, older couple. Money is not an issue. They have a runabout and a small aluminum fishing boat, but admit that much of their time will be spent simply sitting on the dock watching the birds and boats go by. Both recognize that there is a chance one of them may eventually be confined to a wheelchair. Occasionally, the grandchildren (all in their teens) drop in for a visit, a swim, and to cruise the lake in Grandma and Grandpa's boats.

The Shoreline

A south-facing cliff overlooks a small, glacial lake having steep sides and a rocky bottom that drops off sharply from shore. Depths are at least 25 feet, probably more. The space between the water and the cliff is narrow, at times nonexistent, and consists of large, random boulders. The steep slope to the water makes it impossible to put in or remove docks from the waterfront.

The lake is quiet, unaffected by strong winds or large waves, and water levels are stable.

A Solution

This is a good situation for a suspension dock. Usually, such a cliff-faced waterfront leaves little or no shore for sunbathing or other beach activities. In this case, the dock becomes the beach. If the narrow shoreline permitted the construction of a sizable deck, a 10- x 25-foot dock might be adequate, otherwise go bigger (such as 12- x 45-foot) to accommodate the grandfolks and third generation of splashing swimmers. A stairway, and person lift if the budget permits, is necessary for easy access to the waterfront. The lift is a better choice if much fishing gear will be carted to and from the dock, and will be appreciated more and more as the couple ages.

If the lake freezes during the winter, adding a lift to the suspension dock will get it angled up out of harm's way.

Alternative Solutions

A cantilever dock embedded or pinned to the rock cliff also is an option. In this case the dock would run parallel to the shore rather than out from it, extending only a few feet out into the water. This would provide room for both mooring and swimming, but no protection for either (not a problem here). Total dock width, including the land-based portion of the cantilever, should not be less than 8 feet.

A large, floating dock, using the same dock plan as the suspension dock, would be a less expensive alternative. Ice conditions might require that a floating dock be towed to a protected bay for the winter; otherwise, it could be left in place with its ramp detached from the shore-based deck.

A Solution for Waterfront #6

Steep cliffs, especially prominent around glacial lakes, present a challenging obstacle. The suspension dock takes full advantage of the tiny shoreline and actually becomes the beach. In addition to the dock, a stairway is necessary to make the dock accessible.

 A Few What-Ifs

If the cliff were shale or limestone, a cantilever dock might not hold in the rock. Unstable rock can also erode and break off, making any shore-based deck a potential hazard. In this situation a large floating or suspended dock would be preferable, moving activities away from the cliff. Life's tough enough without getting bonked on the head by a piece of your own property.

Preserving Aquatic Habitats

Aquatic life includes fish, crustaceans, waterfowl, amphibians, and aquatic vegetation. Our shorelines are often considered prime real estate by this diverse group — in other words, it's essential habitat.

Shorelines provide spawning areas where eggs are laid, a nursery where the young find food and protective shelter, and a two-way restaurant where the patrons may find themselves on the menu. Shorelines also serve as thoroughfares and stopovers, for both seasonal migration and daily travel. For aquatic vegetation, the shallower depths typical of shorelines provide energy from the sun (in the form of photosynthesis) and nutrients from shore runoff.

Unfortunately, the requirements of one species are often incompatible with those of another. Therefore, alterations to this shared environment will often benefit one species, or a particular facet of one species' life, at the expense of another. So while large pipe or floating docks can provide shade and shelter for fish, smaller versions of the same docks will allow sunlight into the water, thereby encouraging vegetation. The vegetation in turn provides food, protection, and spawning areas for fish, waterfowl, and other forms of aquatic life. For this reason, in situations where you must pass over a vegetated area to get to your boat, legislation often limits your choice in docks to a narrow pipe-dock or pile-dock gangway.

Many waterfront residents want to eradicate these "sea weeds" from their aquatic landscape because they feel so yucky against the legs when you go swimming. Unfortunately, getting rid of the vegetation also destroys fish habitat, and often spawning areas.

Considerable confusion clouds the concepts of "habitat" and "spawning area." Habitat is where fish feed and congregate, but not necessarily spawn. And while docks often provide a dandy habitat, spawning areas are sometimes destroyed in the process of creating that habitat. And of course the new habitat is conveniently within easy reach of a worm-draped hook. Increased fishing coupled with decreased reproduction leads to fewer fish and cries for government intervention.

So when you look down into the water surrounding a crib dock and see swarms of fish happily darting about, don't let the appearance of good health fool you — it's quite possible that these fish are up the creek without a spawning bed.

Dock Types

And now, the secret of what differentiates one dock type from another is revealed in detail. Read the chapter pertaining to your dock of choice. You'll find that it's chock-full of design tips and options illustrating how best to maximize that dock's benefits to your individual situation. Again, it's your shoreline, your activities, and your dock. Take whatever time you need to make it your solution — preferably before you build it.

Although not necessary, you are also encouraged to read the other chapters in this section before proceeding to section 3, The Art of Dock Building. The more you know about docks in general, the greater the likelihood of building that ideal solution.

To bring some order to this section, I have arbitrarily assigned all the docks mentioned in the preceeding chapters to four, admittedly broad, categories: floating docks, pipe docks, permanent docks (which includes cribs, concrete piers, and permanent pile docks), and specialty docks (cantilever, suspension, and lift docks).

The emphasis here is on the do-it-yourself-friendly varieties, but even the stuff best described as hobby hostile is not forgotten.

floating

docks

As the name implies, a *floating dock* keeps its deck above water by relying on flotation, a trait it shares with any boat moored at its side (see The Theory of Flotation on page 42). Because the dock floats on the water's surface rather than being supported by solid land, freeboard doesn't vary as water levels rise and fall — the deck's distance above the water's surface remains constant (although the deck's relationship to the shoreline will change). And, in common with boats, fluctuations in freeboard can result from overload — mounds of fishing gear piled up in the corner of the dock, for instance, or a waterlogged float, or heavy-duty deck chairs, or even extra-large meals, whether carried onto the dock in coolers or in stomachs. Fortunately, any freeboard fickleness on a well-designed floater is minor.

A consistent freeboard is an asset for most dock-based activities including boating, swimming, or simply dangling one's toes in the water as the sun slips away into an evening's mist. A floating dock also maintains its as-installed look, with no seasonally exposed skirts or ugly algae covered undercarriage. And because a floating dock doesn't depend on submerged lands to hold it up, there is no maximum water depth to concern yourself with.

Floaters can be adapted to many uses. They can even be used as makeshift barges to transport heavy and bulky stuff to waterfront locations lacking road access. One local dock builder (who specializes in floating dock sections that weigh 2 to 3 tons each) told me about a client who floated a full-sized, industrial backhoe out to an island cottage. Come to think of it, he never mentioned anything about floating the equipment back . . .

Where ice conditions prohibit a four-season dock, the floating dock can be removed from the water for the winter (albeit with no small effort in some cases). Some well-built floaters routinely survive mild ice conditions that would destroy more susceptible types.

Although floating docks are the overall versatility champs, they won't work everywhere. For instance, a pipe dock is often a better choice in shallow water. For a floater to function, it must have sufficient draft to keep its floats resting on water, without bumping into submerged lands (which can harm both the dock and aquatic habitat). A depth of 3 feet at low water is the normal accepted minimum; less is possible if the water level never varies and the area is not subject to harsh wave action.

Oceans have a love-hate relationship with floaters. On the love side, we have the floater's ability to maintain a constant freeboard; welcome tidings where tides constantly alter water levels. However, when submerged lands slope gradually out to sea, breaking waves can come toppling down on floating docks, pounding humanity's best handiwork to pieces. Even in the absence of such rude behavior, retreating tides can leave a floating dock high and dry on the exposed land. Although the returning tides will float the dock once again, harm can come to the dock, shellfish, and their habitat. For this reason, some jurisdictions (such as South Carolina) will not issue permits to install floaters if the dock is subject to bottoming out, while others (Washington State, for example) will permit floaters when equipped with "stops" designed to keep the dock's floats from resting on the submerged lands during low tide, thereby minimizing the area of contact.

Types of Floats

Floats are the life jackets of dock building — they keep the floater from becoming a sinker. They come in enough types and sizes to refloat the lost city of Atlantis. So, to impose a bit of arbitrary order on the chaos, I will assign all the residential dock floats of the world into the following four categories: dedicated dock-flotation devices; floating frames; floating decks; and floats to avoid.

Dedicated Dock-Flotation Devices

Devices in this category have but one function — to float. A dock using these devices has a separate deck (normally of wood or plastic) with some sort of structural framing (wood or metal) to hold the deck and floats in place. The floats are secured below the deck and framing.

The plastic foam billet. Often incorrectly referred to in a generic sense by the trade name Styrofoam, the plastic foam billet is usually made from expanded polystyrene (EPS). During the manufacturing process, a foaming agent is added to molten polystyrene, causing it to expand as the plastic cools. This is how those million or so tiny air pockets or bubbles are formed within the plastic. Manufacturing techniques and foam formulas are altered to make either closed-cell EPS or open-cell EPS, and when it comes to docks, the difference is crucial. As the name implies, with closed-cell EPS each cell is an isolated, or closed, unit, resulting in a more rigid foam with lower air and water permeability. The foam coffee cup that you see blowing across the street is of closed-cell construction; otherwise, it would not have held

liquid prior to being tossed away. Also true to its name, the cells of open-cell EPS are always open for business, letting air and water enter the maze of foam cells, which in turn gives it much higher water absorbency than its closed-cell cousin (see Floats to Avoid on page 40).

A further distinction between varieties of EPS can be made between molded closed-cell EPS and extruded closed-cell EPS. During the extrusion process, the polystyrene molecules tend to align themselves in one direction, creating a stronger, less permeable material. Styrofoam, the blue stuff made by Dow, is an extruded, closed-cell, EPS foam. In comparison, molded billets (normally white) are more fragile, possessing about a third of the strength of the superior Styrofoam billets.

Because any EPS foam consists of countless little pockets of trapped air, puncture a foam float and it still remains afloat. But if a float should break up as a result of abuse from ice, nasty weather, animals, or a clumsy boat operator, remnants of EPS will bob about the surface of the water and along shorelines for a very long time to come. Molded EPS (typically white) will crumble into beads on impact. Styrofoam, an extrusion, breaks into easier-to-gather chunks.

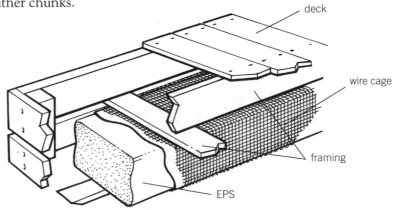

Comprised of expanded polystyrene, plastic foam billets are remarkably buoyant. Structural framing holds the float in place, while the wire cage protects the foam from the sharp teeth of pesky rodents.

One potential advantage of any foam billet as a flotation material is that it can be carved into all sorts of shapes, allowing the dock builder to tailor flotation placement and quantities. Cutting molded EPS creates a mess of EPS beads; Styrofoam produces a much tidier and smaller pile of polystyrene sawdust. Regardless of type, all forms of EPS are susceptible to damage from sunlight, oils and gases, and abrasion (such as from ice).

Some dock designs leave the billets dangerously exposed to abuse and abrasion, particularly when the dock is left in the ice all winter. A better alternative is to encase any foam billet in a subframe below the normal structural framing. This protects the foam from direct contact with anything but water and also secures the billet in place. The subframe, if designed correctly (see chapter 18), can also serve as a skid to support the dock if it's dragged up onto land for seasonal storage.

Although it is not a common practice, polyurethane is sometimes used in the manufacture of foam flotation billets. Compared to polystyrene, polyurethane has greater compression strength — assuming equal densities — absorbs half the water of open-cell EPS, has slightly more buoyancy, and has greater resistance to damage from oil and gasoline spills, although it's more susceptible to wear by abrasion. It's also more expensive than EPS or Styrofoam billets, and not as strong or water resistant as Styrofoam, which accounts for its rarity. However, polyurethane is a good choice for secondary flotation (see below).

The dedicated plastic float drum.

Not to be confused with the industrial plastic drum (see Floats to Avoid on page 40), the dedicated plastic float drum is manufactured specifically as a dock float. Basically, it's a molded-plastic container designed to keep out water. The material of choice for such drums is high-density polyethylene (HDPE). Although less prevalent and not as damage resistant, fiberglass drums are also available.

Dedicated float drums are manufactured in a variety of shapes and sizes. Typically, bolts attach them directly to the underside of the dock frame. Some designs include bolt holes for this purpose, or the bolts may run right through the lip at the float's upper perimeter. Some variations place the mounting lip lower, the float in this case being designed to work either-side up. An off-center lip gives dock builders an option between two different freeboards depending on which side is up. But be forewarned that any increase in freeboard without a proportionate increase in weight and flotation will result in a decrease in stability (see The Theory of Flotation on page 42). Other floats are molded to facilitate vertical stacking when additional buoyancy is required, such as to support the weight of a heavy ramp or a diving tower.

Unlike foam billets, dedicated floats require no subframe below the normal structural framing. While eliminating this subframe partially offsets the additional cost of dedicated float drums, it also reduces weight where it is needed most — down low.

Dedicated plastic float drums are available either as hollow units or with some form of enclosed secondary flotation. The drum's hard, waterproof shell means that open-cell EPS foam can be used for secondary flotation without risk of the float becoming waterlogged. Because open-cell EPS is the least expensive foam suitable for this application, it's the prime choice among manufacturers. If punctured, however, any open-cell-EPS-filled drum will lose some of its buoyancy. (Enclosed EPS is permitted in jurisdictions that otherwise ban its use as dock flotation, because even a punctured enclosure will prevent the foam from dispersing over the water.) Fortunately, both closed-cell-EPS and polyurethane-filled drums are also available. With these, you probably won't even know if the drum has been pierced. Regardless of foam type or whether the drum is HDPE or fiberglass, float drums are stronger when filled with foam. The foam acts as a shock absorber. This can be an advantage whether dragging a float-drum dock onto land for seasonal storage or leaving it to sit in the ice — comparable hollow units run a much greater risk of collapsing under the weight of the dock or crushing ice.

That said, it's difficult for consumers to know if two floats are truly comparable. Because the foam filler adds strength to the drum, some manufacturers have opted for a less expensive means of producing the floats (blown molding instead of rotational molding, for instance). Often, this reduces wall thickness. Thinner walls make the shell of the drum more prone to cracking and more difficult to repair when it does crack (thicker material being easier to plastic-weld). One solution is to look for floats that meet U.S. Army Corps of Engineers regulations, al-though not all quality floats are stamped with this seal of approval.

Tests have shown that when foam-filled drums are left in the water over winter, the ice forming along their bottoms is thinner than ice surrounding the float. This is not the case for hollow drums. The insulating qualities of the foam are credited with preventing the ice from forming. Together, the greater strength and lesser ice buildup seem to give foam-filled drums an advantage for icebound floating docks.

Foam-filled or hollow, float drums with sides that converge slightly toward the bottom have a tendency to rise up out of ice, rather than being crushed by it. This makes them less susceptible to damage than straight-sided units.

Regardless of how it happens, punctured polyethylene and fiberglass are both easily repaired (see chapter 17).

An interesting nonfoam type of secondary flotation is found in an HDPE float drum called the Enviro Float. In lieu of foam, 80 individual "plastic pressure vessels" — a clever euphemism for recycled, clear plastic 2-liter pop containers, all pressure tested and sealed — are stacked within the outer shell like bottles in a wine cellar. The plastic shell, made from the polyethylene leftovers of industry, is molded to hold the pop containers in place. The result is a float drum that looks like it

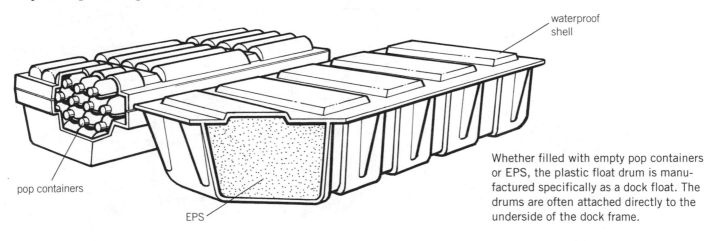

pop containers

EPS

waterproof shell

Whether filled with empty pop containers or EPS, the plastic float drum is manufactured specifically as a dock float. The drums are often attached directly to the underside of the dock frame.

has come down with the mumps. Even if the shell and a couple of "plastic pressure vessels" get punctured, the remaining 78 bottles will keep it afloat. (Sounds like a variation on an old camp song about bottles of beer on the wall.) Also in common with other polyethylene floats, the punctured outer shell can be repaired.

The foam-filled, recycled tire. A recycled car tire provides another way to enclose EPS. Generally, each tire is filled with foam, then a pressure-treated wood "hubcap" is placed on either side and held in place with bolts that also attach the float to the dock.

In common with the float drum, the subframe is eliminated. In this case, however, the floats are heavy enough to make up for the weight loss. One advantage to the tire float, unforeseen during its development, is that the pattern and shapes produced by the tires attached to the underside of the dock attenuate wave action.

Tire floats are reasonably durable but impossible to make watertight. Until recently the sole choice of foam has been EPS, which takes on water and quickly deteriorates from spilled gas or diesel fuel. This could be from the slick drifting over from a nearby marina or a sloppy neighbor. Individual tire floats tend to loose buoyancy at differing rates, leading in turn to the dock developing a permanent list. Fortunately, there is a reasonable solution — the Enviro-Buoy.

Enviro-Buoys are also recycled tire floats, using the same tire size (14 inches) and bolt pattern as the original EPS-filled tire floats. In fact, Enviro-Buoys share all the traits of the standard recycled tire float except one — the type of foam. Instead of open-cell EPS, Enviro-Buoys use Dow Styrofoam blue flotation billets — carved into circles from the standard Styrofoam flotation billets. Using special tooling, this foam "cookie" is squeezed into each tire and, in common with the waterlogged tire float it replaces, the whole shebang is bolted together using pressure-treated wood hubcaps. Which means that Enviro-Buoys easily bolt on as replacements for standard waterlogged recycled-tire floats. And because the flotation is blue Styrofoam and not white EPS, Enviro-Buoys won't take on water and sink.

A lesser problem than a sinking dock is that tire floats remain visible from the side. While a set of new

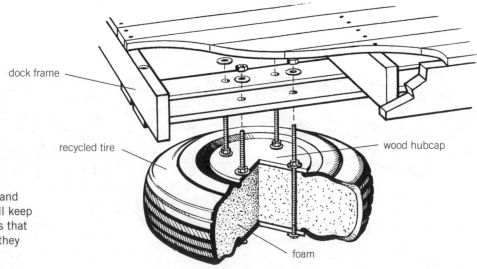

dock frame

recycled tire

wood hubcap

foam

A car tire filled with Dow Styrofoam and bolted to the underside of a dock will keep the structure afloat. Avoid using tires that have been filled with EPS, because they tend to get waterlogged and sink.

tires on the family jalopy might be a welcome sight, a collection of bald, used ones attached to your dock may disqualify it from the Annual Dandy Dock Decor Award. Concerned folks could try ordering whitewalls only.

So the recycled-tire float has a split personality — EPS-filled tires sinking into my category of Floats to Avoid, while the Enviro-Buoy version is certainly a float-type worth considering.

HDPE pipe. A relatively new flotation material is *HDPE pipe,* not to be confused with the standard polyethylene pipe often used for household water-intake lines. The ends of these large pipes are capped — sealed airtight using industrial plastic-welding techniques (also known as fusing the plastic).

An HDPE pipe float can be clamped to the dock's frame, can be placed to fit snugly between two framing members, or can serve as both flotation and framework (see HDPE pipe-frame docks in Floating Frames). The pipes are typically used in pairs, one per side. When clamped in place or tucked into the frame, the float functions like flotation billets or dedicated float drums.

The frame for clamped-in-place pipe is usually made of steel, or wood when the pipe sits between framing members.

Standard HDPE pipes come in diameters of up to 42 inches for dock use, accommodating a variety of dock sizes, projected loads, and boat types. In larger sizes, these docks are proving to be about as strong as steel-tube floats for residential use, the approximately 1-inch and up wall thicknesses of the larger pipes absorbing some fairly harsh impact without denting or cracking.

A nifty variation on the HDPE theme is the corrugated HDPE pipe manufactured by a company called Big O. An outer circle of ribbed HDPE is fused to the inner pipe as the product is extruded at the factory. Corrugation adds strength to HDPE pipe just as it does to cardboard. The outer ribbed ring protects the inner pipe from damage while increasing the pipe's rigidity. As a bonus, each rib seals in a separate air chamber, increasing flotation. In common with standard HDPE pipe, the ends of Big O are fused airtight, and the floats are then secured to the dock in the same manner.

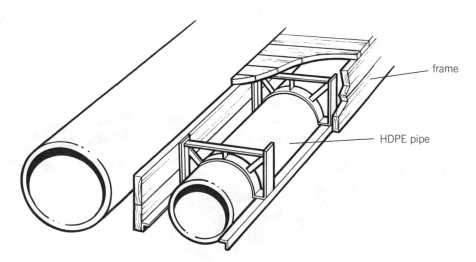

frame

HDPE pipe

Once the ends of these polyethylene tubes are capped, they are airtight and buoyant. They are often clamped to the dock's frame or braced between framing members.

Floating Frames

Floating frames are double-duty flotation devices, serving as both float and structural framing. A separate deck is still required, and at least enough framing to hold the deck together and secure it to the floats. Floats in this category come air filled or foam filled, fat or skinny, long or short, but usually with some combination of pronounced bumps, indentations, sharp angles, or curves. All these oddities are there, in most cases, to facilitate the attachment of decking and its subframe. One result of this apparent design anarchy is different docks for different floats — in other words, each variation often dictates a unique design of dock, so dock plans must be obtained from the manufacturer or retailer when you purchase the float.

The float drum with framing aspirations.
These floats fit somewhere between the dedicated plastic float drum and the floating frame, stretching the definition of the floating frame to its limits. Since each does more than simply supply flotation, however, they end up in this group. At a minimum, each incorporates some method of holding the framing members in proper alignment as the dock is being assembled.

An example of this minimalist philosophy is the Drag-on float manufactured by Great Northern Docks. The Drag-on opts for topside bumps to position the deck framing, giving the frame a modicum of additional support while making it easier to build a dock with square corners. However, this does limit your options for float placement within the dock's frame. The Drag-on also boasts molded-in-place tunnels running through the depth of each float, which allow for the easy attachment of a skidboard. Unlike plastic foam billets, a skidboard is not usually considered essential equipment on float drums. This is especially true with stronger, rotational-mold drums such as the Drag-on. However, with the Drag-on design, the strength of the entire dock is increased when the skidboards are bolted in place. And if dragging the dock out of the water at the end of each season is a must — particularly over rough shoreline — skidboards can be a welcome bonus, the skidboard making the task less laborious while reducing the odds of float damage. Also, at some tidal zones (such as in areas of Washington State), skidboards are required by law in order to lessen the percentage of dock that could potentially end up resting on — and therefore damaging — shell beds and the like.

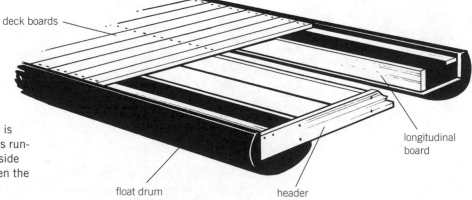

The Techstar Series I is a float drum that is also a part of the dock framing. Two floats running parallel to each other act as the outside stringers. The deck planks stretch between the two floats, secured to boards that fit into molded longitudinal slots.

deck boards

longitudinal board

float drum

header

Aside from these design quirks, the Drag-on looks and acts very much like a standard, dedicated, plastic float drum.

At the other end of the spectrum, a float that assumes a share of the structural duties is the Techstar Series I. Each float is 2 feet wide by 8 feet long. The floats act as the outside stringers (longitudinal structural members) for the dock. Boards are bolted into each float's two longitudinal, molded-in slots. Headers and deck boards are then fastened to these boards. Depending on desired dock width, one or more additional stringers may be required between the floats. Techstar also offers some "center floats" if additional flotation is required (for ramps, etc.). The Series I floats fit flush with the decking, which makes securing mooring cleats from under the decking impossible. On the plus side, the sides of the floats protrude beyond the deck's edge to act as dock bumpers, eliminating that optional expense.

Techstar floats are for light-duty docks, adequate for small runabouts and light loads, but they lack the stability of heavier-duty floating options.

Steel tubes. The dedicated steel-tube float is the traditionalist in the floating-frame class. Awkward and heavy to handle on shore, it is also the most abuser friendly of any flotation device. Since this float makes for a big, heavy dock, steel tubes are well suited to mooring boats that verge on floating houses and coping with extreme conditions, such as high winds and big waves. The tube can be designed specifically for application as a float, or a length of steel pipe can be modified for the task by a reputable dock builder.

Generally, one tube running down each side of the dock is all that is required. Mounting brackets for the deck framing should be welded directly onto the tubes and the tubes linked together with a welded, steel bracket at each end. Since steel will rust, expect leaks after about 25 to 35 years (less in saltwater environments). A few manufacturers are filling their tubes with foam to eliminate this potential problem (sometimes only after the leaks are discovered). Fortunately, protective coatings can be applied to steel to increase its resistance to corrosion (see chapter 7).

As with any hollow float, a punctured steel tube without secondary flotation will sink, possibly taking the dock with it. Punctures usually occur when the shore ends of the tubes are permitted to rub on submerged rocks as water levels drop, a situation often made worse by the breakup of spring ice. Fortunately,

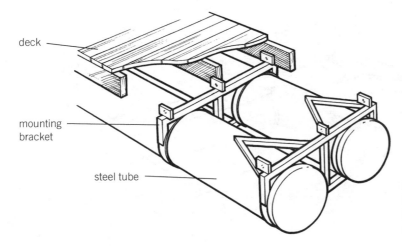

deck

mounting bracket

steel tube

Although extremely heavy on dry land, steel tubes are sturdy and abuse-resistant in the water. Mounting brackets for the deck framing are welded directly onto the tubes.

in common with polyethylene floats, punctured steel floats also can be repaired, although not by the average do-it-yourselfer. Repairs can involve either shortening the tubes or welding on patches. Shortening the tubes will result in some loss of flotation, but because steel-tube docks tend to be considerably heavier and somewhat longer than average (40-foot sections are not uncommon), a couple of feet lopped off the end of the dock is likely to go unnoticed.

HDPE pipe-frame docks (see also HDPE pipe). These come in two flavors: heavy duty and light duty. Regardless of flavor, all pipe ends are sealed and, in common with steel-tube floats, all mounting tabs and brackets to attach the decking are fused (plastic-welded) in place. Heavy-duty versions use at least 16-inch-diameter pipe and are very similar in layout to the dedicated steel-tube float, but HDPE won't rust. The result is a large, durable dock with less weight than the traditional steel-tube dock.

In a typical light-duty version, 10-inch-diameter HDPE pipe is used. Often longitudinal pipes are linked to cross-pipes, the finished frame forming a gridwork pattern of black pipe. Occasionally, some or all of the pipes are filled with foam. With or without foam, what you get is a dock suitable for small boats and limited exposure to nature's wrath — not because the dock lacks strength but because stability is compromised by modest weight and modest buoyancy. For loungers who prefer not to risk spilling the lemonade when the neighbor's boat motors by, stick with the heavy-duty versions.

Floating Decks

In the floating-deck category, the floats form the entire dock. Separate framework and decking are history, along with any of their related maintenance — or choice of materials, for that matter.

The plastic float cube. The polyethylene float cube is a variation on the dedicated plastic float drum, except in this case a collection of floats constitutes the entire dock. Typically, each float weighs about 14 pounds and is about 20 inches square on the top by about 16 inches deep. The shape of the dock is limited mainly by your cubist imagination and the number of floats on hand. However, because all hardware, including cleats, ladders, bolts, float connectors, anchor connectors, and sometimes even the tools required to assemble the pieces, comes from one source — the float's manufacturer — your financial and design options are limited.

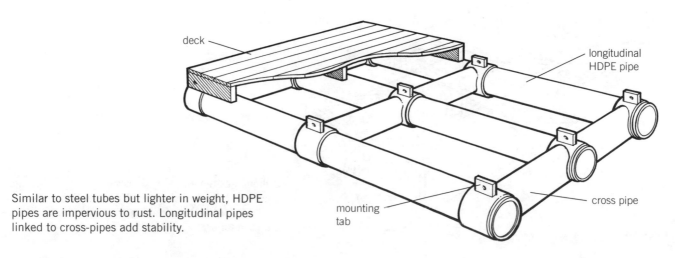

deck

longitudinal HDPE pipe

mounting tab

cross pipe

Similar to steel tubes but lighter in weight, HDPE pipes are impervious to rust. Longitudinal pipes linked to cross-pipes add stability.

Cube docks are easy to assemble and take apart. You don't even need to get into the water — simply drop a cube into the drink, then drop in another and bolt them together, then another, and so forth until you run out of cubes. To remove the dock (you must if your shoreline is subject to harsh spring ice conditions), unbolt the dock into groups of cubes small enough to comfortably handle, lifting each section out of the water as you go along. Depending on load, the connected cubes may slowly undulate underfoot as you traverse the dock, an unnerving motion that can also be instigated by wave action. Usually, a nonskid pattern is molded into the exposed skin of each cube.

While the marriage of flotation and deck can be one of convenience, only you can decide whether a shoreline draped with quilted charcoal gray plastic squares appeals to you. It could put your membership in the Antique Boat Owners' Society at risk.

Plastic float cubes are primarily for light-duty docking.

Floating concrete. Admittedly, "concrete float" seems to contradict itself. Anchors are made out of concrete, right? True, but any object will float if the weight of the water it displaces exceeds the total weight of that object (see The Theory of Flotation on page 42). So, yes, we could have concrete floats held in place with concrete anchors.

The typical concrete float is actually a large block of EPS foam encased in a reinforced concrete shell. The result is a ready-made, floating, concrete sidewalk delivered to your shore. The large floats (normally the full width of the dock by at least 10 feet long) are linked solidly together upon arrival to create your choice of dock size and shape. Concrete floats are expensive and extremely heavy (both the floats and your payment usually require launching by crane) but they offer strength and stability on a par with most land-based sidewalks.

The conventional concrete-float dock owes much of this welcome immovability to its draft — routinely at least half the depth of the float. So not only does any load on the dock (whether from nature or humanity) have to overcome the inertia of almost 2 tons of float (with a minimum of two floats required for a 6- x 20-foot dock), but it must also push aside all that water surrounding the half-submerged float before the dock will

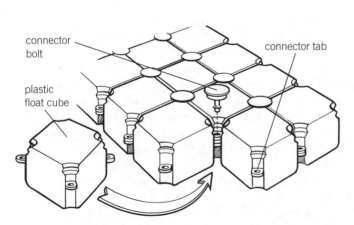

Once they are fastened together, polyethylene cubes actually become the dock. While easy to assemble, the connected cubes undulate underfoot and should only be used for light-duty docking.

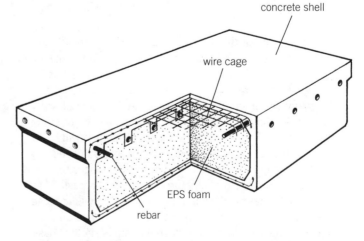

Expensive and heavy, concrete floats are both strong and stable. The EPS foam center is encased in a concrete shell. Often, a wire cage and rebar further strengthen the sections.

move. It's certainly not impossible, but neither is it likely if the floats are installed properly.

It's questionable whether concrete floats are suited to waterfronts subject to seasonal freeze-up — especially in those areas prone to harsh ice conditions during spring breakup. To my knowledge, no concrete float has undergone any long-term testing in this kind of environment.

Concrete floats are well suited to oceanfront locations where fluctuating tides and high waves often play havoc with other floating docks. The floats can be anchored in place, but are more often secured to pilings or stand-off arms. And, at risk of stating the obvious, these floats are overkill for mooring small boats in all but extreme conditions. This is a do-it-yourself type of dock only if writing a check is your idea of active involvement.

Floats to Avoid

Few people in the world are as parsimonious as me — just ask my friends. Yet even I know that the following devices should not be used as flotation devices.

Industrial drums. The recycled industrial drum is available in steel or plastic. Steel drums are bulky, prone to corrosion and leaking, a pain to repair, and make the dock difficult to remove from the water for winter. They're also a great deal uglier than even recycled car tires. If you've really got a hankering to recycle steel drums, spare the dock and form a Caribbean-style marimba band. Plastic drums also are easy to puncture, at which point the dock lists to one side or sinks. Neither type of drum was designed to handle the abuse a dock float is subjected to, either by humanity or nature, and such drum docks are not as stable as other alternatives.

By the time an industrial drum migrates to the residential dock, more often than not industry has found it unacceptable for further use. And you can bet that traces of strange substances still cling to its walls — toxic chemicals, to name one likely candidate.

But surely plastic drums that once held food-grade or biodegradable substances are okay? Nope. While it can be argued that the residual chemical or food product

---

The Dilemma of Caution

The sad reality of the dock-building business (and small business in general) is that while most dedicated dock floats have no trouble keeping afloat, it's not always possible to say the same about the manufacturers and distributors. There are many clever solutions to dock flotation, some of which even make the job of dock building much easier. Regrettably, the more unusual the float, the more difficult it will be to find a replacement should the float become damaged or you want to expand the dock. The float may no longer be in production even if the manufacturer is still in business.

I realize that by offering this caution, I may lead some readers to spurn some of the more unusual floats on the market. And therein lies the dilemma: support cleverness and risk being stranded or stick to the established solutions and stifle innovation? The choice is yours.

The safest route is to buy from a well-established supplier or pick a flotation device that is easily replaceable. For instance, choosing dedicated plastic float drums with standard North American construction measurements such as 24 inches wide by 48 inches long by 12 inches deep is a safe option. Styrofoam-brand flotation billets are also a safe purchase — if a company the size of Dow Chemical goes down the tubes, it's likely we're all sunk. And speaking of tubes, both steel tubes and HDPE pipe are universal and repairable.

Universal availability, durability, and do-it-yourself-ability were the factors that led me to specify Styrofoam-brand billets and generic, foam-filled, dedicated plastic float drums for the floating docks presented in chapter 18.

still residing in a barrel might help alleviate some supposed water problem, only the agencies in charge of water quality in the pertinent jurisdiction can make that judgment. And in many jurisdictions you can be subject to steep fines if you're found responsible for adding *any* substance to the watershed, even if indirectly via a seeping industrial drum. The best thing you can do for the water at your shoreline is to not put any substance into it.

Even in the areas where these barrels are not banned as dock flotation, why would anyone trust such a diabolical device to support the family dock? Or let the kids swim around it? Or drink water from the same lake that these things temporarily float on, and often sink in? Ask the man who owns one, for it's beyond me.

Open-cell EPS billets. Often referred to as "beadboard" in the construction trade (because it's made from, and easily breaks apart into, small beads of EPS), *open-cell EPS* is usually white and is very fragile; it should never be used for dock flotation. It was never intended to function as a flotation billet, and many jurisdictions have banned its use as such.

Although all forms of EPS will absorb water and hence suffer a corresponding reduction in flotation, open-cell EPS is the real villain here, capable of increasing its weight tenfold within two years of waterborne service. If the contained water freezes, the billet usually breaks apart, drifting up on beaches and choking waterfowl.

The pontoon boat. At first glance, the pontoon boat seems a reasonable alternative to the steel-tube dock. Yet, although more costly, it lacks the strength and stability of its dedicated dock cousin. Nor does the pontoon boat make for a very tidy-looking dock. The pontoons (those steel- or aluminum-tube floats underneath) protrude beyond the end of the decking about 4 to 5 feet in the front — a necessity for navigation.

Admittedly, the boat seems to have potential as a multifaceted servant, functioning variously as a dock, mobile fishing platform, barge, and traveling party deck. But to maintain that versatility, all submerged-land and shoreline connections (anchors and ramps, for instance) must be disconnected in order to switch from a dock to a boat. Such temporary connections are incompatible with long-term dock durability or stability. And when somebody takes the dock out for a cruise, what's left at the shoreline for others?

The pontoon boat works best when you can make good use of its mobility (as a boat/barge) and already have a well-constructed dock to securely moor it to. This floating platform can then serve as an extension to the dock when needed, much as your backyard might become an extension to the house when a rousing party needs more room on a warm, dry evening. And while the backyard might serve admirably in that situation, few folks would choose it as their only living room. Ditto for the idea of pontoon boat as dock.

Illegal in many jurisdictions, industrial drums tend to leak dangerous toxic chemicals into the water.

Over time, EPS billets, which are very brittle, break into tiny beads and frequently wash up on beaches.

As a general rule, boats should not be used as docks. They are unstable, and when they go out for a cruise, the dock leaves with them.

From an environmental point of view, a floating dock's biggest asset is that its only direct disruption of submerged lands is from anchors, spuds, or pilings. In fact, if secured only to the shore, there may be no contact at all with submerged lands. This is good news for fish habitats and their corresponding spawning areas. However, because floating docks must be wide and long for stability, they blanket a relatively large area of the water's surface. See page 28, Preserving Aquatic Habitats, to discover why this can be good news or bad news for aquatic life.

In areas with significant littoral drift, any large floating object anchored in place on a semipermanent basis, such as a floating dock or floating breakwater, can cause erosion and aggregation around the object as well as upstream and downstream from it. And the dock doesn't have to be in contact with the submerged lands for this to happen.

Deciding whether a floating dock will be environmentally benign or harmful tends to be more area specific than site specific, which explains why in some jurisdictions floaters are the only residential dock option while other jurisdictions don't permit them at all. That said, in the majority of situations the floating dock is looked upon favorably. Just check with the appropriate local authorities to ensure that your waterfront isn't one of the exceptions.

The Theory of Flotation

Although evidence suggests that floating objects have been around since water was first invented, give or take a few millennia, it was Archimedes, the third-century B.C. Greek mathematician and part-time dock builder of enduring renown, who first made note of the natural law of flotation. Subsequently known as Archimedes' principle, this law applies to any object placed in water, be it a floating dock, a boat, or a rubber duck. What Archimedes noticed was that the weight of a floating or submerged object (such as you swimming) exerts a downward force on the water, which is met by an opposite upward force equal to the weight of the water the object displaces (that is, the amount of water your immersed body pushes aside). This upward force is known as *buoyancy*. If buoyancy is greater than the total weight of the object (such as you wearing your water wings), the object will float. If buoyancy is less (such as is the case with your run-of-the-mill cement boot), the object will sink. (see Calculating Required Buoyancy on pages 44 and 45).

Buoyancy acts on the center of gravity of the displaced volume of water — that theoretical point lying in the center of the space that used to be occupied by the now displaced water. From the standpoint of stability, ideally that point should coincide with the horizontal center of the dock. For example, if everyone should move with drinks, magazines, and deck chairs to one side of a floating dock, the upward force now pushes more on one side of the dock — the unoccupied side specifically — than the other. If it pushes up hard enough, the dock will tilt, perhaps enough to even

dump its load, after which the dock will be in balance once again (although the dumped load might be a bit upset).

And we don't need a bunch of dockside party animals to observe this phenomenon. It happens even when a single individual steps onto a floating dock — the end you step on sinks while the opposite end rises (although hopefully to a lesser extent than in the example above). And the farther away that opposite end is and the more heft it has, the greater the odds that the dock won't even acknowledge your intrusion. So generally, long and wide is good.

At the other end of the stability spectrum, your presence is immediately acknowledged on a skinny floater, especially one with a high center of gravity — much as it is when you stand at one end or to one side of a canoe. (Do not attempt this at home.) Having a brave volunteer present at the other end of the diminutive dock (or canoe) can help, adding heft at the opposite corner to partially offset your arrival — but it's better to count on a well-designed dock than on the generosity of others who may derive some form of perverse delight in witnessing your dunking.

The vertical location of both the dock's center of gravity and the center of gravity of the volume of the water displaced by the dock are also important stability factors. Basically, the lower either point sits, the greater a floating dock's stability. For a floating dock to react to any force exerted upon it (such as you stepping onto it), that force must not only move the dock itself but also displace the water surrounding any submerged portion of the dock, and water isn't pushed around as easily as air. The keel on a sailboat takes full advantage of this principle in order to resist being capsized by

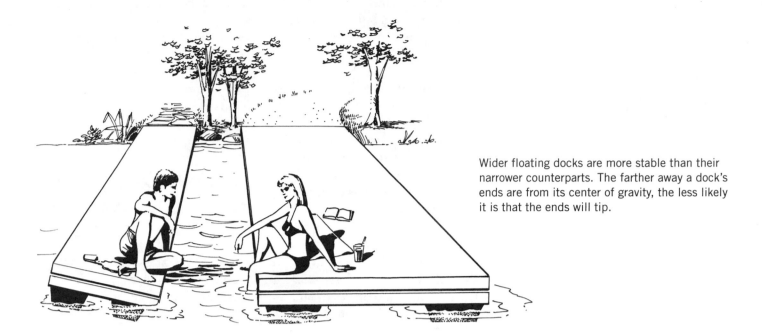

Wider floating docks are more stable than their narrower counterparts. The farther away a dock's ends are from its center of gravity, the less likely it is that the ends will tip.

the force the wind exerts against the sail (as I so astutely explained to a friend of mine after flipping his sailboat). And so too do the concrete floats in this chapter (which is what my friend suggests I try sailing the next time).

Essentially, lowering the center of gravity (whether of the dock or displaced water) has the same effect as increasing the width or length of the dock — it becomes more difficult for humanity or nature to upset the floating object's balance, much as sitting down in a canoe makes the canoe less prone to capsizing.

The total weight of the dock also affects stability. The heavier the floating dock, the less influence the weight of humanity has on it. It's simply a matter of percentages — getting everyone in the family to go on a diet might accomplish the same thing, but it's not nearly as much fun as stuffing ourselves with all sorts of calorific snacks while constructing or moving a hefty dock. Granted, the benefits of a prize heavyweight may seem debat-

able when struggling to either install or remove the dock, but at worst those potentially laborious activities will intrude on only two weekends — once in the spring and once in the fall for those of us located in the seasonally frozen North. For the remainder of the year, you will be grateful for the dock's stability every time you step on it.

A floating dock works best when it adheres to that credo that nearly sank the North American car manufacturers during the 1970s: Make it long, wide, low, and heavy. The consensus among dock builders points to a 6-foot-wide x 20-foot-long dock as the minimum size needed for a stable floater, this single section weighing in at about 1,000 pounds minimum. Six feet is also the maximum permissible dock width in several jurisdictions (although a few restrict widths to a mere 4 feet), which accounts for the widths of the docks built in chapter 18. That said, from the standpoint of stability 8 feet wide is even better, so feel free to adjust those plans (and bills of material) if local conditions permit.

Of course, there are always exceptions to the rule. Finger floats are, by definition, long and narrow and are used only for access to a moored boat (the finger floats in turn are moored to a larger dock). The width of a finger float should not be less than 10 percent of its length (and never less than 1 foot wide). With finger docks, stability is sacrificed for increased space for boat mooring.

If you are building a swim raft for the kids you can chuck stability into the drink because one of the highlights of youth is a bouncy and tipsy raft. For this reason (or lack of reason), swim rafts should not be bigger than 6 x 6 feet, and forget about keeping the weight low. Then, when your neighbors suggest that your offspring are not playing with a full deck, you can agree, and be proud of it. Just don't use the raft for mooring your boat.

Calculating Required Buoyancy, The Engineer's Way

Although a float's claimed buoyancy should reveal how much each float will support (in pounds or kilograms), there is no industry standard

Flotation Location

Placement of flotation also affects dock stability. If a dock is going to rock and roll, you will notice it first at the edges. (Obviously, the center of a dock is never the first part to dip into the water.) Any force applied to the perimeter of a dock — like jumping off the end to splash fellow swimmers — will cause the dock to rotate on its "roll axis," a theoretical point located roughly in the center of the dock. If flotation is distributed equally under a dock, the center of the dock gets a boost in buoyancy, which raises the height of the roll axis,

which in turn increases the dock's tendency to rotate. So for maximum stability, place the flotation around the perimeter of the dock, the area most likely to react to external forces (those people jumping off the end, for instance). Points of extraordinary loads — such as where a ramp joins the floating portion of a dock — are often good places to add an extra dose of flotation. These loads typically act on the dock like a lever, prompting it to rotate.

for determining the amount of buoyancy required to keep you and your dock afloat, or even how to measure it. Industry recommendations range from 20 to 35 pounds of buoyancy per square foot of decking, the variables being the type of flotation you choose and the weight of the dock. At the lower end of the weight scale, the buoyancy provided by any wood in contact with the water should be part of your calculation. At the upper end, it's not a simple matter of more is better — too much buoyancy will result in an unstable dock with high freeboard. And of course salt water yields slightly more buoyancy than fresh water, which may affect your calculations.

That confusion aside, in order to compare the claimed buoyancy of various floats, each must be measured in the same manner. Unfortunately, they aren't. For instance, Marv's Marvellous Float Co. may claim its float holds more than the model produced by We Try To Be Honest, Inc., but Marv may be measuring the ultimate buoyancy of the fully submerged float while Honest Inc. may be measuring the "working" buoyancy at 50 percent submerged. Which float has the most buoyancy? You don't know.

Ideally, we need to know not only how much weight each float can float, but also what the freeboard will be when the float is loaded up with differing amounts of weight. While this information occasionally can be coaxed out of the manufacturer, I'm only aware of one that makes it freely available to the public — Follansbee Dock Systems. For every different float in the company's catalog, you'll find the buoyancy corresponding to various depths of submersion — such as 4,

6, and 8 inches. The load the float is capable of supporting increases as the float is pushed farther into the water.

Of course, even when blessed with the thoughtfulness of Follansbee, you still need to calculate both dead load and live load. *Dead load* is the weight of the structure itself — all the boards and bits that go into making it, such as the framing, decking, the hardware that holds everything together, and even the floats themselves. Dead load is relatively easily to calculate. *Live load* consists of all the other loads a dock is likely to experience, a lengthy list of variables that includes people, weather (such as wind, rain, and snow), waves, currents, boats tugging on mooring lines, boats bashing into the dock, and wakes. Live load is a pain to figure out.

If this engineer's method seems intimidating, read on.

Calculating Required Buoyancy, The Quick Way

Ask. After deciding on your flotation system, check with the manufacturer or dealer about the quantities needed for your particular dock. Some float manufacturers offer plans for building docks using their floats, which would seem to make the task much easier. Unfortunately, some of these plans (even a few from well-known manufacturers) fail to meet the minimum standards set out in this book for a durable, safe, and stable dock. The solution is to compare any plans to those in this book and upgrade where necessary, or simply follow one of the plans in chapter 18.

Flotation Options

Type of Flotation	Description	Quantity Needed (approx. 6' x 20' dock)	Typical Size and Weight	Availability	The Quick Review	DIY Rating
Styrofoam BB	Blue polystyrene extruded-foam billet, closed-cell construction	4½ billets	7" x 20" x 96", 14 pounds and up	Building supply stores and dock builders	Light, reasonably strong when handled, easy but messy to cut; extruded closed-cell construction retains buoyancy; damaged by abrasion, chemicals, and fuels; not approved in all jurisdictions	DIY friendly
Dedicated plastic float drum (generic)	HDPE shell, usually black, empty or filled with secondary flotation, such as plastic foam or recycled pop containers	Varies greatly; average 6 floats	12" x 24" x 48", 15 pounds and up	Building supply stores, dock builders, and direct from manufacturer	Available in many shapes and sizes; durable; make a subframe unnecessary, offsetting the added expense of these floats; models with secondary flotation generally more durable	DIY friendlier
Steel tubes (generic)	Long steel tubes, sometimes foam filled	2	19" diameter x 24' long, 25 pounds per linear foot	Dock builders	Heavy, awkward to handle, expensive, very durable; no subframe required; overkill for small boats except in extreme conditions	Flotation must be assembled by dock builder, but decking can be DIY
HDPE pipe, heavy-duty (HD) and light-duty (LD) generic versions	Black HDPE pipes; corrugated versions have ribbed exterior; light-duty versions usually linked together to form a gridwork, sometimes foam filled	HD: usually 2; LD: varies greatly, average 6	HD: 16" diameter x 24' long, 6 pounds per linear foot of pipe; typical LD: 10" diameter x 20' long, 35 pounds per linear foot of assembled gridwork	Dock builders	HD: comparable to steel tubes but less awkward, larger sizes also overkill for small boats except in extreme conditions, can serve as part of the framework; LD: strong and light, modest buoyancy, suitable for small boats	Flotation must be assembled by dock builder, but decking can be DIY
Concrete float	Large EPS cube enclosed in reinforced concrete, usually with dimensional timbers bolted to the side top edges, securely linking the floats together	2 floats	3' x 6' x 10', approximately 65 pounds per square foot of deck	Dock builders	Extremely heavy, stable, and expensive; overkill for small boats except in extreme conditions	Definitely not DIY; nothing to do but park the deck chairs

pipe
docks

The *pipe dock* is basically a portable deck on stilts. Also referred to as a *portable, stationary,* or *portable stationary* dock, this category is a bit of a catchall, the common denominators being the dock's relatively light weight (and therefore portability) and vertical legs to keep the deck above water. Sometimes, wood or square metal tubing is called upon to serve as leg material but normal practice is to use round metal pipe — hence the "pipe dock" name tag even when the dock uses no pipe.

Pipe legs are usually 1½ to 3 inches in diameter and should not be confused with spuds or the much larger-diameter piles. While *spuds* are about the same diameter as pipe legs, spuds are driven into the ground in order to moor a dock in place horizontally; they do nothing to support the dock vertically. And while both piles and pipes can support the decking, *piles* are large, heavy-duty "legs" driven into the earth for the long haul while pipe legs usually rest upon the earth's surface, and are therefore easily moved.

Sure-Footed Notes

When pipe or square tubing is used, each leg usually has some form of plate at its base so that the weight supported by the leg is spread out over a larger area. This not only lessens the legs' tendency to sink into the earth, but it also gives the legs a better grip on most submerged surfaces. Hard-packed sand, stone, or rock bottoms do a much better job of supporting legs than clay (which offers minimal strength when wet) and mud, both of which invite legs to sink into the subaqueous mire. And as the legs sink, in nature's endearing and anarchic fashion no two corners of the dock ever sink to the same extent. Often such settling is not severe enough to constitute a safety hazard, but once in a while a deck gets twisted enough to qualify as a carnival ride in the local fall fair.

For those with soft bottoms (submerged lands, that is), placing a 2-foot-square concrete patio stone under each leg will often cure a leg's tendency to sink. If the dock

Pipe Docks
At a Glance

Best feature: Most versatile dock for shallow water, minimal environmental impact

Freeboard: Varies as water level changes but has some limited adjustability

Suitable sites, best: Less than 6½' depth at high water, firm bottom, waves, small boats (large with marine railway or boat lift), wetlands

Suitable sites, worst: Mooring large or heavy boats, any ice, deep mud, deep water (greater than 6½')

Winter hardiness: Remove if water may freeze

Size limits, small: Width not less than water depth, never less than 3' wide

Size limits, large: As big as you want to make it, assuming local laws permit

Environmental impact: Minimal (best)

Relative cost: $$

Building skills: Basic carpentry for wood versions; metal-framed versions not do-it-yourself friendly, but decking can be

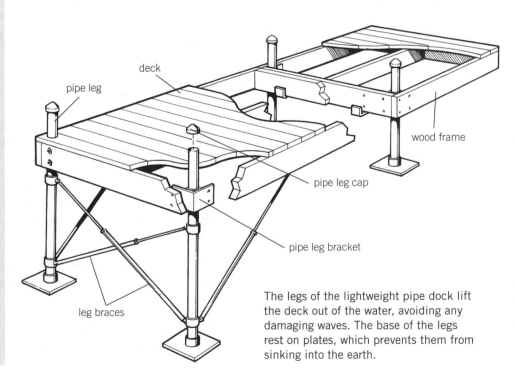

deck

pipe leg

pipe leg cap

wood frame

pipe leg bracket

leg braces

The legs of the lightweight pipe dock lift the deck out of the water, avoiding any damaging waves. The base of the legs rest on plates, which prevents them from sinking into the earth.

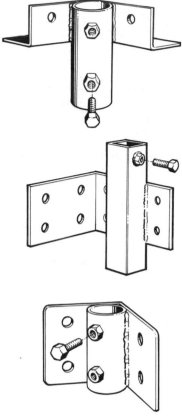

When brackets are used to fasten the frame to the pipe legs, the deck can later be raised or lowered according to fluctuating water levels.

is removed for the winter, these squares make dandy markers, resolving any springtime arguments about exactly where the dock resided the previous summer.

Leg Hold

The best way to secure the dock's legs to the framework is with adjustable clamps or special pipe-leg brackets with built-in cinch bolts. Sometimes legs are either bolted or screwed directly into framework, or even nailed in place where wood leg meets wood frame (to the delight of wood-destroying fungi everywhere; see chapter 17 for the rotten review). Regardless of leg type (round pipe, square tube, or even the poor choice of wood), clamps and pipe-leg brackets give a more durable dock plus the ability to adjust leg height.

It's this adjustability that elevates the pipe dock above its dock brethren, making it possible to maintain a level deck as the legs settle, and to lower or raise the deck to preserve a preferred freeboard. So while a pipe dock's freeboard changes with water level, proper pipe-leg brackets allow you to at least compromise with nature on freeboard (within the practical limitations of dock stability discussed below). This allows some leeway to set freeboard to suit the demands of the activity, making a properly constructed pipe dock the most versatile dock type for shallow-water applications. Without adjustability, you lose this advantage (such as is the case with nails or bolts).

Ready for Action

Very little of a pipe dock's deck and framing are exposed to the water because they remain elevated above it. A good, sturdy pipe dock is therefore largely unaffected by moderate wave action, the waves washing under the platform. This makes the pipe dock a good candidate for situations with plenty of surface activity, such as busy river channels where the wakes from passing boats may be a problem. However, because waves are allowed to pass under the dock unobstructed, boats moored to the opposite side or swimmers paddling about will be

Getting Your Sea Legs

While legs can provide excellent vertical support for whatever lies above them, not even sturdy legs are immune to the horizontal forces that push and tug on the load above. We experience the same forces when attempting to walk in a strong wind. In the case of a pipe dock, the frame, the deck, and any onboard baggage (such as people and fishing gear) are subject to constant horizontal attacks from wind, waves, and perhaps the abuse of barbarian boaters. The size of boats already tied up to the dock also contributes — the bigger the boat, the greater the force. The effect of these forces increases in proportion to the length of the dock legs — the longer the legs, the more leverage in the hands of the forces of destruction. What you notice on the dock is more sway.

The dock notices more wear. The vibration and constant pushing and shoving (nature is not very polite) stress the joints, particularly where legs meet framing. This problem is more pronounced on wooden-frame pipe docks (wood being both soft and heavy), although metal docks are certainly not immune.

To counter these forces, most dock builders recommend that any pipe dock in more than 3½ feet of water and all wooden versions (which are heavier) be equipped with leg braces.

exposed to the full brunt of wave action. So a pipe dock is a poor choice for creating protected areas, either for watercraft or for people.

Severe wave action, which often occurs in shallow water facing a large exposure (an ideal situation for a pipe dock, by the way), can put some of the lighter, aluminum-tube-frame docks at risk. And any lightweight dock is a risky choice for mooring large boats, or for mooring any boats in an area subject to severe wave action. It's a variation of the tail-wagging-the-dog theme, the boat wagging the dock in this case. Granted, such shenanigans don't seem to bother my dog, Martha, but they can make a mess of your pipe dock, bending legs (Martha's are designed to bend) and loosening joints because the legs resist bending.

Lightweight pipe docks have their place, nevertheless. Lighter construction usually costs less and requires less labor when it comes time to install or remove the dock. In the right situation — a protected bay, for instance — lightweight pipe docks are certainly up to the task of mooring smaller boats.

There are ways around the dilemma of dock weight versus safe mooring. For instance, when a pipe dock is used in partnership with a boat lift or marine railway, the boat can be dry-docked for overnight or long-term parking, or when threatened by nasty weather on the horizon (see chapter 16).

On a slightly different note, if your shoreline abode is in an area subject to seasonal freeze-ups, be aware that the slightest amount of ice movement can fold up a pipe dock like an accordion. Then you must face the music and replace the dock (to the tune of many dollars). So lightweight or heavyweight, it's essential that any pipe dock in an area subject to freeze-up be removed from the water for the winter. Removal requires getting into cold water in all but a few cases, such as with wheel-equipped pipe docks or lift pipe docks. While cold water can be quite a shock to those of us who tend to get into hot water, the actual task is lightened by the comparatively light weight of pipe-dock design (see chapter 14 for dock-removal tips).

Give Yourself a Raise

Adjusting the height of a pipe dock's deck can be done manually — which often means getting into the water, loosening set screws or removing pins, and then muscling the decking into place while retightening screws or inserting pins — or with a pipe-leg leveler.

Most leveling devices incorporate a winch placed on top of a leg. With a cable or chain hooked onto the deck, the dock owner loosens the set screws (or removes pins) while standing on the deck, then turns the winch handle until the deck moves either up or down to the preferred location. (I suppose you don't have to make it level — some folks might enjoy the funhouse thrills of a twisted deck.)

Another option is to get a Dock-A-Vator 750. Its most obvious advantage is price — about half that of other levelers. It's also a wonderful work of simplicity, basically a screw-jack. A screw-jack works something like a meat grinder — turn the screw, the screw remains where it is but the meat moves. With screw-jacks, it's usually your car that moves. In

the case of the Dock-A-Vator, it's your dock. As with other leveling devices, you set it on top of one leg and hook a chain around the deck. Then, using a T-bar-shaped handle, you simply turn the screw (after set screws have been loosened or pins removed), the deck rising or lowering in unison with the threads of the screw. Retighten the screws (or insert pins), move on to the next leg, and soon you're on the level again. The Dock-A-Vator 750 is designed to work with pipe legs having a 1.9-inch outside diameter, which means most 1½-inch pipe (pipe at this size being labeled by its inside diameter) and a few thin-walled 1¾-inch pipe legs. If the legs on your pipe dock differ from this, the manufacturer can in some cases provide a custom leveler for a small additional charge.

Regardless of which method you use — manual, winch, or Dock-A-Vator — to avoid damaging your dock, it's best to raise the deck in increments — perhaps 3 to 6 inches (depending on dock design), one leg at a time, until the dock is where you want it. (See Rules for Size and Stability on page 50.)

Rather than being secured to a dock's frame, removable decking is assembled in small, relatively lightweight panels held in place by gravity. Such a dock weighs more than the fixed-deck version, but it's easier to install or remove because the deck sections and the separate frame are individually lighter and easier to handle.

Removable decking usually makes a better-looking dock because the ends of the deck boards and the deck fasteners are hidden from view (see chapters 9 and 18 for details). As a bonus, wood-destroying fungi have a harder time settling in for a meal because the surface isn't punctured by fasteners. Also, you can gain access to the height-adjustment screws on pipe-leg brackets by simply lifting out a removable decking panel. On the downside, there is more labor and material involved in building this type of dock. This means more cost, especially if you're paying for the labor.

Rules for Size and Stability

Since a pipe dock is propped up on legs, in theory you can build it smaller than a floating dock and still have acceptable stability. That said, I have experienced the terror of pipe docks that sway underfoot so badly that walking in a straight line becomes impossible. What turns theory into reality?

The basic rule for pipe-dock stability is that the width of the dock should not be less than the depth of the water, and never less than 3 feet. The maximum depth suitable for pipe docks is about 6½ feet at high water. Floating, cantilever, suspension, or even permanent pile docks are better choices for deep-water applications. For pipe docks, total dock height will not exceed the depth of the water plus freeboard; so dock height is restricted by practical freeboards. Recommended freeboards for residential docks fall between 12 and 24 inches. And as mentioned in Room and Freeboard (see chapter 2), the lower the freeboard, the more stable the dock.

The distance between supporting legs also plays a significant role in stability. This distance should not be greater than 10 feet for wood frames, 12 feet for aluminum frames, and 16 feet for steel.

Because it relies on legs for stability, a pipe dock can be a good choice in shallower areas where tight quarters or sensitive aquatic vegetation make a wide, stable, floating dock impractical. Pipe docks also can serve admirably as steady walkways over shallow areas to larger sections of pipe dock, or perhaps to a floater anchored out in deeper water. In common with floating docks, the modular nature of most pipe docks makes it easy to attach sections together into enough configurations to satisfy the needs of most waterfront residents.

Individual sections can be held together using bolts, J- or U-shaped pipe-dock section connectors, or dock hinges.

Regardless of water depth, leg braces contribute strength and stability to a pipe dock. Leg braces are struts that run from the lower end of the pipe leg up at an angle to the dock platform, or to the leg on the opposite side, making an X or up-side-down V between pairs of legs. Secured at both ends, the braces form sturdy triangles, restricting movement at the leg-to-frame joint. Some braces are secured to the dock legs using one-piece sleeves, in which case the sleeves must be installed before the feet are attached to the bottoms of the legs. Other sleeves are of a two-piece design, allowing them to be installed after the dock is in place. This type is the best bet for retro-fitting. In all cases, telescopic braces make the tasks of installation and periodic adjustment easier, the struts being easily adjustable for length.

In common with most dedicated dock hardware, the type of brace your local supplier deals in is likely the type you will end up with; but be aware of your options should local materials not seem up to snuff.

Types of Pipe Docks

Pipe docks come in two basic flavors — wood frame and metal frame. Beyond that, the variations are almost as endless as the varieties of floating docks.

Wood-Frame Pipe Dock

The wood-frame pipe-dock category can be further divided into those with fixed decking and those with removable decking. In both cases, the decking material usually consists of wood but could be plastic, a wood-and-plastic composite, or even metal.

The two wood-frame pipe docks in chapter 18 are solid, economical, and easy to build. However, wood docks are heavy compared to aluminum ones, which adds stress to the joints where the pipe-leg brackets attach to the wood frame and to the joints of your body when the dock needs moving. Yet for the do-it-yourselfer only a crib can be less expensive to build than an all-wood, fixed-decking pipe dock, and the crib is certainly more labor intensive (see chapter 5).

While wood is an easy material to work with, making virtually any wood pipe dock well within the skills of the average proud owner of a hammer and saw, wood should never be used for the legs (see chapter 7).

Metal-Frame Pipe Dock

Climbing up the ladder of the pipe-dock hierarchy, things start to get a bit blurred (must be those heights). There are all-steel pipe docks, all-aluminum pipe docks, and versions of both with wood, plastic, or wood-and-plastic composite decking, usually in removable sections. In common with their wood counterparts, metal-frame pipe docks with removable decking provide easy access to height-adjustment screws, usually have a tidier appearance, are easier to install and remove, and take more labor and material to build than fixed-deck versions.

Steel is stronger than aluminum, but aluminum is lighter. In either case the frame should be an open, triangulated web structure, which provides maximum strength while presenting the least amount of surface area for waves and wind to push around. Any steel-frame pipe dock

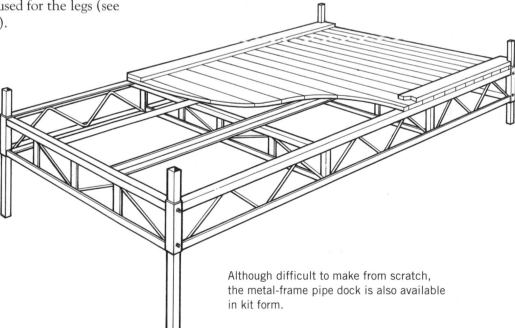

Although difficult to make from scratch, the metal-frame pipe dock is also available in kit form.

For a variety of good reasons, the pipe dock has become a favorite among many government agencies. Consider the advantages from the environment's point of view. First, the only part of a pipe dock to touch submerged lands is the foot at the base of each leg, a very small area of disruption. Since the feet and legs are the only part of the dock in continuous contact with the water, danger to aquatic life from paints or treated wood and metal is minimal as well.

A pipe dock's open undercarriage allows water to flow freely, again minimizing disruption to aquatic life and the natural processes of erosion and accretion. And because a stable pipe dock can be smaller than a floating dock, it shades submerged lands less (usually, but not always, an advantage; see chapter 2). Finally, fewer materials go into a pipe dock than a floating dock (at least in wood versions), so there's less pollution from manufacturing the materials.

Of all the dock types, a simple pipe dock is the least disruptive to the environment.

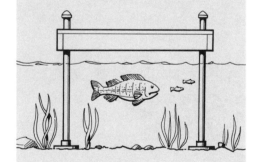

should be blessed with a protective coating to resist corrosion (see chapter 7).

Since few folks have access to welders, jigs, or galvanizing equipment, a metal pipe dock is not the stuff of basic do-it-yourself workshop projects. Although simple in appearance, metal-frame pipe docks are more difficult to construct well than all-wood docks. Fortu-nately, metal pipe docks are available in kit form, with either you-bolt-it-to-gether frames or stronger, more expensive, welded frames. Often, the decking is left to the purchaser, so even dedicated tinkerers can usually keep themselves amused.

Roll Out the Pipe Dock

If your shoreline and submerged lands are reasonably firm and form a gentle gradient, wheels on a pipe dock can make installation and removal much easier. Instead of lifting the dock in or out, you can simply roll it around, much as you would a wagon or wheelbarrow. You might even attach a trailer hitch to the dock and move it with an ATV or the family vehicle, making the job even easier.

While wheels can be installed on all four corners of a heavy-duty, all-steel pipe-dock section, a pair of wheels at just the deep end is more customary. A wheel-equipped pipe dock can also solve a problem with seasonal fluctuations in water level — just wheel the dock in or out as the water rises or falls.

Wheels can be installed directly onto the legs in lieu of base plates, the dock resting permanently on the wheels. Leg braces are essential for such docks. Or a pair of wheels can be attached to an independently mounted swing axle, in which case you guide the dock into position with wheels down and then raise the wheels and axle up off the submerged lands, usually by turning a handle. This lowers the dock down onto a normal set of legs and base plates. Come time to remove the dock (or relocate, or adjust the leg height), turn the handle in the other direction and the wheels and axle lower onto the submerged lands, raising the dock off its legs. Usually, the raised-wheel version is more stable.

permanent docks

The term *permanent dock* describes a human goal, not a reality — the sad truth is that nature doesn't recognize the concept. Nevertheless, blessed with sound construction techniques and appropriate conditions, a dock can be made nature resistant, serving faithfully for several generations, or at least for a few good storms.

Permanent docks are designed not to move. As a result, freeboard varies only with fluctuating water levels. Since this can make mooring a boat a tricky task, particularly when tides are at play, permanent docks are frequently used in conjunction with floating docks.

Residential permanent docks can be divvied up into three types: cribs, concrete piers, and permanent pile docks. Occasionally, governments regulate the choice, sometimes using lake size as the basis for their decisions. For instance, in Minnesota a lake must be greater than 500 acres in area before a permanent pile dock can be installed, and greater than 2,500 acres if a crib dock is to be considered. Or the composition of the submerged lands may determine

the choice, calling for cribs on bedrock and piles elsewhere. In many jurisdictions, new concrete piers or crib docks are either discouraged or banned outright because of their impact on submerged lands. So if you like the concept of theoretical permanence, find out what's acceptable to your local dock police.

The Crib Dock

A *crib* is a container; in the context of waterfront construction, a crib is a container for rock and stone. Cribs should not be confused with gabions (see Wired for Disaster on page 54). A proper crib is usually made from new, square-cut timber, but never from wire or driftwood or round logs wired and tacked together with hope. In some cases, concrete curb-like castings or steel are used instead of wood timbers, but this is not the stuff of do-it-yourself projects. The timbers are assembled into a slatted boxlike affair as shown in the illustration below. The crib is then filled with rocks, providing the necessary mass for submersion.

Crib Docks At a Glance

Best feature: Most economical and easy-to-build permanent deck for do-it-yourselfers

Freeboard: Varies with water level

Suitable sites, best: Less than about 8' of water, firm bottom, stable water levels, waves; makes good attachment point for floating or lift dock

Suitable sites, worst: Deep water, severe ice, fluctuating water levels, sensitive aquatic habitats, solid rock bottom unless pegged in place

Winter hardiness: Generally resistant to most ice conditions

Size limits, small: Height equal to width

Size limits, large: Budget and legalities (local laws)

Environmental impact: Extreme

Relative cost: $–$$$$ (do-it-yourself vs. contractor installed)

Building skills: Basic carpentry, but labor intensive; only strong backs need apply

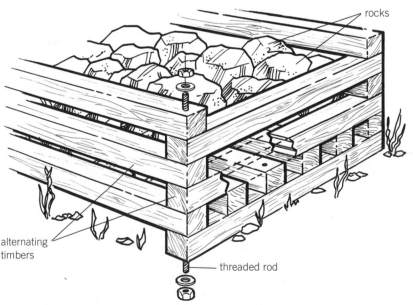

rocks

alternating timbers

threaded rod

Alternating timbers are bolted together to form the crib. The structure is then filled with rocks to hold it underwater and keep it from drifting. Two or more cribs that share a common deck make a sturdy dock.

Environmentally speaking, cribs leave a lot to be desired. Most of the problem results from a crib's size, since a corpulent crib is necessary for both stability and durability. Unfortunately, extra-large cribs leave a crushing footprint on the submerged lands and obstruct the flow of water and natural sedimentation. Owners often exacerbate the problem by installing vertical planking between cribs to hide the exposed deck structure as water levels drop. While it's true that the spaces between timbers and contained rocks provide useful habitat, the net result is a loss (see page 28, Preserving Aquatic Habitats).

From an environmental standpoint, cribs work best when placed above the high-water mark, using the strength of the crib as an anchoring point for structures such as floating and cantilever docks, or pipe docks.

Typically, two or more cribs are connected by a deck and its substructure. Ideally, the top timbers of a crib should extend to and overlap any adjoining cribs. While a series of cribs with a shared deck is most common, cribs also work well in other configurations. Sometimes the crib is built right into the shore, becoming the juncture between the shoreline and other dock types — such as a pipe dock or floating dock. A crib can be used as a breakwater, creating a nature-resistant harbor where none existed before. Incorporating a crib into existing shoals can take advantage of local topography to increase a dock's odds of surviving nature's tantrums. And a single crib with its own small deck can provide a landing or attachment point for one of the other types of docks.

A crib's principal nemesis, slipshod building practices notwithstanding, is ice. As the water in and around the crib freezes, it gets a firm hold on the crib. When water levels under the ice change, the ice pulls on the crib. If the water level rises, the ice can actually lift the entire crib, rocks and all. If the crib has been properly built (see Cribbed Notes, chapter 9) with a floor capable of holding the weight of the rocks, and the cribwork is well secured to shore, it will usually lower back down, intact, as the ice melts or the water level drops. If the water level drops, the crib must be able to carry the weight of the ice clinging to it without breaking or capsizing.

Another trick to longevity is to angle the crib so that it faces into the prevailing winds, the direction of which should be determined when the waterfront is at its nastiest (spring breakup, for example). The decking above remains in the desired orientation to shore; it's only the cribs below that are angled. Ice and heavy waves are therefore not as likely to get a purchase on a crib's corner, the weakest point, butting the crib broadside instead. (The stress is then transferred and shared between two corners instead of just one.)

Rules for Size and Stability

The width and length of a crib should be at least as great as its height. In other words, if the water is 4½ feet deep and we want 18 inches of freeboard at high water,

Wired for Disaster

Gabions are inexpensive wire- or plastic-mesh baskets designed to hold 4- to 8-inch (approximately) stones, rocks, or chunks of broken-up concrete. Gabions are ugly, and strong currents, waves, and ice will distort their shape, causing them to sag and flatten in time. Meanwhile, they do a good job of tearing the skin of a passersby.

Perhaps it's not surprising that many jurisdictions are becoming increasingly wary of gabions as a solution to waterfront problems. Washington State's Department of Ecology sums up the gabion's attributes as "limited durability and a potential hazard to shore users and the shoreline environment," while Ontario's Ministry of the Environment and Energy claims that "gabions have proved unsuccessful in harsh wave environments," including breakwall and retaining-wall applications, which is where they usually turn up.

When you consider the difficulty of attaching any sort of decking system to these heinous devices, you might ask why gabions continue to break out like pimples along North America's shorelines. The answer lies in their comparatively low cost.

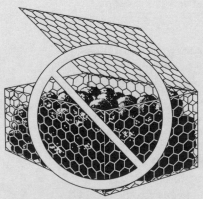

Gabions are ineffective breakways and are of limited durability. Refrain from using them.

the minimum crib size would be a 6-foot cube (the width and length typically being equal). Yep, that's a fatty for sure, containing a ton or two of rocks for both you and the ice to move. Perhaps this is why some professionals and most do-it-yourselfers make narrower cribs. Unfortunately, these easier-to-build slender jobbies give nature too much leverage, putting the crib at risk during spring breakup or a pounding storm, either of which can jostle a crib or topple the whole thing over. Disturbed cribs can twist a deck into a slope so steep that roofing contractors will drop by to bid on installing shingles.

Obviously, the height-width rule makes cribs unsuitable for deep-water applications.

Material Considerations

Wood is the best choice for do-it-yourself crib construction, preferably hemlock, Douglas fir, or a comparably strong and decay-resistant species. And since you can't play crib without a full deck, a crib needs to be topped off with both a subframe and decking. Both are usually wood too, although there is no reason why plastic could not be used for the deck if your material preferences bend in that direction.

A few very experienced professional dock builders have been making cribs out of steel, the crib slightly tapered as it rises, the bottom corners pegged into submerged lands. What results is an extremely strong and nature-resistant crib. It is also both expensive and beyond the requirements of most residential waterfronts.

Rock-Bottom Bargain

Years ago, filling the crib was a simple matter of diving into the surrounding water and hauling up the rocks. Okay, so it wasn't that simple. But speaking from experience, it was still good fun for a young lad with visions of building the eighth wonder of the world. Since then, we have realized the error of such ignorant enthusiasm. Liberating rocks from submerged lands destroys fish habitats and crucial spawning areas, which is why it's illegal in many jurisdictions to remove rocks or soil from below the high-water mark. So whether legal or not, no rocks should be taken from the water but from above the high-water mark instead. Both the fish and your chiropractor will thank you.

Concrete Pier

The *concrete pier* holds few secrets, for what you see is what you get — a big, monolithic block of concrete, often with an integral boat ramp. The dock's "deck" is simply the monolith's top surface.

In common with cribs, concrete piers can be merged into shorelines to provide a shoreline juncture for other types of dock, or they can create safe harbors, either in conjunction with the natural topography or in spite of it.

Working with concrete projects of this size is a job for a contractor with experience in waterfront concrete formwork. However, it has been my experience that contractors will occasionally let do-it-yourselfers watch, and sometimes even help, if desperate. When a concrete delivery truck sank up to its axles in the spring mud next to our cottage, the contractor let me use my backhoe to get the concrete from the truck to the far end of a foundation pour. He even gave me a hat with the company logo on it so I could feel like part of the crew. (Both hat and foundation are wearing well.)

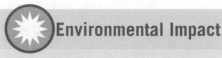
No dock does a better job of disrupting currents and littoral drift than the concrete pier. Erosion of the submerged lands at the base of the pier can often be a problem too. And unlike the slatted sides of the crib, the concrete pier provides no substitute home for refugee aquatic life. From an environmental point of view, the concrete pier is the worst dock you can inflict on your shoreline.

Heavy Going

Keep in mind that concrete trucks are extremely heavy, awkward to maneuver ("You don't want that tree there, do you?"), and that ready-mix concrete should be out of the truck and into the forms within 90 minutes of adding water to the dry ingredients. This obviously places practical limits on where a concrete pier can be built, though barges can sometimes ferry the trucks to a waterfront site (at an additional cost, of course).

If this is beginning to sound expensive, that's because it is. But if your enthusiasm for concrete prevails over budgetary concerns, make sure you specify a nonslip surface for the deck. The sides, however, should be as smooth as possible to deter the growth of any slimy varieties of aquatic vegetation.

Like the crib, the concrete pier is not suitable for deep water. Although stability comes with width, the substantial bulk of concrete piers can help them survive being narrower than cribs installed in comparable depths, particularly when the pier's reinforcing rods are pegged into the bedrock below (talk to a good contractor).

A well-made concrete pier is arguably as close to permanent as you'll get, presenting a heavy, formidable front against nature. But it is not indestructible.

The Permanent Pile Dock

The *permanent pile dock* is a heavyweight, long-term version of the pipe dock — still a deck on stilts, but definitely not portable. And unlike pipe docks, pile docks are not do-it-yourself with the exception of perhaps the decking and framing. Instead of resting on the surface of submerged lands as the legs of pipe docks do, piles are driven, jetted, or socketed (see below) into earth. The barges and pile drivers required for this job are not the stuff of home workshops.

In shallow water, the concrete pier is about as stable and permanent as a dock can be. Ask the contractor for a nonslip surface for the deck, or you will be spending an awful lot of time on your back.

Piling, whether supporting a permanent dock or mooring a floater, is a good choice where wind, waves, or wakes are at their worst behavior, and the water is not too deep for piling to be installed. So how do you determine what type of pile works best for a specific location, or how far the piles should be sunk into the submerged land, or if the submerged land is even suitable to hold a pile? Let me answer with a quote from the best textbook on commercial marinas: "The methodology employed in the analysis is not universally agreed upon by active practitioners in the field of structural design." Which is an engineer's way of saying that they really don't know what's going on. Basically, there's a lot of guesswork (educated or otherwise) involved. Here are a few guidelines to consider, gathered from engineers and the tradespeople doing the actual installations.

Silt and mud are poor choices for piles unless better soil lies within a reasonable distance below. At the opposite end of the soil-hardness scale, hard, solid rock works great, but it must be drilled and the piles socketed in place to provide the necessary leverage.

Exposed Piles

Any portion of a pile sitting above solid earth — including any part of the pile exposed to soft mud, water, or air — is subject to lateral movement. The more pile exposed, the more leverage nature has to try and wiggle it loose. Braces added between the piles can help control lateral movement just as they do on the legs of pipe docks — the longer the exposed portion of the piles, the more necessary the bracing. Exposed lengths greater than 25 feet can make piles a very expensive or impractical proposition.

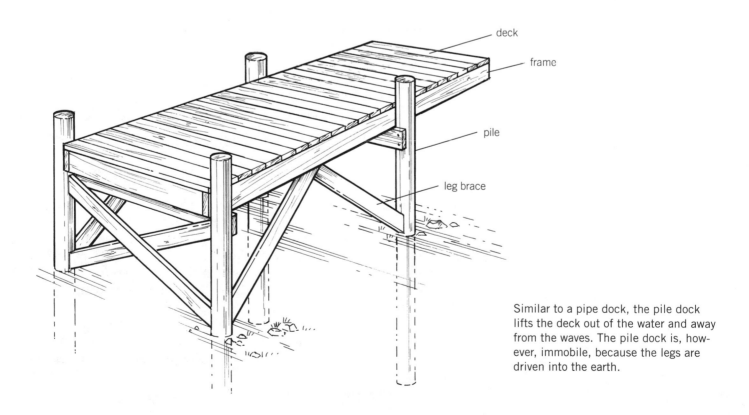

deck

frame

pile

leg brace

Similar to a pipe dock, the pile dock lifts the deck out of the water and away from the waves. The pile dock is, however, immobile, because the legs are driven into the earth.

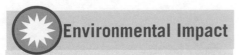

How far a pile must be sunk down into the earth depends on the makeup of the submerged lands, the dock's exposure to destructive forces, and the size of boat you expect to moor there (the bigger the boat, the greater the stress on the piles). As a rough guide, a pile should be sunk into the earth at least 15 feet, but 20 to 40 feet is better. The distance between piles is normally about 10 to 15 feet.

Installation Methods

The traditional method for installing piles is to pound them in, just as you might do with a couple of wooden stakes for an impromptu game of horseshoes. However, since piles are somewhat larger than horseshoe stakes, a huge machine known as a pile-driving hammer is substituted for the household mallet — hence the term *driven piles.* Driven piles work in most geological formations, including limestone, but not in hard, solid rock such as the Precambrian rock of the Canadian shield found along much of the eastern border region of Canada and the United States.

A *jetted pile* is pushed down into the earth as a high-pressure stream of water clears a path immediately below it. Give a garden hose to a child in a sandbox and you'll soon see how well a stream of water can move earth. In both cases, the trick is control — too big a hole and the pile will wiggle around. Jetting works best in soils that are easily pushed around, such as sand.

A *socketed pile* is placed into a predrilled hole, like a lightbulb into a lamp. This system allows piles to be installed into hard, solid rock, although socketing is occasionally used in more permeable types of rock that can be pile-driven, such

as shale and limestone. Because of the drilling process, this is a very expensive operation. Socketed piles can be "glued" into place with grout, sometimes using reinforcing rods that extend into the surrounding rock. Nature at its nastiest may be able to bend or break off a grouted pile, but the part secured into the rock will likely give the pyramids of Egypt a good run for longevity.

Reset Routine

Neither driven nor jetted piling can boast of such tenacity, both having a tendency to rise out of their homes over time. Rising piles must therefore be periodically *reset* — meaning pounded back down — so it's a good idea to plan for this possibility when designing the dock.

Ignoring the problem of ice, which can lift a pile entirely out of the ground during the course of one winter, the distance that piles will rise in your neck of the waterfront is dependent on local soil and weather conditions. Speak to your contractor and neighbors who have pile docks to get an idea of the frequency, cost, and inconvenience of such ongoing maintenance.

Material Considerations

Piles can be made of wood, steel pipe, steel H-beams, concrete, or HDPE pipe. Both steel and HDPE pipe can be filled with concrete for added strength. A good contractor will advise you on which material and installation method is best suited to your waterfront and budget.

Framing materials are usually metal or wood, while the decking can be of wood, metal, concrete, or plastic. Wood is the best choice for do-it-yourselfers.

specialty docks

Specialty docks include cantilever docks, suspension docks, and lift docks. All three are dramatic to behold, rare, and usually expensive. While there are similarities between specialty docks and the docks discussed in chapters 3, 4, and 5, cantilever, suspension, and lift docks are much more complex, often beyond the skills of even professional dock builders. So be forewarned: These docks do not lend themselves to the average tinkerer, although some variations can be installed without their decking, leaving at least this part of the building task to folks determined to exercise sacred build-it-yourself rights.

Cantilever and Suspension Docks

Taken to their design extremes, cantilever and suspension docks are perhaps the most visually stunning of all dock types. In both cases the dock juts out over the water, seemingly supported by nothing but a layer of air. No part of the dock touches the water; no part of the dock touches submerged lands. The deck simply hangs in space, unaffected by waves, wakes, or currents,

held there apparently by magic. So what's the trick?

The *cantilever dock* works in the same manner as an overhanging balcony, the dock's frame stretching from shore out over a support (the fulcrum point) and then overhanging the water. The maximum length of the dock, and what proportion of that length is land based, is determined by how well the land-based end is anchored to the shore. It's the land-based end that supports the load. Customarily, a cantilevered dock has 2 feet of onshore dock for every foot overhanging beyond the support. That said, I have seen well-anchored cantilever docks supported at their midpoint, and even closer to their shore end when that end is embedded in concrete. Minimalist land-based cantilevers such as these usually employ triangulated bracing for additional support, the braces running from under the overhang back to the support.

The *suspension dock* has more in common with a suspension bridge than a balcony. Picture one half of the Golden Gate Bridge. What you get is the Golden Gate Dock. Instead of connecting two bits of land together, it ends out over the water.

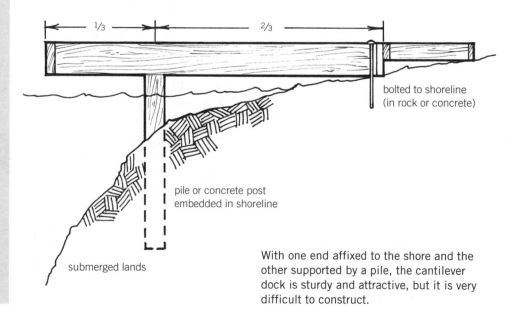

With one end affixed to the shore and the other supported by a pile, the cantilever dock is sturdy and attractive, but it is very difficult to construct.

Of all the dock types, cantilever and suspension docks cause the least disruption to the water or submerged lands — it's difficult to disrupt what you don't touch. However, in common with floating docks, the shadow they cast over the aquatic environment could be either beneficial or harmful to aquatic life (see page 28, Preserving Aquatic Habitats, for clarification). Assuming that shade is not harmful, a well-designed, -constructed, and -installed suspension dock can have negligible environmental impact. A cantilever dock, on the other hand, will disturb the uplands because it depends so much on the shoreline for leverage. This in turn can disrupt both aquatic and land-based life.

Unlike the cantilever dock, a suspension dock's deck does not extend onto the uplands beyond the shoreline. Instead, it's attached to a shore structure with super-duty hinges. A tower shaped like an inverted U, approximately the width of the dock and typically about 10 feet high, is permanently attached to the dock frame at the hinge point (the fulcrum). Twin cables or rods run from an on-shore anchor over the top of the tower to the dock frame, approximately three-quarters of the distance out along its decking. The onshore anchor is located about the same distance back from the hinge point. Voilà, a demi-bridge.

Since both cantilever and suspension docks remain out of the water, neither demands a minimum water depth for installation. However, because freeboard varies only with water level, cantilever and suspension docks are not the answer for waterfronts with extreme changes in water level.

Neither dock type is immune to the wicked ways of ice. During spring breakup, pack ice can collect under the deck and lift it right off

its mounting. And wind-driven spray during freezing weather can create so much ice on the deck's undercarriage that the weight can collapse the dock. Fortunately, most suspension docks are also lift docks (see below), so the deck can be raised to avoid such shenanigans. A cantilever dock does not share this advantage. On the other hand, that long, continuous frame of the cantilever avoids a suspension dock's ugly cables, stays, or towers that can spoil the view.

Both dock types have practical limits to the length of overhang — about 8 feet for the cantilever, usually with about 16 feet of onshore decking and about 50 feet of total dock length for the suspension dock. Greater distances are not considered cost effective.

A short, cantilevered overhang of about 1 to 2 feet can work very well along bulkheads (see Glossary), cribs, breakwaters, and the like. And when a large, shore-based deck is desirable (such as over a boulder-strewn shoreline), the cantilever dock again becomes a reasonable option.

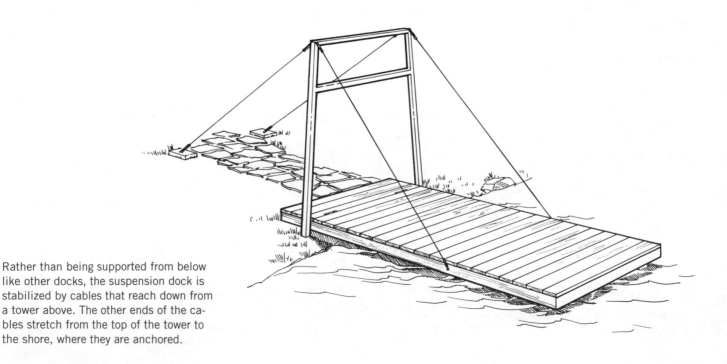

Rather than being supported from below like other docks, the suspension dock is stabilized by cables that reach down from a tower above. The other ends of the cables stretch from the top of the tower to the shore, where they are anchored.

Lift Docks

Lift docks come in a trio of flavors — lift pipe docks, lift floating docks, and lift suspension docks. The freeboard of each depends on the type of dock being lifted (see the related sections on each dock type).

The lift-dock concept is much like that of a classic drawbridge. While the drawbridge of a castle was raised to keep out unwanted weekend guests, the lift dock is raised for its own protection, hoisting it out of the reach of winter ice.

To avoid damage from ice, the lift dock must have its mounting point (which is also the lift's pivot point) beyond the reach of ice buildup. Obviously this mounting point also must be strong enough to support the weight of the hoisted dock. (Only the lift suspension dock uses this mounting point for structural support when the dock is lowered.)

To raise nonsuspension versions, a lightweight tower is attached to the dock at the pivot point, cables are run over the tower and secured to the far end of the dock, and a land-based winch then raises and lowers the dock. (The lift suspension dock keeps the required rigging year-round.) Towers and cables are never candidates for shoreline beauty pageants and often are downright ugly, especially when obstructing your or your neighbor's favorite view. Keep this in mind when deciding where to locate the dock.

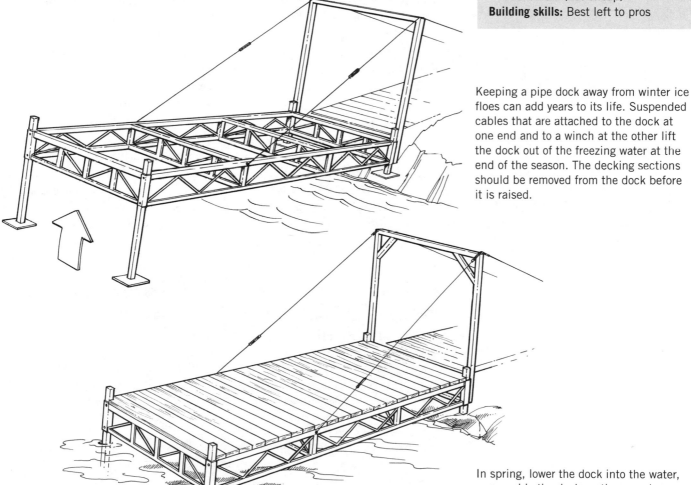

Keeping a pipe dock away from winter ice floes can add years to its life. Suspended cables that are attached to the dock at one end and to a winch at the other lift the dock out of the freezing water at the end of the season. The decking sections should be removed from the dock before it is raised.

In spring, lower the dock into the water, reassemble the deck sections, and you are ready for another season of fun and enjoyment.

Decking sections are normally removed from a lift pipe dock for winter storage. Once raised, the skeletal frame points skyward at about a 30-degree angle to keep the legs out of ice. In the spring, simply lower the dock, disconnect (or lower) the tower and cables, and re-install the decking. That's as close as you need to get to the water.

For either floating or suspension types, the decking is usually not removed before the ceremonial raising of the dock, but left as installed (another advantage for those not keen on manual labor). Since there are no legs left dangling below, the angle necessary to keep the dock out of the ice is often half that of the lift pipe dock. (Obviously, such a dock has to be designed to cope with any expected snow loads, a good reason to leave lift docks to the pros.) Dock ladders must be either pivoted back onto the deck or removed to prevent ice from grabbing hold and pulling the dock down to its destruction. Lower the dock in the spring, disconnect (or lower) the tower and cables if it's a pipe or floating version, then get out the deck chairs and suntan lotion — or an umbrella if you're blessed with my weather luck.

High winds can increase loads at the mounting point of any raised lift dock, but especially for docks longer than about 20 feet. To reduce this potential stress, install *sway cables* or *telescopic braces* from each side of the dock back to a shore mount.

Where wave action is strong or access to a boathouse is required, lift pipe docks can be combined with marine railways. Sometimes, twin pipe docks straddle the railway for easier docking and launching of the boat. Come winter the entire dock and the end section of railway are hoisted up as a unit. (Lift marine railways with no attached dock are also available from some dock builders.)

Seasonal waterfront residents who rely on the lake or river out front for their water supply may be able to attach their water-supply line to the lift dock, hoisting both the dock and water line out of the water as one. This eliminates any need to get into cold spring or fall water. However, I know of one person with such a setup who goes for his mandatory first swim of the season immediately after lowering the dock and water line. Pride molds some of us into do-it-yourselfers and others into do-it-the-first-timers. I fall into the former category when facing frigid spring waters. To each his own.

A Dock Only Its Builder Could Love

I have seen do-it-yourself versions of lift pipe docks. At the risk of offending their proud owners, the ease of use, longevity, and aesthetics of these home-crafted wonders are no match for the work of the professional dock builder. With nonlifting floating or wooden pipe docks, it's possible to come close to a dock builder's efforts. The same cannot be said for lift docks, ingenious use of boat-trailer winches and recycled lumber notwithstanding. However, as I personally know all too well, the pride of building your own plus any real or imagined savings often outweigh the disadvantages of owning an ugly-duckling dock. Just curtail your do-it-yourself instincts to lift pipe docks, not floating or suspension versions.

The Art of Dock Building

I n past chapters, we examined your shoreline and considered the various methods to successfully merge that shoreline with your activities. Your shoreline, your solution. Now we delve into the materials, tools, and techniques required to realize that solution — in other words, the art of building a well-crafted dock.

Chapter 7 introduces us to the materials of dock building and how these materials perform in a waterfront environment. Understanding construction materials allows us not only to choose the right materials for the task, but also to make the best use of a material's properties. Chapter 8 looks at the tools, hardware, and nuts and bolts of dock building — both the necessities and the niceties — reaffirming that we don't have a screw loose for insisting that our dock be screwed (and bolted) together

properly. Chapter 9 combines the information from chapters 7 and 8 along with some interesting tricks of the trade that make our dock both easier to build and more soundly constructed. Chapter 10 is the token inspirational chapter, a portfolio of design ideas to whet your waterfront desires, with comments as to why each works (or doesn't work). These chapters everyone should read. Even if not intending to follow the do-it-yourself path, understanding the makings of a good dock allows you to knowledgeably judge the work of a professional.

And finally, in acknowledgment that art is admittedly, and regrettably, also work, chapter 11 examines the alternatives to doing it all yourself, from just dabbling in the arts to being a full patron of the art of dock building — in other words, how best to deal with the pros.

the materials of dock building

The basic ingredients of docks are wood, metal, plastic, and concrete. In one form or another, wood and metal find their way into most residential docks, so the sections and asides related to these materials should be considered essential reading. The sections on plastic or concrete are worth reading even if your plans don't call for their use because they may reveal a better method of handling some aspect of your dock. (Personally, I always glance at the entire menu before making important decisions.)

All materials — even nature's own rock — are under continuous assault from two very destructive forces — stress and decay. Not even the pyramids are impervious to the ruinous ways of these two powers. Nevertheless, even though we can't prevent dock degeneration, we can at least slow the process.

The secret to limiting the effects of stress is to distribute the loads (a technique that also holds true for humans). This applies to the entire dock, from connectors to anchors to joints — the load must be shared by as much of the structure as possible. (See chapters 8 and 9 for more on relieving your dock's stress; see your doctor regarding your own.)

Failure due to stress is greatly hastened by decay. Wood rots, plastic degrades, concrete spalls and cracks, metal corrodes, rock erodes — it's all part of the regenerative process we call nature, the nutrients and residues of decomposing materials or species giving shape or life to those materials and species that follow.

Generally, decay thrives in an environment of warmth, a little moisture, and a little oxygen, all readily available at your local shoreline. Too much or not enough of any of these ingredients and decay moderates its attack. The secret to longevity therefore is to take advantage of this weakness, using good design and appropriate materials to discourage the onset and growth of decay. (See chapter 17 for ways to deal with wood rot once it has taken hold.)

Wood

Wood is the most common material for residential docks. It is relatively easy to work with, reasonably priced, and has some *give*, allowing it to bend slightly under duress. It's also at its strongest under short-term loads, a decided advantage to waterfront structures that tend to get clobbered by every uncle who buys a new ski boat. And things made of wood usually are rebuildable when nature proves the better of humanity once again.

Wood is a renewable resource, allowing us, theoretically, to grow new trees to replace those we cut down to make docks or books about how to make docks.

Wood exposed to climatic change (all wood not continuously immersed in water) constantly expands and contracts at the caprice of nature, and not in a uniform fashion. In fact, wood is at its worst behavior down at the waterfront — wet and fat one moment; drying and on a diet the next. Therefore, joining pieces of wood in dock building requires different techniques than the accepted practices of house and general carpentry (see chapter 9). This adds a bit to the cost of construction, but without it any dock will suffer premature failure.

With the exception of perhaps a few private sawmills, wood suitable for construction is square-edged, dressed lumber known as *dimensional stock*. It is sold in standard sizes, theoretically measured in rough-sawn condition before planing takes place. This is why a nominal 2 x 4 measures only 1½ inches by 3½ inches, and so on.

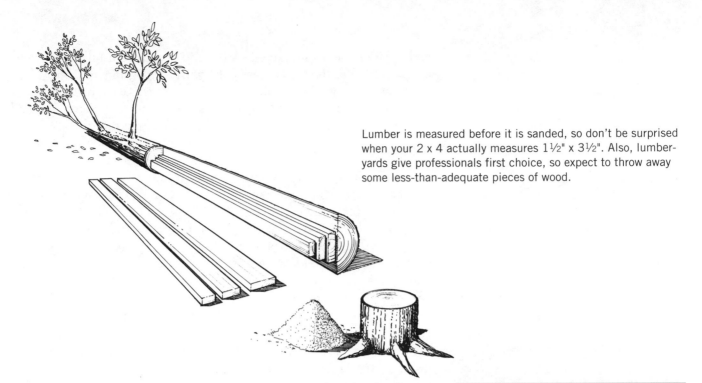

Lumber is measured before it is sanded, so don't be surprised when your 2 x 4 actually measures 1½" x 3½". Also, lumberyards give professionals first choice, so expect to throw away some less-than-adequate pieces of wood.

Recently, planks that are a full inch thick after planing have become a popular choice for decking. Known as "⁵⁄₄" (spoken "five-quarter"), this material costs less than nominal 2-inch stock. Although close in strength to the nominal 2-inch-thick stock, it's also more prone to warping and splitting. In fact, you really need to predrill ⁵⁄₄ stock to avoid split ends.

When it comes to getting quality wood, the do-it-yourselfer is always at a disadvantage. Understandably, the choice goods usually go to the best customers, the professionals who buy lumber year in and year out. And lumberyards don't want you to pick through their stocks for the better pieces — it leaves them with a lot of junk. Budget for about a 10 to 20 percent rejection rate.

For most dock construction, western red cedar, redwood, cypress, and eastern white cedar (in that order) all offer reasonable longevity and beauty, especially in concert with the appropriate hardware (see chapter 8).

The exception is cribs and piles. For either, it's tough to beat the strength of Douglas fir. Fir is much stronger than the softer decking species, such as cedar, but lacks the same degree of natural resistance to rot. Hemlock and tamarack also work reasonably well for cribs, but both are more prone to warping. Western larch, pine, and even spruce can be used for piles if fir is not available.

Due to the continuous immersion in water, wood treated with preservatives, including the pressure-treated green stuff, is generally not recommended for cribs or piles. In some jurisdictions, it is illegal to use such biocides and toxic compounds for cribs and piles. Others will allow their use if you can prove that no feasible alternative to toxic treatments is available, while still others don't care. Check with local authorities. Or better yet, just avoid chemically treated wood in these instances. (See Deterring Rot with Chemical Preservatives on page 66.)

Wood of any variety is a poor choice for pipe-dock legs. The fasteners where the legs meet the frame are under heavy, highly concentrated stress. This causes wear, which causes the dock to sway, which causes more wear, and on

General Dock-Decay Deterrents

Perhaps the greatest threat to the life of a wooden dock is rot. A few simple precautions, however, can deter potential decay.

- Provide ventilation under the dock (avoid completely enclosed undercarriages) and through the decking (one of several good reasons to leave gaps between decking boards).
- Provide for surface runoff and avoid creating pockets or areas that can trap water (such as by leaving gaps in the decking, slightly sloping a concrete deck, and not creating "dams" along the perimeter of any deck or where materials join).
- Don't load the dock with excess trim — materials pressed together hold water, air, and warmth. This is one reason why wood rots and fasteners corrode so frequently around mooring hardware.
- Minimize butt ends such as where the ends of decking boards meet over framework, another dandy place for water to seep in but not escape. Wood decking is particularly prone to rot in this situation because water is naturally absorbed through the highly porous end grain.

and on. Metal legs with pipe-dock brackets transfer the load to more of the frame and therefore are not as prone to wear around bolt holes.

Wood Rot

Because decay needs oxygen, wood continuously immersed in water (the colder the better) will last longer than wood exposed to air and water. The consensus among professional dock builders gives 40 to 50 years for the submerged stuff versus 15 to 25 years for any wood from the waterline to the top of the deck, the worst area being right at the waterline. Wood piles and cribs in areas experiencing daily fluctuations of water level generally have a rotten time of it.

Painting and staining

A dock is one of the toughest tests for paint and stain. A coating on a dock routinely endures UV degradation, blistering hot rays from the sun, acid rain, seasonal temperature extremes, snow and ice, melting snow and ice (which can scrape paint right off the wood), and a cycle of wash, rinse, and dry that dutifully carries on with Maytag-like reliability. Below deck, restricted ventilation, seasonal temperature extremes, and continuous exposure to high moisture and humidity all conspire to strip coatings from surfaces. Heck of a world, ain't it?

Despite all this, most folks paint or stain their dock. When new, these coatings can look great and appear to protect the dock from decay. However, once paint and stain begin to fade and peel (and they all do), the dock looks really bad. Damaged coatings (whether damaged by humanity or the forces of nature) can actually trap water between the coating and the wood, creating an ideal spot for a wood-destroying fungal family to take up housekeeping. So once committed to paint or stain, you're in it for the long haul, recoating the dock every few years. Some folks actually enjoy this task. Some folks enjoy pain too, I've heard.

Choose a coating specifically formulated for outside decks (or docks). For docks, a finish that is absorbed into wood will last longer and is better for the wood than a

Deterring Rot with Chemical Preservatives

Products containing creosote (CRT), pentachlorophenol (PCP), and copper chromated arsenate (CCA) all have the potential to extend the life of wood. These toxic chemicals discourage the growth of wood-rotting fungi and attack by wood-boring insects and the like. Unfortunately, there is some evidence to suggest that the murderous ways of these wood preservatives are not restricted to the target fungi or bugs, but also can cause health problems in other living things, such as humans.

The legalities regarding the use of these chemicals vary throughout North America, the more environmentally concerned jurisdictions often restricting or banning the use of all or some of these wood preservatives.

Even where their use is permitted, never lose sight of the fact that these products were designed to kill. Treat them with the same respect as you would a loaded gun. One of the primary rules of safe gun handling is to never point a gun at anything you don't want to kill, so don't let these chemicals touch anything you don't want to kill. Don't let the chemicals slop or spill onto the ground (and possibly seep into the groundwater), and don't let them touch your skin. Never apply chemicals or cut treated wood near water. And when working with chemicals or even when cutting the treated wood, wear rubber gloves, coveralls, and an appropriate mask (most manufacturers and governments recommend at least that much). Also, all treated wood should be thoroughly dried (some jurisdictions suggest 6 months for CRT) and then be scrubbed and wiped to reduce residual oils prior to being placed in the water. And never sand or rout treated wood — the dust can be lethal.

finish that forms a film on top of the wood (the inevitable scratches and blisters that form in the film will trap water, creating the ever-popular domicile for decay). If you settle on a gloss finish, also invest in some SLIPPERY WHEN WET signs to reduce the odds of guests landing on your dock with a thump.

"Au naturel"

In my view, painting or staining is too much work when there's swimming, fishing, and dockside lounging to be done. I let the wood go gray naturally.

Nature supplies the preferred decking species with their own naturally decay-resistant resins, good for about 15 to 25 years, no nasty chemicals or warranty needed. Left to their own devices, these species will all weather to a mellow, soft gray and you won't have to refinish the dock every couple of years. The entire exterior of my house, decks included, is "finished" in this manner because I'm not big on creating maintenance where none is needed. (And, yes, this philosophy of letting it gray naturally also extends to my hair.)

The natural preservatives in some woods, such as cedar, do have a corrosive effect on some unprotected metals — steel, for instance — which in turn can create black stains around the area of the metal. The solution is to use only metals with a protective coating or that are inherently resistant to corrosion (see Metal on page 68).

Pressure-Treated Wood

One method of minimizing contact with toxic preservatives during construction is to use *pressure-treated* spruce or pine, that Kermit-green alternative seen on countless decks,

playground equipment, and docks. Copper chromated arsenate (CCA) is the pesticidal ingredient here.

Pressure-treated pine or spruce is about 20 to 30 percent less expensive than the preferred decking species, such as cedar, but because the grades of lumber set aside for treatment are usually at the bottom end of the lumber scale, pressure-treated wood is much more susceptible to warping and cracking when exposed to weather than the untreated decking species, and even some of the structural species, such as fir. So expect a high percentage to be unsuitable for decking and perhaps even framing. In my experience, the rejection rate for pressure-treated wood is much higher than the 10 to 20 percent rate for cedar.

Look for pressure-treated wood marked as *S-DRY*, which is kiln-dried before and after its chemical bath. *S-GRN* (much easier to find) is treated when the wood is green, and therefore the CCA is not absorbed into the pores of the wood as well.

Most manufacturers of pressure-treated wood guarantee the product anywhere from 40 years up to the life of the original purchaser. But these warranties are difficult to take advantage of. (How long do you hold onto your receipts, a requirement for making a claim against a warranty?) Should the wood fail in service, and you've kept all those receipts, the manufacturer will supply you with a new piece to replace the rotted one. The removal of the old, installation of the new, and repair of any associated damage is your problem, as it is with nature's own varieties. And apparently in some cases the manufacturer's warranty is void if the wood is immersed in water (read the fine print).

When cutting CCA wood, not only do you expose yourself to toxic

dust, but you also void the warranty unless the cut ends are sealed with an approved preservative (again, keep those receipts). This of course exposes you to the nefarious, raw chemicals you may have been hoping to avoid by using the pre-treated wood in the first place.

Pressure-treated wood works better as a structural material than it does as decking if only because it's hidden, reducing the exposure of dockside users to CCA, CCA-impregnated splinters, and the visual blight of low-grade wood. There are, however, saltwater applications where decay and destructive marine organisms are so severe that pressure-treated wood becomes the best choice for wood used in dock construction. It's all a delicate balance of longevity, environmental concerns, cost, and human preferences.

Metal

Both steel and aluminum are used extensively in the dock-building biz. They both come in a seemingly infinite variety of forms, including plate, pipe, tubing (both round and square), angle, and channel, and in an equally dazzling array of lengths, widths, diameters, and thicknesses. And this doesn't even mention castings and extrusions, which are only limited by a fabricator's imagination or customer's wallet.

Making metal docks is not basic do-it-yourself territory. It requires a knowledge of both dock building and metal fabrication, not to mention a big assortment of expensive tools. However, metal is often used only in the frames of residential docks. Wood and plastic are the preferred materials for decks because neither gets particularly hot under the midday sun, and both are do-it-yourselfer friendly. And of

course metal is the material of choice for hardware and fasteners, regardless of the materials being joined together.

Steel

Steel is the most common metal: inexpensive, stronger, more durable, and heavier than aluminum. However, steel will rust without any protective coating, and look ugly, and possibly corrode away before you do, particularly when exposed to salt water.

The simplest way to extend the life of a steel dock is to use thicker steel. Not only is as little as an extra ⅛ inch in thickness stronger, but the outer layer of surface rust that develops actually slows the corrosion's migration to the core of the material. It still looks ugly, but the required strength is not compromised by that outer layer of ugliness. This technique works well in areas where protective coatings are either hard to apply or apt to wear off quickly, such as on steel piles.

Protective coatings deter corrosion by preventing moisture and air from contacting the steel in the first place. Typical coatings are paint, epoxy, ceramics, galvanizing, and powder coating. Paint is the least expensive option, the least durable, and most easily scratched (just check the doors of your new car after you've owned it for a month). But applying paint demands little in the way of talent or tools, just time. Paint works well for parts that are too big or awkward to treat otherwise, such as steel-tube floats and large framing members.

The remaining coatings are not suited to home workshop application, but all provide superior protection. Epoxy has excellent adhesion and corrosion resistance, is very durable, and is expensive. Ceramic coatings are even tougher and more expensive. Both are excellent coatings for deck screws, the only place a do-it-yourself dock builder is likely to run across them.

Galvanizing is less expensive than epoxy or ceramic coatings but arguably just as good, making it the most popular coating other than paint. Galvanized steel has a coat of zinc bonded to its surface. A minimal coat of zinc can be applied using an electroplating process, producing a very thin, smooth, shiny layer. Because it is so thin, plating is only appropriate for small items like screws (although epoxy or ceramic coating is a better choice for this application). Larger pieces like dock hardware should be hot-dip galvanized. In this process, the object is totally immersed in a bath of molten zinc, producing a thick, gloppy, dull silver finish considerably more rust resistant than mere plating. *Double-dipped* is just as the name implies — a second dip in the zinc bath — and is even more resistant to corrosion and wear. Typically, bolts and nuts are simply plated, but hot-dip galvanized versions sometimes can be had from local dock builders. Plated bolts and nuts eventually will seize from corrosion; I've yet to see hot-dip galvanized bolts and nuts do the same.

Galvanized steel should be painted for saltwater applications. The paint protects the zinc from salt corrosion. (Galvanized steel in fresh water also will last longer if painted, just in case you want to leave some of your dock for your great-grandchildren.) A galvanized surface must be completely degreased and treated with an "etching" primer before painting for the paint to develop a long-term bond with the zinc.

Powder coating is an interesting system that is finding increasing industrial use. The item to be coated is heated to above the melting point of the powdered coating material. The powder then melts and adheres to the object on contact. The powder, often a vinyl resin or polyethylene, can be sprayed onto the heated object, or in a manner similar to hot-dip galvanizing the object can be immersed into a vat of the powder. The result is usually a very smooth, reasonably durable coating (depending on the powder material and thickness). Pigments are usually included in the mix to add color. Less expensive but not as durable as hot-dip galvanizing, powder coating is being used on some dock hardware.

Any coating, from paint to galvanizing, should be applied after fabrication to minimize cracking of the coating, and preferably after any cutting so that all surfaces remain protected. The metal must be clean, rust-free, and of high quality if the coating is going to adhere properly.

Aluminum

Another way to cope with corrosion is to choose a metal less prone to corrosion, such as aluminum or stainless steel. Aluminum forms a thin oxide film on its surface, making its own protective coating. Lighter than steel, aluminum must be of thicker stock to duplicate the strength of steel. Extrusions are also used to increase strength, the shapes often designed to provide for the easy attachment of floats or decking. Aluminum in dock building is frequently used where light weight may be an advantage, such as where docks must be removed for the winter. It's about three times more expensive than hot-dip galvanized steel plate.

Aluminum is susceptible to corrosion at connectors, usually because there's not enough space

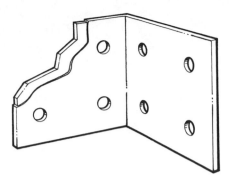

With a protective coat of zinc bonded to its surface, the galvanized bracket is impervious to corrosion.

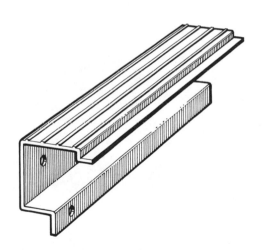

An aluminum extrusion makes attaching decking simple. Better yet, aluminum is rarely susceptible to corrosion.

between the connectors for oxygen to recoat the surface. Aluminum can also fall victim to electrolytic corrosion, a form of corrosion that occurs between dissimilar metals in an electrically conductive environment like water, especially salt water. Steel connectors should never be used on aluminum-frame docks, only aluminum or stainless-steel connectors. When exposed to salt water, use only a marine-grade aluminum, such as the 5000 and 6000 series of alloys (for example, 5052, 5083, 5086).

Stainless Steel

Stainless steel is expensive — at least five times the price of hot-dip galvanized steel. It's also very strong, and because of its high chromium and nickel content, it won't rust, and will likely last generations longer than the wood around it. Stainless steel is a good choice for dock ladders — strength and resistance to corrosion being particularly important in this application. And because of the small amount of material required to make a ladder, the added cost — if any — is minimal. Other than that, reserve stainless steel for connectors on aluminum docks in salt water, or for places where it will show (otherwise, no one will ever know you've spent the extra money).

Plastic

Although a wide variety of plastics can be found around the waterfront today, the focus in this chapter is on dock-construction materials: polyethylene (PE) and polyvinyl chloride (PVC).

PE and PVC date back to the beginnings of plastics. PE is now the most widely used plastic in the world with PVC running a close

second. Both are waterproof and decay resistant, certainly an advantage when it comes to dock construction. Both can be formed into virtually any shape that takes an engineer's fancy — a potentially scary thought.

Compared to most woods, metals, or concrete, PE and PVC are low in strength, subject to creep (stretching), and lack hardness. These shortcomings rule them out for structural duties (at least at the time of this writing — who knows what the future will bring?). But PE and PVC are both good candidates for properly supported decking.

Examined up close, most plastic decking neither looks nor feels like wood; it looks, feels, and smells like plastic. But before you dismiss it solely on that basis, remember that the same can be said for most pleasure boats.

PE comes in five different grades plus a foam, but only two grades are generally of concern to waterfront residents — low density (LDPE) and high density (HDPE). LDPE is the weakling, the most flexible and the least expensive. HDPE is the strongest and, in keeping with the tough-guy image, also the least flexible. HDPE is the only poly suitable for dock-flotation devices. PE is easily repaired (see chapter 17) and easily recycled.

PVC holds its shape better than PE, but is not as flexible and therefore not as resistant to bashing. PVC also can be repaired using "welding" techniques similar to those used on PE (see chapter 17).

All plastic decking has a tendency to sag. U-shaped and similar extrusions sag less than dimensional stock look-alike variants, but no plastic decking (again, at the time of this writing) can extend across the traditional spans of all-wood dock designs. So the standard 24-inch

Most plastic-decking manufacturers bash wood in their brochures. This is to be expected, I suppose, but keep in mind that wood holds most of the world's plastic decking in place. Those same brochures also brag that plastic decking doesn't splinter and that you can work on it with standard home power and hand tools. However, I have never been punctured by a splinter from any deck made of a quality grade of wood, and wood shares the same tool advantage. Another claimed advantage is that plastic decking doesn't require finishing or treating, which eliminates that ongoing labor and exposure to harsh chemicals — again true. But it could be argued that the same applies to several good, quality grades of wood.

As for pricing, it's a bit of a mishmash. Certainly pressure-treated wood has the advantage, being the least expensive decking material. But many variations of the recycled plastic-based decking are at least price competitive with the preferred decking species (cedar et al.), and some are noticeably less. And at the high end of the scale sit the virgin plastics, such as PVC decking.

Within its design limitations, plastic decking offers a life expectancy of at least 100 years, and likely much longer. That is certainly longer than you can expect from wood. That's both good and bad news. Because real, unadulterated wood rots, the sawdust and scrap created from cutting it can be burned in the fireplace or left to rot and become food for other life forms. The same cannot be said for plastic lumber. True, in theory plastic can be recycled, yet more often it is not, and even when it is, energy is consumed. Nature looks after its own, but has a great deal of difficulty coping with humanity's mess.

spacing of framing members may have to be reduced to 16 inches. This means more framing members will be required. This can increase costs and weight unless the dock is designed to take advantage of the reduced spans by using smaller dimensional stock for stringers and headers (such as 2 x 6s on 16-inch centers instead of 2 x 8s on 24-inch centers — check with the decking supplier for allowable spans and framing sizes).

Most plastics become slippery when wet, although all the manufacturers of plastic decking that I am aware of have incorporated a nonslip surface, either by adding an abrasive material to the plastic or by molding in a tread pattern. The result is traction at least on par with similarly soaked wood. Just make sure the decking you are considering incorporates this feature.

Plastic decking can be lumped into two broad categories. The first is made from recycled materials and extruded into standard dimensional "lumber" so you can simply substitute it for wood. The other is made from virgin plastic (new plastic, not yet recycled), which is usually extruded into some variation on a squared-off U- or W-shape and sold in standard lengths (8 feet, 10 feet, etc.). Normally, the virgin variety is PVC. The recycled variety comes in two distinct compositions: 100 percent recycled plastic, usually PE, and a mix of recycled PE and some sort of filler, such as recycled wood.

Plastic Degradation

Most plastics tend to become brittle at low temperatures, which makes them susceptible to failure when the thermometer dips down toward freezing. At the other end of the thermometer, plastics soften as temperatures rise. They then lose stiffness and sag. And while plastics don't rot the way wood does, they will break down in the sun, a process known as UV or photo-degradation. Normally, a plastic with a place in the sun will change color and become brittle, its impact strength will decrease, and, eventually, it will break up into small pieces. Different plastics have different rates of degradation, so their life expectancies vary too. That said, most manufacturers of plastics destined for dock duty add *UV stabilizers* to the formula (a plastic's answer to sunscreen.) For instance, carbon black added to PE will extend the probable service life to long after any surrounding wood has begun to rot.

Speaking of carbon black, dark colors are inherently less susceptible to UV degradation. Dark surfaces also become hotter in the sun, so be cautious when using darker shades where bared feet are likely to contact them, decking being the most obvious example.

PE and PVC are largely unaffected by fuels and similar petroleum-based solvents, and, in general, plastic-based decking is not prone to warp, twist, or cup — something that cannot be said of any wood decking.

Virgin PVC Decking

A good example of a quality virgin PVC plastic decking is that made by Brock Dock. The company's decking is an extruded, upside-down W-shaped "plank"; the top surface is flat with a molded-in nonslip texture.

Brock's decking is not noticeably affected by the sun or freezing temperatures. However, in my experience it "stays clean" as the company claims only if the owner takes the trouble to clean it (admittedly not a difficult task). I don't find the thin gray film that accumulates on the Brock-equipped docks that I have seen to be a problem. I suspect that I would not have even noticed it had I been looking at the light gray or tan decking rather than the white decking.

Brock Dock decking is one of the most expensive decking options on the market, but what you get in return is a durable, minimal-maintenance, good-looking deck. (See chapter 9 for an overview of installation.)

Recycled PE "Lumber" Decking

Recycled plastic decking, plastic "lumber," is heavier than standard decking woods — more like oak than cedar. This can be an advantage with floating docks (see chapter 3) as long as sufficient buoyancy is added to offset the increase in weight and loss of freeboard (extra floats also mean extra cost).

In my experience, recycled decking is more prone to splitting than even pressure-treated wood. This can be overcome by drilling for each screw, but obviously this increases the workload. I've also heard complaints that this material shrinks in cold temperatures, but I have not

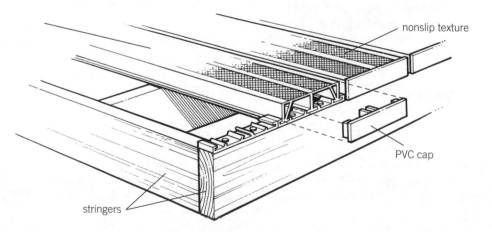

nonslip texture

PVC cap

stringers

PVC decking is strong, light, and warp-resistant. It also comes with a molded-in texture that allows better traction.

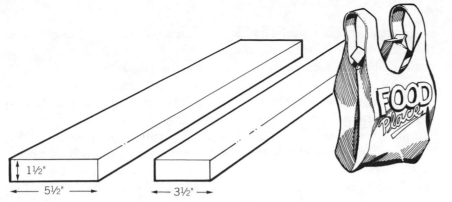

"Lumber" no longer refers only to wood. Manufacturers now offer 2 x 4s, 2 x 6s, and other plank sizes that are comprised of recycled grocery bags and other reclaimed plastics.

experienced this personally. On the plus side, plastic "lumber" can be shaped, routed, and ripped to fit the design.

There is one more potential concern with recycled plastic "lumber": Staying in business seems to be a problem for many manufacturers, just as it is with the manufacturers and distributors of dedicated dock floats. This is not a reflection on the ethics of the industry, but on the difficulties they have with consumer acceptance and perhaps with obtaining sufficient financing, often a regrettable fact of life for small businesses.

Plastic-Based Composites

Most plastic-based composites suitable for use on residential docks are made from recycled plastic and waste wood. However, there is much research being done in the plastic-based composite category — including the unlikely combination of recycled plastic and the shredded remains of junked cars — so don't be surprised to discover composites of different origins and characteristics doing duty on some shoreline.

As with most plastic-based decking, normal woodworking tools are fine for working with wood-and-plastic composites. However, wood-and-plastic composites tend to chip easier than either all-plastic decking or wood decking, and therefore require some extra care during construction.

One composite decking that has been on the market for a few years is Trex. Trex is made from reclaimed LDPE (such as plastic shopping bags) and waste hardwood purchased from furniture manufacturers and the like. The plastic and wood are shredded and ground up (the wood more like a fine powder than chips or sawdust), then mixed and heated to the melting point of the plastic. The wood powder absorbs the molten plastic and the two dissimilar products unite. The composite is then extruded out into solid dimensional "lumber" (such as 2 x 4s).

Trex shares many characteristics of other plastic "lumbers," such as heavy weight and a tendency to split when you fasten without first predrilling suitable holes. Yet because Trex does contain real wood, it will accept paints and stains if you want to change its color, although this is not necessary. Left untreated, the natural shade of Trex will weather to an even, light gray (just as cedar does). In fact, because it's recommended most wood-and-plastic composites be allowed to age before staining, even should you choose to stain it you will get to see it go gray first. Trex also comes in a colorfast dark brown for those who don't like gray or the job of staining or waiting for things to age.

Another product similar in concept to Trex is ChoiceDek. In

contrast to Trex, ChoiceDek uses both LDPE and HDPE as its plastic base, and cedar chips for the wood element.

One composite that differs substantially from the rest is The Bauhaus Composite Decking System, manufactured from a wood-and-plastic composite known as NexWood. As with similar composites, NexWood is made mostly from postconsumer waste, 98 percent in this case. Forty percent is recycled LDPE, and 58 percent of the remainder is some sort of cellulose-based filler, usually sawdust. This gives NexWood the highest content of filler for any LDPE composite lumber. The higher the filler compound, the closer the properties of the material are to wood, which is the key to NexWood's strength and workability. And the filler doesn't even have to be wood — any cellulose-based material will do, such as ground-up peanut shells, sugarcane, or even hemp.

But the big difference between this NexWood-based system and its principal competitors, including wood, is that Bauhaus Composite Decking is a ribbed, hollow-core, boxed-in extrusion, open only at the ends. (Picture a harmonica with its holes installed lengthwise

instead of sideways.) In common with the frame on a car, the Bauhaus decking gains its strength from shape as much as the material. Yes, PVC decking is similarly extruded, but with the PVC variants, both the bottom of the decking board and its ends are open, one of the reasons it lacks the structural strength of the Bauhaus system.

Bauhaus Composite Decking has a brushed texture on its two horizontal surfaces, allowing it to be installed either side up. Besides making installation easier, this means that should a plank become chipped or cracked from dockside abuse, it can be flipped over and left looking as good as new. Special clips are required for installation. Fortunately, the clips are both inexpensive and easy to use.

Speaking of costs, because less material is used in the manufacturing process of Bauhaus Composite Decking compared to its composite companions (which are typically solid planks), the Bauhaus variation undercuts cedar in both price (about 10 percent less) and weight (also about 10 percent less).

And, begrudgingly, I have to admit that the brushed exposed surface on this decking (which

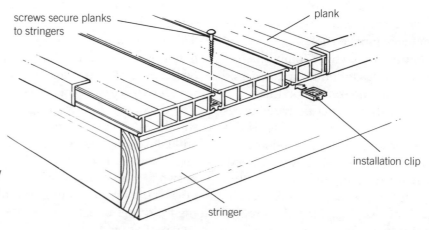

Bauhaus Composite Decking is gaining in popularity because of its strength, light weight, and versatility. Special, easy-to-use clips make installation of this wood-and-plastic composite decking a snap.

provides traction and a surface for paint and stain to bond) does provide a very woodlike appearance. Only without the risk of warping and rot.

And finally, a very important note on plastic-based decking of any type: Regardless of which plastic or composite decking you choose to use, do not vary from the manufacturer's recommendations, particularly when it comes to spans and installation techniques.

Concrete

Concrete is composed of Portland cement, aggregate, and water. This means it's cheap, certainly an asset for the spending-challenged among us.

Concrete will flow into all sorts of shapes and sizes, just like molten plastic or metal. This opens up a Pandora's box of potential curves and angles — anything is possible as long as the form can be built. Radical departure from the standard construction rectangle isn't always practical when it comes to waterfront structures, but certainly there's potential for unconventional approaches to shape. Unfortunately, working with concrete is labor intensive. This can make it expensive when you have to pay for the labor.

Concrete's Weakness

While concrete possesses impressive compressive strength, the ability to support what's above it without deforming, it is not big on tensile strength, the ability to resist being bent or pulled apart. And when the forces of nature conspire to move concrete, there's seldom anything left worth salvaging (a disadvantage not shared with wood).

Concrete's Crutch

Fortunately, concrete can be reinforced, adding tensile strength and distributing loads over large areas. The most common reinforcing material is steel, either reinforcing rods (usually referred to as *rebar*) or concrete reinforcing mesh (sometimes referred to as welded wire fabric). You should not choose the cheap route — recycled chunks of metal rod, pipes, angle iron, fencing, bits of cast-off castings, or undesirable labor leaders. Steel must be clean for the concrete to stick to it, and it must be linked together if it is to provide satisfactory tensile reinforcement. Separate pieces of metal, even proper reinforcing rod, do little to distribute loads unless they are tied together with wire wherever they intersect. Where mesh mats meet, they must overlap and also be wired together.

Sometimes vertical rebar is embedded into submerged or dry lands, either pounded into place or set into holes drilled into the rock. I have used this technique on several occasions to keep concrete pegged to rock. In fact, that's what is holding my house in place as I write this, and hopefully still as you read about it.

Another, more recent, concrete reinforcement is chopped fiberglass. Mixed in with the other dry ingredients, this reinforcement is finely and evenly distributed throughout the mix. The result is known as glass reinforced concrete, or GRC. The solar slab in my house is made from GRC.

Knowing the limits and capabilities of dock-building materials removes much of the guesswork from choosing what will work best for your dock and your situation. Next, we investigate the tools and hardware best suited to converting these materials into a dock.

Concrete Blocks

Don't confuse poured concrete with concrete blocks. Even in 12-inch widths, and with the spaces between the webs filled with concrete and reinforcing rods, blocks are not suitable for waterfront projects. They are too easily torn apart by the forces of nature — both the blocks themselves and the mortared seams that join the blocks together.

the tools, hardware, and fasteners of dock building

You need tools to assemble dock-building materials into a solution to your docking needs. You also need fasteners and, to do the job right, dedicated dock hardware.

Tools

According to some evolutionists, the use of tools is what separates man from the apes. My father didn't buy this, maintaining that it was not hard to find an ape using tools. I've also come to believe the old saying, "It's a poor workman who blames his tools" — mostly because good workmen have learned to avoid poor tools.

The tools you'll need to build a dock are all general-purpose tools — you can use them for an endless list of other projects. Most handy folks already own most of them. I inherited the majority of my hand tools from my father, who inherited them from his. When my grandfather acquired them a century ago, tools were made by craftsmen for use by craftsmen. Having been exposed to well-designed and well-made tools all my life, I've grown to value quality tools — they work, and they last.

No tool — hand powered or electric — should be uncomfortable or awkward to use. Unfortunately, cheap tools often are. While some door-crasher specials are fiscally attractive, reach for the tool before you reach for your wallet. Pick it up and feel how it fits in your hand. Is it balanced to minimize the strain of its weight on your wrist and arm? Does the handle feel "right" when held in working position? Quality tools last longer and conform to the quirks of human anatomy. Cheap tools break in use, seriously testing your self-control. They also wear quickly. You don't need to buy the very best for occasional use, but do yourself a big favor and avoid cheap. Your body will thank you, and in the long run so will your wallet.

Most of my power tools are "industrial" or of a similar quality. Each tool has given me excellent service over the years. For casual use, though, industrial-grade tools may be overkill. Choose a name-brand line between the industrial stuff at the high end and the "homeowner" stuff at the bottom. When comparing power tools, the higher the amp rating, the more powerful the motor. Also look for features such as ball or needle bearings, long cords, large sturdy "feet" on circular saws (the platform that rests on the wood), and easy-to-use adjustments such as the reverse switch on drills and the depth and angle adjustments on saws.

Hand Tools

Tape measure. One 25-foot tape for measuring the long of it, and two 16-foot tapes for measuring the shorter of it. I find the 16-foot tape less awkward to use — a good investment for dock building when most measurements are less than 16 feet. (You need two, one for the tool belt and one to temporarily misplace.)

Carpenter's pencil. This flat-sided marker is sufficiently accurate for dock-building duties. It leaves a nice fat line that's easy to see outdoors on dark wood, and it is easily sharpened on the job site using a utility knife.

Utility knife. Sharpens pencils and whittles sticks into toothpicks or useless folk carvings while musing over what to do next. It also cuts away splinters at the edge of saw cuts and drilled holes, sometimes necessary when trying to align dock hardware with bolts and the dock's frame. Get one with an easily retractable blade (such as an Olfa L-2).

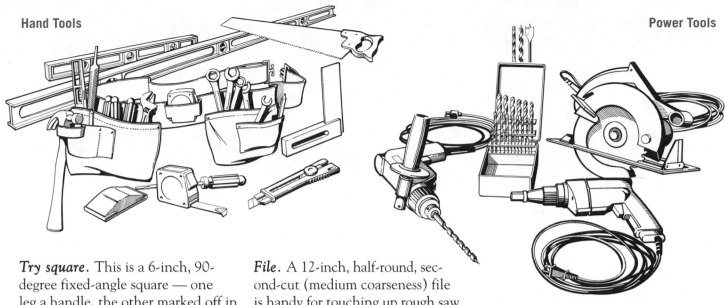

Try square. This is a 6-inch, 90-degree fixed-angle square — one leg a handle, the other marked off in inches. Use it to mark perpendicular lines for cross-cuts in framing and decking. Mine has a lovely rosewood handle; modern versions often have metal handles.

Level. I have 6-inch, 2-foot, and 4-foot levels, but the 2-foot is the most versatile and the one to buy if buying only one. You'll need this tool for leveling concrete forms, shore mounts, and pipe docks once they're installed. (*Note:* A level is a relatively fragile instrument — bumped hard it will no longer measure on the level.)

Hammer. My preference is a 16-ounce claw hammer with a hickory handle. Hickory has some spring to it, which metal lacks, making it easier on the elbows. A good hammer should be well balanced; when held at a 30-degree angle it should want to fall neither forward nor back. Always hold a hammer at the end of the handle to maximize your leverage.

Handsaw. There are places a power saw just won't fit, and sometimes a power saw doesn't cut deep enough to slice right through the wood. Then you need a handsaw. A cross-cut saw, with 8 to 10 teeth per inch, will prove the most versatile.

File. A 12-inch, half-round, second-cut (medium coarseness) file is handy for touching up rough saw edges or smoothing and rounding corners of rough cuts. A sanding block will also work for such tasks, it's just slower.

Wrenches. Five combination box and open-end wrenches in sizes from ⅜ to ⅝ inches in 1/16-inch increments, and an 8-inch adjustable (an adjustable wrench is classified by its total length) to deal with sizes not covered by the combination wrenches. You will need these wrenches to bolt brackets and accessories onto the dock.

Screwdrivers. I recommend #1 and #2 Phillips (cross head), at least one slotted (a ¼- x 6-inch blade is the most versatile), and if you live in Canada, probably #1 (green handle) and #2 (red handle) Robertsons (square head).

Power Tools

Circular saw. A 7¼-incher, with a carbide-tipped "framing" or "deck" blade (about 20 teeth) for general sawing. For cleaner cuts in softwoods, such as when cutting cedar decking, a fine-toothed blade (40 teeth) is a good second blade to have.

Renting infrequently used tools such as power augers for digging holes for placing concrete tube-forms, or a portable cement mixer, can make sense if you have a reputable rental outlet in your neighborhood. The trouble is that most rental tools quickly deteriorate from abuse and lack of maintenance. I have yet to rent a tool that worked as well as its designers intended. Luck of the draw, perhaps, but the last tool I rented — a battered and badly worn concrete drill — was in such poor shape that it broke during use. I could have lived with this inconvenience but the staff of the rental company claimed that the breakage was my fault (a not uncommon tactic for this shady outfit, I later discovered). I'll spare you the details of my reaction, but they didn't get a new drill from me and I don't rent from them — or anyone — anymore. I buy, or borrow from Cheap Neighbor Dave.

If you do decide to rent, refuse to accept any tool that looks too unfit for a garage sale. Also, get in writing the exact total cost of renting. Many outlets will obligingly supply you with all sorts of "extras" — often essential for operation — all for an additional cost that they tell you about only when you return the tool.

It's a renter-beware market.

Electric drill. A ⅜-inch chuck, variable speed, with reverse. The minimal list of drill bits includes ⅛ to ⅝ inch in ⅛-inch increments. The only practical choice in the smaller sizes is the traditional twist drill. For faster and not-so-tidy drilling of holes ½ inch in diameter and up, get spade bits. They're reasonably cheap, fast, and rough. For cleaner and still-faster holes, get the more expensive auger bits.

Screw gun. Variable speed, with clutch, reverse, and magnetic bit holder to hold the screw on the driver tip. This is an essential item if you intend to screw your dock together. If your budget won't allow a screw gun, at least get a dimpler for your variable-speed electric drill. This is a cheapo attachment that converts drills into mediocre screw guns, sort of.

Miscellaneous

Leather carpenter's tool belt. Adjustable to fit your waist size. Ideally, it should have pouches or holsters for a hammer, utility knife, try square, tape rule, plus two pockets for nails, screws, and hand-carved toothpicks.

Friends. To consume your food and drink while helping to flip the dock during construction, offer dumb advice, and later help install the dock.

If your site lacks electricity you will need a brace and bits for larger holes and a hand drill and bits for smaller holes. You might also want to consider a 20-ounce framing hammer since you will be nailing the decking in place. (A framing hammer is easier on the elbows if you're doing much hammering.)

Optional Tools
Hand Tools
Sliding bevel. This nifty tool is like a try square but is for marking cuts at angles other than square. If your dock doesn't have any oddball angles, you don't need it.

Combination square. Similar again to the try square but with fixed 90-degree and 45-degree angles plus a movable head. It doesn't carry in a tool belt as well as the try square, nor is it as nice to use, but the movable head with a built-in notch for a pencil point at each end of the 12-inch arm allows it to function as a marking gauge — great for marking a lengthwise cut on those last pieces of decking that don't quite fit.

Chisels. A few would be nice; a ½-incher will probably do, for chiseling out chunks when things don't fit or making square insets for carriage bolts and the like.

Hand plane. Great for chamfering and rounding edges.

Pipe clamps. I have a pair of ½-inch x 3-foot-long clamps and a ¾-inch x 8-foot-long pair. Both ease the task of drawing warped decking (or framing) into line.

Socket set. Much easier and quicker for bolting things together than wrenches (but you'll still need at least an adjustable wrench to keep the other end of the bolt from turning).

Power Tools
Router. A quick and noisy way to round edges (swimming near docks can be a contact sport and round edges are easier on bodies than sharp, square edges). You also can make decorative edges or rout your name into the decking.

Sander. If you intend to stain a non-pressure-treated wood dock, you'll want either a belt sander (fast and prone to gouging the wood if you're not careful), a disk attachment for your drill (not as fast or quite as likely to gouge the wood, and the least expensive power sander), or a palm sander (slow and safe) to remove company logos stamped on the wood before sealing them in place under the finish. Hand-operated sanding blocks will also do the job, but that's a lot of work. Left unstained or unpainted the company logos usually fade away.

Mitre saw/chop saw. Depending on your point of view, this is either a portable radial-arm saw or a circular saw mounted on an arm. It makes fast, accurate cuts, and is most appreciated when cutting angles to either side of 90 degrees.

Sabre saw (portable jigsaw). Cuts round holes for pipe-dock legs and finishes cuts that are too deep for circular saws. Mine (my only cheapo power tool) is broken, so I borrow Cheap Neighbor Dave's the few times I need one.

Cordless screw gun and/or drill. Eliminating the cord has some advantages but you'll want an extra battery pack so you don't have to halt work while waiting for a tool to recharge. Taking a break to recharge is great, but I prefer to take a break when I need one rather than when a tool needs one. The most powerful tools usually have a cord attached.

Cordless screwdriver. This is my one cordless tool. Cordless screwdrivers are small and not much use for big decking jobs, but for those few occasions when there's just not enough room to squeeze in the

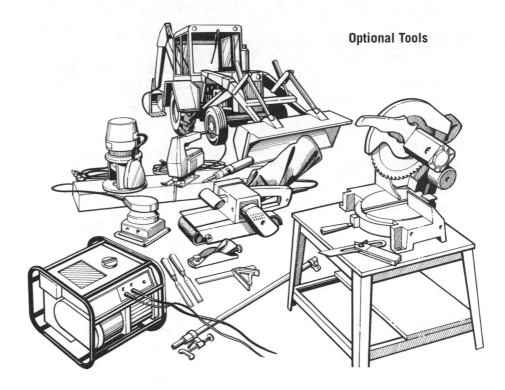

screw gun, they work great. It's also the screwdriver I reach for first for quick jobs around the house, which is what it really was designed for.

Miscellaneous

Generator. For sites without electricity.

Backhoe. I called mine Waldo. It could lift whole docks into the air, dig big holes in the ground for building concrete piers, and do all sorts of backbreaking stuff at the flick of a lever — especially stuff I never thought needed doing until I bought it. But be forewarned: People will continually stop by to ask if you want to earn a few bucks doing a "simple" job for them (it's never worth it) or ask if you want to sell Waldo. To the first question, I always said no; to the second I quoted a ridiculously high price, until some cad said, "Sure," and Waldo was sold. Now whenever I spot a backhoe sitting in someone's yard I stop by and ask if they want to sell it. Invariably the owner wants too much.

Any cutting tool must be kept sharp. Most of the preferred decking woods, including cedar and redwood, are very soft, susceptible to splintered edges when cut with dull tools. Sharp tools also put less strain on the tool and operator since both work less to get the job done.

With saw blades, the more teeth, the cleaner the cut, and the longer it takes. Less teeth make for a faster, rougher cut.

Carbide-tipped blades on circular saws last up to five times longer than "high-speed" steel blades before requiring sharpening. And for reasons known only to merchandisers, good carbide-tipped blades can often be found on sale, which is when Cheap Neighbor Dave and I buy them.

A crosscut is a cut across the grain, which in most cases means cutting at an angle to the width of the board, rather than along its length. To cut lengthwise in the direction of the grain is known as *ripping*. It's reasonably easy to follow a straight line marked on the wood when making the typically short crosscut. When ripping, however, the cut is often 4 to 10 feet long. Holding a circular saw straight over that length, no veering allowed, is not easy. Most people, professionals included, use a saw guide for such long cuts.

You can buy a saw guide if you're keen on spending money, but any straightedge of an appropriate length will do. I use a 10-foot aluminum door-jamb that Cheap Neighbor Dave salvaged from a renovated commercial building. The guide is positioned so that the foot of the saw abuts it when the blade is in line with the cut line, then clamped in place.

Dock Hardware

Dock hardware is that bewildering array of metal brackets (usually steel) used to brace corners and joints, connect dock and ramp sections, hold the legs of pipe docks in place, and basically add strength to any dock connection under load. Technically, it doesn't fasten stuff together; it leaves that task to the nails, screws, and nuts and bolts (see The Fastener Debate on page 83). Instead, once fastened in place with nuts and bolts, dock hardware shares and transfers loads, diminishing stress at crucial junctures. For example, when a dock hinge is bolted through a dock's end header to a corner bracket, much of the load placed on the dock hinge is transferred via the corner bracket to the dock's longitudinal framing members, rather than dumping it all on an already overworked end header. Nailed or screwed corners pull apart, and while complicated joinery may impress your neighbors and perhaps the fish, you had better get them over quick for a viewing because it won't last if it isn't backed up with good dock hardware.

Good hardware will outlast any wooden framework or decking. It doesn't make sense to waste your time and money on second-rate alternatives whether of your own creation (sorry) or designed for less demanding duty. (The list of hardware not up to dock duty includes joist hangers made for residential construction, eye bolts, barn-door hinges, and even "econo" hardware from some mass-merchandising outlets.) Whether buying individual pieces or acquiring the hardware as part of a completed dock or kit, buy hardware from an established dock builder. It's an expense you'll never regret. (Naturally, all exposed dock hardware should be resistant to corrosion; see Steel, chapter 7.)

There are several manufacturers of dock hardware to choose from. Generally, it's best to stick with one brand of hardware where the pieces have been designed to work together. Each piece should be pre-drilled using the same bolt pattern, allowing structures to be assembled like Lego. Corner brackets for floating docks should bolt to pipe-leg brackets, which should bolt to connectors, which should bolt to hinge plates, and so on — although who knows what might result from this bizarre combination. But it does illustrate the importance of using integrated hardware: How you use it, for docks, decks, or whatever, is restricted mainly by your budget and your imagination.

That said, suppliers occasionally will develop different solutions to particular docking problems, and sometimes market hardware for special uses. In this case using pieces from more than one source might prove advantageous. For instance, you can get hardware specifically made for diamond- or octagon-shaped docks from one manufacturer, and brackets that flare the ends of finger docks where they connect to the main floater from another.

Hardware that joins dock sections should be designed to disconnect with relative ease. You should never have to remove hardware from the dock in order to disconnect dock sections. Removing hardware not only creates unnecessary work, but it also increases wear around the bolt holes, increasing the possibility of the bracket moving under stress, creating more wear, weakening the structure, and creating yet another cozy little home for rot.

Corner Brackets

A rectangle wants to become a parallelogram under stress. The best and easiest way to curtail this unruly behavior is with braced, metal, inside corner brackets. (Some manufacturers also offer an outside corner bracket to be used in conjunction with an inside bracket for particularly heavy-duty applications.) Corner brackets that include built-in slats for the anchor chain are a nice touch. When these are used, the dock design should allow easy access to the chain for adjustment (see chapter 18). If your dock requires chains attached to the sides of the dock you can get special anchor brackets for just this application.

Hinges

Hinges hold sections of dock laterally in place; that is, they connect the sections and keep them in line. They do nothing to stop the ends of the sections from moving up and down. In fact, the primary purpose of a hinge as opposed to a connector (see below) is to allow such vertical movement. That's why they work so well for joining the dock to the ramp and the ramp to the shore. Here at the juncture of land and water most docks need some freedom to move, because land is not as inclined as a dock to jiggle about in response to wave action, fluctuating water levels, and boat-mooring anarchists with bad attitudes.

Most hinges designed specifically for dock use are heavy duty, easy to install, and easy to disconnect at season's end — simply pull a couple of pins in many cases. At least one high-end dock hinge places the hinge pin bolts in nylon bushings, reducing pin wear while eliminating metal-to-metal squeaking as the hinge responds to dock and ramp movement. When installing a hinge, keep in mind that it works best when the hinge pin is close to center of the height of the dock's framing. Usually two hinges will suffice, one at each corner of the ramp,

but on wide ramps — greater than 10 feet wide, for instance — it's a good idea to add a third hinge in the center for additional strength.

The common practice is to hinge floating sections together. Big mistake. This allows free up-and-down movement at the ends of each section, setting the stage for the infamous roller-coaster effect as each section tends to rotate about its own roll axis when you travel from one end of the dock to the other. What you get is an aquatic teeter-totter, which is great if that is what you were after. If not, the hardware of choice is a dock connector.

Connectors

Dock connectors tie sections of a floating dock together both laterally and vertically, thwarting the tendency for the sections to rotate on their individual axes. The whole dock reacts as a single unit. When you step on this corner over here your weight has to move the entire dock, not just the section you're standing on, before any corner dips down and an opposite end rises. Good dock connectors turn a bunch of little sections into one big, stable dock while still providing for easy disconnection and removal at season's end.

Dock connectors come in several guises, including neoprene cushion mounts (Techno Marine), overlapping stringers (Bellingham Marine), double pin connectors (Bauhaus Docks), and male/female corner brackets (Great Northern Docks). The easiest type to install when building from scratch is the Bauhaus unit, while the connectors from

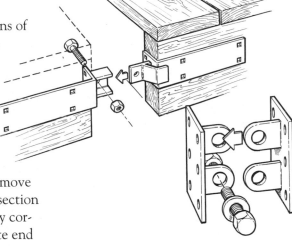

corner bracket   hinge

A metal corner bracket helps the structure maintain its shape when stress is added. A hinge serves a very different function, allowing verticle movement between two attached structures. Because they are constantly moving and creating friction, hinges must be extremely durable.

Connectors join together sections of the dock into a single, stable unit. It is important that connectors secure the sections tightly, to prevent both vertical and horizontal movement.

Great Northern are likely the best bet for retro-fitting an existing dock.

If finances are tight, or the local dock builder does not stock dedicated dock connectors, you may be able to turn dock hinges sideways to serve as quasi-connectors. But be forewarned: Most hinges are not designed to work in this manner and therefore will not accommodate the change in direction of stress, eventually leading the hinges to break. An acceptable candidate for quasi-connector status is the "pin"-style hinge. Here, a long L-pin or bolt slides through sleeves welded to both halves of each hinge bracket, the sleeves fitting together so as to form one long sleeve for the pin. Now unable to pivot vertically, the two hinges also restrain each other from lateral movement (their pivot points no longer aligned on a common axis). So check with your supplier to determine if this is considered acceptable use for the hinge style on your dock. Another possible solution — if connectors are not locally available — is to double up on the hinges, pairing one above the other, which would prevent vertical movement yet still allow for easy disconnection.

Pipe-Dock Hardware

A pipe-leg bracket's primary purpose is to attach pipe legs to the frame of a pipe dock. But good pipe-leg brackets do much more. Often, the bracket will act as a corner bracket as well, doing its bit to share and transfer stress, which can be considerable at this crucial juncture of leg, header, stringer, and perhaps ramp or additional dock section.

A good pipe-leg bracket also provides a means to easily adjust the height of the deck, either with built-in cinch bolts or pins that slip into predrilled holes in the legs. In either case, if the dock shows an inclination to slouch as legs settle and sink into submerged lands, it's no big deal to relevel the decking.

Pipe-leg brackets come in two basic varieties — those that mount on the outside of the frame and those that mount on the inside. Outside versions are easier to install, particularly if retro-fitting — just bolt them on. On the other hand, they tend to bruise boats and swimmers unless dressed in protective sleeves (the brackets and pipe legs, that is, not the boats and swimmers). Also, outside pipe-leg

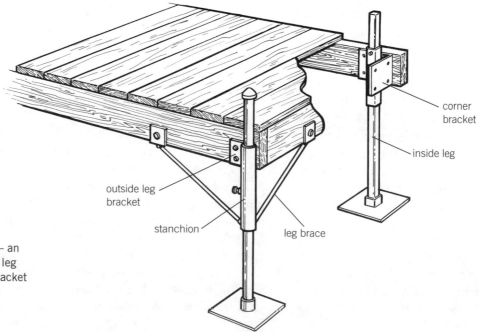

corner bracket

inside leg

outside leg bracket

stanchion

leg brace

Two variations of pipe dock hardware — an outside leg bracket with stanchion and leg braces, and an inside leg and corner bracket combination.

brackets rarely serve double duty as corner brackets. Pipe-leg brackets that mount inside the frame eliminate both of those shortcomings, and the dock looks better too. Depending on inside-bracket design, however, it's possible that leg-height adjustments cannot be made without ducking under the dock and getting your head wet. Not a problem when the weather is hot but . . . (See chapter 4 for pipe-dock levelers, one solution to dry pipe-leg adjustments.)

Leg braces work best when the lower ends are installed as close to the feet of the legs as possible, thereby providing the maximum bracing leverage against nature's attacks. To maintain this preferred positioning, whenever the heights of pipe legs are adjusted the leg braces must be adjusted too. Telescopic braces make this task much easier, the braces simply sliding in and out (like a telescope, actually) to facilitate the change in leg length, no unbolting and moving of brackets necessary. If you can't get telescopic braces, installing standard braces in an upside-down V configuration between the legs — rather than crossing them in an X, the braces typically pinned where they cross — will make it easier to keep the bottom end of the brace near the leg's foot as adjustments are made throughout the season. On the other hand, if the water levels at your shoreline aren't subject to seasonal fluctuations, and the leg's feet are not likely to sink into submerged lands, then install the braces once and forget about them.

An interesting variation on the conventional pipe-leg bracket is the *stanchion*, an outer pipe through which the pipe leg slides. Cinch bolts hold the leg vertically in place. With metal leg braces attached to the outer sleeve instead of to the leg itself, you can adjust the height of the legs without having to also adjust the position of the metal leg braces.

Homebrew versions of dock hardware abound, usually making use of old pipes, barn-door hinges, U-clamps or similar scrap-yard ingenuity. Unfortunately, of the literally hundreds of variations that I have seen, none work nearly as well as the typical hardware sold by a good dock builder. There are better places to save money.

The Fastener Debate: Nails versus Screws versus Bolts

Fasteners join materials together, such as hardware to the dock and decking to the frame. The short list of fasteners includes nails, screws, bolts, and nuts.

Screws and bolts have several advantages over nails, the foremost being threads. In the case of screws and lag bolts, threads allow us to draw materials together (decking or float drums to the frame, for instance). Machine bolts and carriage bolts hold pieces together in compression (such as when hinge brackets, dock framing, and corner brackets are bolted together). If parts loosen up as new wood dries and shrinks around the hardware, threads make it easy to retighten the works using a wrench or screwdriver. And speaking from experience, wrenches and screwdrivers are less inclined than hammers to bash thumbs and other body parts.

Continuing with this nail-bashing theme, as wood expands and shrinks with the weather, and nature continuously wrestles with the dock, nails inevitably loosen their grip on the wood. The heads then sit proud off the dock's surface. This weakens the structure of the dock; wiggling pieces pull and tug at nails. Further,

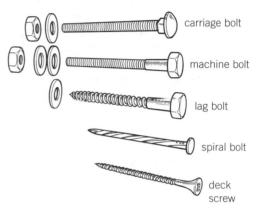

carriage bolt

machine bolt

lag bolt

spiral bolt

deck screw

Never use a pneumatic nailer for dock building. Pneumatic nailers are the machine guns of carpentry. True, you can shoot in a whole whack of nails in the space it takes me to tell you about it, with an accuracy comparable to an AK47, but the nails these things spit out lack sufficient holding power for dock use — less even than old-fashioned, hammer-driven nails. It's also very difficult to avoid denting the wood. The pneumatic nailer drives the head of each nail slightly below the wood's surface, leaving little hollows for water to gather and initiate the rot process. And good nails for a pneumatic nailer are considerably more expensive than standard nails suitable for dock building. Being a tool freak, I do own a pneumatic nailer, a very good one. It's great for house framing, installing subflooring and sheathing, and impressing people who have never seen one in use, but it never sees duty on decks or docks.

If speed is important, buy a quality autofeed canister for your screw gun. QuikDrive is a good choice. (If you do, keep in touch — I may need to borrow one.)

wood fibers are pushed about, creating an ideal location for a waterfront condo of wood-destroying fungi. It's also a loudly voiced fact that raised nail heads attract bare toes. And of course nails are difficult to remove to fix the construction mistakes made by your helpers (not you, obviously).

Speaking of removing fasteners, using boat-cable grease (or any similar water-resistant grease), lubricate any bolt, nut, cinch bolt, or set screw that you may want to remove later. It makes the task much easier.

For sites without electricity, nails are the only realistic fasteners for decking (screwing the decking in place by hand would turn the elbows of even a top-seeded tennis player to mush). Nails are also about five times less costly than comparable deck screws, and a good hammer is about a tenth the cost of a screw gun.

If you don't have access to a screw gun and money is tight, all is not lost. A dimpler attachment for your drill is comparatively inexpensive and could put the holding power and ease of installation of screws within your reach. But if nails are it, at least insist on hot-dip galvanized spiral nails, not merely the plated variety, which are decidedly more prone to corrosion and staining the surrounding wood (see chapter 7).

Whether for nails or screws, predrilling holes lessens the odds of splitting the wood, particularly at the ends of boards. However, this adds so much to the workload that

few people bother, even professionals or me. Holes for all bolts must be predrilled, including the self-tapping lag bolt. True, a lag bolt can be installed without predrilling, but its large diameter makes the risk of splitting the wood very high. Some professional dock builders use lag bolts without predrilling because we consumers don't want to pay for their time to drill a hole and insert a machine or carriage bolt with nut and washers, which — almost invariably — is the better way to hold things together. Lag bolts are okay in thick chunks of wood — the timbers used to build crib docks, for instance — but even when predrilling, using lag bolts in 2-inch dimensional stock typically provides a temporary hold only.

Install nails and screws with the top of the head flush with the surface; install all bolts with the underside of the head flush. Overtightening screws and bolts or sinking nails below the wood's surface does not make fastening more secure, it simply crushes the wood fibers around the fastener's head, increasing the odds of rot at these points. Standard screws are all plated now, but ceramic baked or epoxy coated (the brown or green ones also known as deck screws) are the best choice for docks.

We have the materials, we have the tools, we have the technology. We are ready to delve into the proven processes of assembly. It took the trades years to learn this stuff. All you have to do is turn the page and read.

the techniques of dock building

This is the nifty-ways-to-put-stuff-together chapter, a do-it-yourselfer's guide to working with the materials, tools, hardware, and fasteners of dock building. Essential reading includes everything related to your dock's platform. If you're burdened with an insatiably inquisitive mind, then read the other sections too. There's no extra charge for satisfying your curiosity.

There are many motives for going the build-it-yourself route. Certainly one biggie is the hope of emulating the work of the top professionals without paying the top price. Another is the opportunity to spend constructive time with family and friends — doing-it-yourself usually consumes lots of time, sometimes stretching out to beyond tedium. Yet from my perspective, the main motive for doing anything that doesn't directly result in a paycheck is simply the enjoyment of doing it, of putting things together and seeing a project evolve from using your own hands and ingenuity.

Some Basics

Before you begin construction, you should familiarize yourself with some of the basic terminology of dock structural members — so you can at least sound like an expert.

The longitudinal pieces of a dock's frame are called stringers (or sometimes joists), headers are the frame's end boards, and crossers (also known as cross-braces) are the pieces running parallel to the headers but within the perimeter of the frame. Skirts are an additional, cosmetic, outer layer of wood that encloses the frame. Stringers and headers (and, hence, skirts) are usually installed on edge (that is, a 2 x 8 with its 8-inch dimension vertical). Crossers are sometimes on edge and sometimes on the flat. Decking, also called planking or deck boards, is what you see on top, typically installed wide-face up. Decking runners are the longitudinal boards that hold a removable decking panel together.

Work Zone Ahead

You can prevent free-falling objects (such as sawdust, nails, hammers, electric screw guns, paint, and nuisance observers) from contaminating that ecologically sensitive area known as your waterfront by building your dock (and stacking your wood) well back from the shoreline. The area should be relatively flat with a clear path to the waterfront to ease the eventual launch. And before beginning to

Max's First Rule of Do-It-Yourself

Save on the labor, not the materials. Regardless of what you are intending to build, buying quality supplies from knowledgeable specialty sources will inevitably make the task easier. The quality of goods sold by a local dock builder, and that builder's honesty and attitude, is more important than any of the differences between hardware, flotation systems, or whatever other dock item you care to name. So if you're lucky enough to have a good dock builder nearby, use the materials sold there and, if necessary, adapt the plans in chapter 18 to suit.

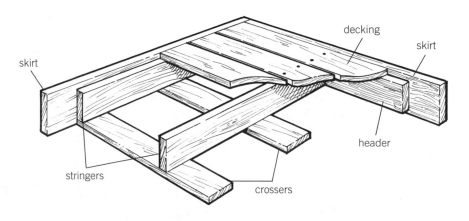

It is important to understand a few basic terms before beginning the construction of your new dock. It will also help you understand the directions in the following chapters.

There's an old adage common to all trades engaged in cutting stuff: "Measure twice, cut once." My advice is to measure more often. When accuracy is crucial (for example, when patching a piece inadvertently cut too short), I measure, mark the cut, nick the mark with my saw, then measure again. At this point, it's still possible to fine-tune the whereabouts of the proposed cut before actually making it.

"Leave the line" is another bit of sage advice. Always cut on the waste side of the line, leaving the line on the piece you'll use. The line, after all, was drawn through the mark you made when measuring the wood to be cut, so the line should be included as part of that measurement. Cutting on the line makes the piece shorter than required. Assuming, of course, that you measured correctly.

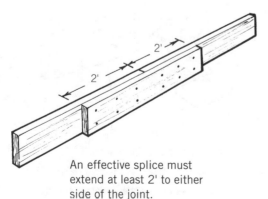

An effective splice must extend at least 2' to either side of the joint.

build, make sure you have enough room to maneuver the dock during construction (some docks need to be flipped over — see Floating-Dock Quirks on page 89).

Working with Wood

Once you've got the wood to your site, sort it in order of building sequence (large framing members first, decking last, for example) to avoid having to hunt through your cache to find that header sitting at the bottom of the pile.

If you've chosen one of the preferred species of wood for docks (cedar et al.), stack the planks with two or three spacers between rows to allow for ventilation. Let the wood sit in the shade for at least a couple of weeks (4 to 6 is better) to dry and shrink prior to installation. For other species and pressure-treated wood, it's best to begin assembling the stuff as soon as possible, securing it into position before it begins to warp and twist.

Yet even with the preferred species, although usually cut straight at the mill, no lumber stays that way. The sad reality is that no piece, even when correctly stacked and dried, is going to remain perfectly straight. A slight curve here, a bit of a twist there, all must be corrected (or at least allowed for) when building.

Working with Ugly Wood

As discussed in chapter 7, it's unlikely you will escape working with bad pieces of wood (knotholes and pieces with "punky," split, or checked sections, for instance). When possible, delegate the ugly stuff to below-deck duties, stacking them in that sequence.

If much of the wood is plagued with bad ends (gouged or split), you may need to trim them and re-

duce the dimensions of your dock accordingly.

Long splits can sometimes be glued back together with the aid of clamps, but getting glue to run into the split can try the patience of Job. (I coax the glue in with splinters and pieces of stiff paper.) Occasionally it's best to split the entire piece along its length, slather the split edges with glue, then clamp the two parts back together to dry. In either case a properly glued member will be as strong as the unsplit stuff.

Carpenter's glue will suffice for repairs to wood destined for above-water applications, but product manufacturers disagree for wood near or below the waterline (which typically includes the dock's frame). To be safe, use a moisture-resistant glue (such as Titebond II).

If you need to splice a piece (too short, badly damaged in the middle, etc.), overlap the joint with a wood backup plate of the same thickness and width as the stringer. The overlap should extend at least 2 feet on either side of the joint. Glue between the backup plate and the stringers will strengthen the splice.

Framing

Examine your stack of framing members, glancing along the edge of each, and choose the straightest of the bunch for the perimeter of the dock's frame. Even these pieces will probably have a slight crook (or bow). The crown or hip edge of the crook should face the top of the dock (deck side). The weight of the dock and associated users will tend to straighten it, or at least not encourage it to sag further as it would if the crown faced downward. Again, try to assign ugly framing members to unseen areas, such as header duties where the dock meets a ramp or another section of dock.

To ensure that decking will fit and the dock won't look like some reject from a carnival funhouse, pause periodically during assembly to monitor the structure for squareness (that is, that those 90-degree corners really are 90 degrees). There are two easy ways to do this.

Easiest: Measure the diagonals of the rectangle. If they're equal, the frame is square.

Almost as easy: The 3-4-5 triangle method. Make a mark 3 units (such as 3 feet) from the corner along one side of an angle and another mark 4 units (4 feet in this case) from the corner along the other side. If the distance between the marks (as the crow flies) is 5 units (5 feet), then the angle between the sides is 90 degrees.

Assuming your dock bears some resemblance to standard geometric shapes (rectangle, octagon, diamond, etc.), it can be visually divided into smaller sections and, using either one or a combination of the these two methods, be checked to make certain that all sides and angles are in proper alignment with each other, if not the universe.

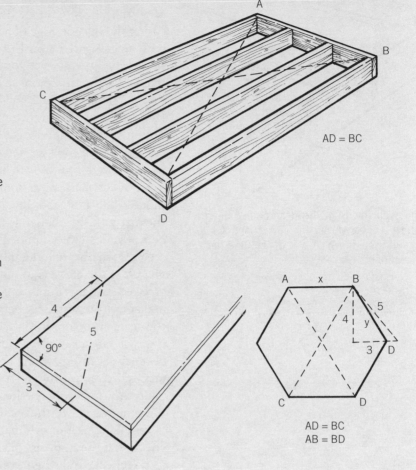

Lay out the perimeter of the frame in your almost-flat work area. Shim the parts so the deck-side surfaces are flush and hold the outside surfaces flush ("Make them feel as one," as my shop teacher used to say), then fasten the corners together using 3-inch deck screws (or nails if no electricity is available). This initial connection is only for laying out the frame — proper corner brackets will be installed shortly. Check that the frame is square, adjust as necessary, check again, then initially fasten any inside stringers in place (remembering to keep the deck side of intersections flush). Check for square again.

If your plan calls for a ramp narrower than the dock (a 4-foot-wide ramp on a 6-foot-wide dock, for instance), place two of the inside stringers so that they line up with the outside stringers of the ramp (4 feet apart in the above example, measured from outside to outside of the stringers). The bolt holes for the stringer brackets and hinges (to be installed shortly) then can be lined up, allowing the load on the hinge to be distributed throughout the dock, rather than just on the end header (see Dock Hardware, chapter 8). If the ramp is the same width as the dock, evenly space the stringers (usually about 24 inches on center for nominal 2-inch decking, 16 inches on center for 5⁄4 decking, and often less for plastic decking — check with your supplier).

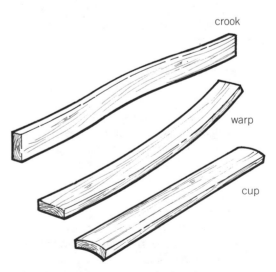

Check wood inventory, assigning the worst of the ugly pieces to out-of-sight, below deck duties.

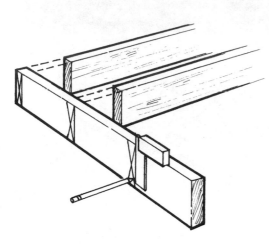

On each side of the header, scribe a line to show stringer placement. A freehand X will remind you on which side of that line the header sits.

Making your mark

Use a try square to mark the location of each stringer on both sides of both headers. A single line indicating the outside edge of a stringer, with an elongated X scribed on the side of the line reserved for the stringer, is the time-honored method of making such markings. (By marking both sides you know not only where the stringer goes, but also where the fasteners go when viewed from the outside.)

Install crossers using similar techniques. This is a good time to use the aesthetically challenged members of your stash of lumber, because crossers usually are hidden from view. Use the crossers to hold any crooked stringers in place. Measure and adjust the distances between the stringers before initially fastening each crosser in place with one fastener per intersection. The distances between stringers should remain the same from one header to the other. Once all the crossers are fastened in place in this manner, check that the frame is square, adjust, recheck, and when everything is "perfect," finish the fastening process (usually two fasteners per 2 x 4, three per 2 x 6 at each intersection of crosser and stringer).

If utilities such as running water or electricity are part of your dock plans, now is the best time (before the decking is installed) to drill the appropriate holes for the pipes and conduit.

If the plans call for a frame skirt, this is usually a good time to install it. Skirts are normally taller than framing members (2 x 10 for a 2 x 8 frame, for instance). They sit above the frame just enough to hide the ends of the deck boards; 1½ inches in the case of 2 x whatever decking. A scrap of decking makes a good gauge to check the position of the skirt as you fasten it in place.

Check again that all is square and then install the corner and stringer brackets (assuming that you haven't already done so). Use each bracket as a pattern to mark holes for drilling. Pay particular attention to keeping the drill perpendicular to the stock (more difficult than it might seem) so that bolts and brackets line up. Dock hardware that includes outside corner brackets usually demands that the corners of the dock be slightly chamfered so that the bracket will fit snug against the frame. A sharp hand plane makes easy work of this. Hinges and dock connectors customarily share bolts and bolt patterns with corner or stringer brackets. Install them together.

At the risk of sounding like a nagging parent, please don't attempt to save a few bucks by skipping the hardware. The elaborate joinery of cabinetmaking, or even the less fancy work of conventional deck building, can't handle the burden of shoreline abuse. A dock needs the added strength dedicated dock hardware provides in order to cope with nature's flair for improv waterfront gymnastics.

Bolting it together

Bolts usually need a slight tap of encouragement to slide through the wood and bracket. But don't clobber them or you will risk damaging the threads. Install the nuts loosly until all the bolts on a bracket are in place, then tighten them gradually, alternating between bolts. This draws the bracket into place without binding on any bolt's threads.

Decking

Decking planks work best when restricted to either 4- or 6-inchwide planks. Wider boards have more wood per plank to shrink, expand, and warp, putting more strain on the hardware that holds the dock together; narrower boards lack strength. Six-inch boards are the industry standard. With fewer boards to cut, it's less work to install, and because the same number of fasteners are used to install 4- or 6-inch planks, material costs are marginally less (see chapter 10 for decking design variations).

If you're using cleats, tension mooring devices, or dock ladders that require a backing plate (stringer brackets are sometimes recruited for this use), it's easiest to install them as you install the decking rather than after all the decking is in place. For example, cleats are often found on the third deck board from the end. Install the two end deck boards. Then, prior to placing the third board, bolt the backing plate and cleat to it (again using the bracket as a pattern for hole drilling). Set the plate back from the board's end just enough (normally 1½ inches) to allow the backing plate to fit snug against the framing member. Fasten the decking in place and then bolt the backing plate to the frame.

But be forewarned: All this work does not guarantee that a cleat, mooring whip, or dock ladder is held securely in place. The pull on any deck-mounted device typically does not fall at the point where it attaches, but at the opposite far end of the decking board or decking panel to which the device is bolted, the bolts and backing plate acting as a fulcrum and the decking a lever (see Leverage Your Purchase, chapter 14). So don't neglect the other end of the dock's decking. Fortunately, because of leverage, it doesn't take much of a fastener to offset these forces — usually the normal quantity of deck screws will suffice; just don't scrimp.

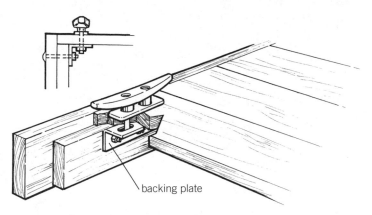

backing plate

If docking accessories require backing plates, install the plates when you install the decking.

Unlike land-based decks, the decking on a dock should not hang over the framing; it should provide a broad, flat contact surface for boat fenders, canoes and small sailboat hulls, and human bodies to rub against. An overhang risks scraping, denting or putting holes in any of these objects, particularly after the decking has aged and the end cuts become more open and coarse. A broad, flat edge also makes it easier to install dock bumpers (see chapter 15).

Filling the gaps

The one possible exception to the no-overhang rule is between attached sections of dock, where an overhang of up to 1¼ inches will reduce the open space between sections while still allowing access to dock hardware.

However, a much better method for filling this unsightly gap is to use a piece of decking known as a filler board. First, some means of supporting the filler board is required. Make a couple of support boards from a 2 x 4, or a scrappy piece of 2 x 6 decking ripped in half (making two 2 x 3 boards). Fasten these supports to the faces of the headers of the adjoining sections. The supports should fit between the header's hinges or dock connectors, 1½ inches below

Floating-Dock Quirks

Floating-dock frames are often built upside down to make float installation easier, then turned over to attach the decking after the floats are in place. In this case, any crooked members must have the crowns facing down initially in order to curve upward when turned over. Similarly, keep the joints between framing members flush at the bottom when assembling them so they'll be flush on the top of the completed dock. (Stand on your head; it'll all make sense.)

The sequence of installing floats, building framing to enclose the floats if applicable, and installing the brackets will depend on the style of dock. For example, the docks in chapter 18 using dedicated plastic float drums are turned after the floats are installed; those docks with Styrofoam flotation billets are turned before the floats are installed (the lower level is built upside down, flipped, flotation installed, then the upper level built, sandwiching the flotation between the two levels). So sometime during the building process you will need to invite friends over for a flipping good party; the more friends, the easier it will be to turn the dock deck-side up, and the better the party. Once you're fully recovered from any overindulgence, check that your dock is still square (again).

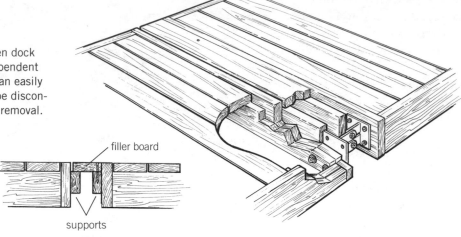

A fillerboard fills the gap between dock sections but still allows for independent movement of sections. Also, it can easily be removed if sections need to be disconnected for maintenance or dock removal.

filler board

supports

the top of the decking. When the dock is installed, fasten a 2 x 6 decking board (the filler board) to one of the supports using two screws, its other edge simply resting on the opposite support. This covers the gap nicely without interfering with the independent movement of the sections. If the dock needs to be removed, simply unscrew the filler board and, voilà, you again have complete access to the hinges or connectors.

Some dock builders rout the upper edges of each decking board before installation. This not only makes the whole deck look mighty purdy, pardn'r, the decking boards are also then easier to paint or stain, and the coating covers better (see Applying Paint or Stain on page 93).

Secure the decking to the framing members (or decking to decking runners if you're building a dock with removable decking) using two fasteners per deck board at each intersection. Leave gaps between decking boards, not only to allow the wood to expand and shrink, but also to allow for under-deck ventilation — necessary to deter rot and mildew — and surface runoff. You could measure each gap to keep them all even and consistent, but

that takes too long and is prone to error. Instead, use twin spacers. Two screwdrivers work great, each with a ¼- to ⅜-inch-diameter shank, such as a #2 Phillips (and/or a #2 Robertson if in Canada, eh?). The handles function as stops to keep them from falling through (one of many reasons not to work over water). Scrap wood of the right thickness also will do.

After the initial deck board is fastened in place, slide the next deck board in place, slip the twin spacers in between the two deck boards — one at each approximate end — push the new board against the spacers, and fasten it down. Pull out the spacers, and move on to the next board.

Every few boards measure from both ends of the last board to the header you are working toward to make sure the decking isn't beginning to skew. The distances should be equal.

The decking will look much tidier if the fasteners are installed in straight lines. Some dock builders use string to mark a straight line for fasteners. Typically, the string is secured to each end of the dock on partially installed first and last deck screws, running above each framing

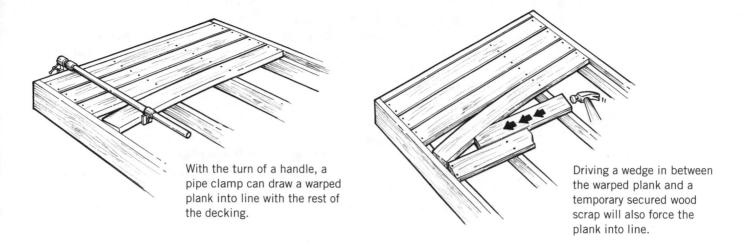

With the turn of a handle, a pipe clamp can draw a warped plank into line with the rest of the decking.

Driving a wedge in between the warped plank and a temporary secured wood scrap will also force the plank into line.

stringer about an inch or so higher than the decking.

Avoid butt joints by using boards long enough to cover the span (for example, 2 x 6 x 8 feet for an 8-foot-wide dock). Butt ends provide a place for rot to begin, or dirt to gather in plastic decking.

A *warped approach*

As framing members are sometimes curved, so too goes the decking. To straighten out these radical members, choose the straightest end and fasten it to at least two stringers (using the twin spacers), curved end pointing outward. Usually you can coax a curve into following a straight line with a good tug (or with the help of a pushy assistant), fastening the remainder of the board down once you have it in place. When a curve proves too obstinate for such subtle persuasion, I reach for my pipe clamps. Using the end of the dock or a gap between deck boards to hold one end of the pipe clamp, I tuck the other end around the rebellious board and simply turn the crank to draw the board into line, then fasten it in place.

Lacking pipe clamps, a home-made wedge also works well. After

securing one end of the plank in place as above, temporarily fasten a piece of scrap wood to the framing in front of the warped board, angled away from the board toward the center of the dock. Cut another bit of scrap to a wedge shape and tap the wedge into the space between the deck board and the fastened-in scrap, slowly driving the deck board into line. Fasten the deck board in place, remove the scrap, and move on to the next board.

It's not uncommon for professional dock builders to have to rip a few boards lengthwise to make things work out right at the end of the deck. Rather than making all of the adjustment in the last board, possibly making a very skinny and noticeable board among the rest, distribute the difference among a few boards. As you approach the end, lay out the last six or so boards, determine the amount of correction needed, divide that by the number of boards required to hide the adjustment (the bigger the correction, the more boards), and remove that much from each one. If the total correction is small, consider slightly increasing or decreasing the gaps between the last few deck boards instead.

Cribbed Notes

Cribs are built of heavy timbers, such as 6-inch or 8-inch-square Douglas fir or hemlock (see illustration, page 53). The choice of size is determined by the crib's exposure. Heavy loads such as huge waves or severe spring ice require the bigger timbers. Begin by laying out two runners, the outer edges a crib-width apart (for instance, 6 feet for a 6-foot-square crib) — the runners eventually will rest on submerged lands. Next, place the floor timbers on top of the runners, 90 degrees to the runners, each member spaced less than a timber-width apart (3 to 4 inches apart for 6-inch timbers, for example). Initally fasten the two

end floor timbers to the runners (toenailing with nails or screws — it's just for temporary positioning), square the crib, then nail the others in place. Long, galvanized spikes (10-inchers for 6-inch timbers, for example) work best for this, the spikes being used primarily for lateral positioning.

What holds a crib together is the ¾- to 1-inch diameter galvanized threaded rods inserted through each of the four corners of the crib. The nuts on the ends of the rods draw the timbers together. The floor timbers are sandwiched between the runners and wall timbers. Drill the holes for the rods before assembling the crib, lining up all the holes.

Removable Decking

Some docks use panels of removable decking to lessen the weight of the individual pieces when installing or removing the dock. The panels lift out in easy-to-handle sections, leaving only the frame to carry out (or raise) as a unit (see A Removable Panel Discussion, chapter 4, for the full review).

To keep the weight of individual decking panels manageable (a particular concern for heavy, pressure-treated wood) the panels are assembled in short sections, measuring approximately 4 x 4 feet for 4-foot-wide docks, or 6 x 2 feet for 6-foot-wide docks. If the dock design calls for any inside stringers (see chapter 18), they must be smaller dimensional stock than the outer framing members to allow the decking panels to sit flush with the perimeter frame. For example, with a 6-foot-wide dock using 2 x 8 outside framing and 2 x 6 decking, 2 x 6 inside stringers would be installed, set down 1½ inches from the frame's top edge. The inside stringers would then help to support the decking panel. (The same 1½-inch set-down applies to all decking-panel supports, ensuring that the entire deck will be flush.)

To build a removable panel, lay the decking out upside down in the dock's frame (ugly-side up, in other words). Decking runners are then fastened to the decking from the "bottom" (the ugly side facing up at the moment). Decking runners are typically 2 x 4s (1-inch stock increases the odds of the panels warping) set in from the sides approximately 4 inches. Use two runners for 4-foot-wide panels, three for 6-foot-wide panels — the center runner sometimes offset to clear any inside stringers. Some dock builders extend the runners an inch or so beyond one end of the panel, the extended bit sliding under the adjacent panel, thereby helping to lock

the panels together. If 1-inch stock is used, these extensions are essential to lessen the odds of individual panels warping.

Attaching the runners to the decking from the bottom leaves the deck side unblemished by fastener pockmarks, making a better-looking deck. (My wife used this technique when assembling our picnic table. It not only looks better for it, spilled hamburger toppings don't get trapped in the fastener indents, a serious disappointment to our dog.)

Where the decking meets pipe legs, cut square holes in the corners of the panels. The holes should be slightly larger than the legs (a 2½-inch hole for a 2-inch-diameter leg, for instance) to clear the leg when the panel is removed.

If the dock is to be stained or painted, do the panels separate from the frame, coating both sides and the ends for increased protection.

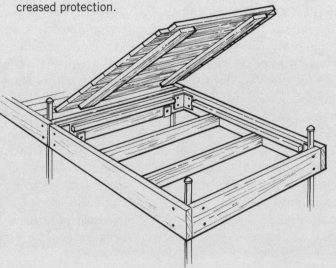

The top timbers, or stringers, should be long enough to reach a subsequent crib or the shoreline, and should be soundly secured at that point. Anchoring the cribs in this manner increases their resistance to waves and ice.

The crib's final resting place must be clear of obstructions to allow the crib to sit level and on all four corners. If the submerged lands consist of sand or mud, get in there and stir things around to ensure that rocks and other obstacles are not lurking just out of eyesight, any of which could prevent the crib from settling level. Also, in such soft land conditions, it's a good idea to dig trenches for the runners to sit in so that the crib floor will rest flat. This increases the contact area, minimizing settling.

Crib on the rocks

When the crib is placed on solid bedrock in areas where wave or ice action is severe, expandable rock pins may be necessary to secure it to submerged land. Professional dock builders have an even better way to battle nature. They drill holes into the rock, glue threaded rods up to 2 inches in diameter into the holes, slide the timbers down over the rods, and cinch them in place at the top with nuts.

Rocks in the crib

When filling the crib, individual rocks should be big enough not to fall out the slots in the sides or bottom. This limits your ability to stuff gaps between big rocks with the little stuff (the little stuff will just fall out). So avoid huge rocks, which leave large gaps, opting for a medium, consistently sized rock. With cribs, such rocks pack better, maximizing the weight in the crib, which makes for a sturdier dock. Fill the crib to the bottom of the top stringers. Then bolt the deck assembly to the stringers.

Applying Paint or Stain

If you have decided to paint or stain your dock (see chapter 7 for the pros and cons), the following offers some general advice common to most coatings for wood, although much of the advice also applies to metal.

Never apply paint or stain above water; only do so when the dock is on dry ground. Shorelines are the most ecologically sensitive part of any body of water, so any chemicals added to water, accidentally or otherwise, can have a profound negative impact on this crucial and delicate narrow band of earth.

The most trying part of applying any coating seems to be reading the manufacturer's instructions, judging by the number of folks who skip this essential task. Be a radical and read them, and adhere to them — you'll be doing yourself a big favor. And don't scrimp on brushes — buy only top quality.

It's fairly common to see folks stripped down to minimal attire, acquiring a swell tan while painting during the heat of the day. This might not appear bad at all if you're a neighborhood spectator but it's hell on the paint. When paint dries too quickly it doesn't bond to, or soak into, the material it's being applied to. The painter will likely be back brushing and tanning much sooner than would otherwise be necessary. For maximum adhesion, avoid painting or staining in rain, high humidity, direct sunlight, or when the surface is hot or very cold to the touch. Fortunately, most coatings have a reasonably wide heat range for application, typically somewhere between 50°F (10°C) and 95°F (35°C).

Apply coatings in the direction of the grain, maintaining a wet edge between the freshly applied sections

To install decking in a 45-degree pattern, begin at one end and fasten the first full-length board in place (that is, the first full-length board running from one side of the dock to the other). Then install the rest of the boards to either side, making your way out to each end of the dock using the same techniques as you would for perpendicular decking.

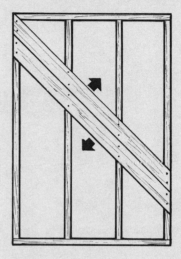

For a 45-degree "herringbone" pattern that meets in the center of the dock — the two abutting boards meeting at a 90-degree angle in the middle of the dock — begin with a pair of boards that reach all the way to the sides, and then work toward the dock's two ends from there. A double stringer at the center of the dock frame will provide better support where decking board meets decking board and allow more room for fasteners.

and the about-to-be-applied areas. Once decked out in its new coat, a dock should be left to dry and cure for about a week before being placed in the water.

A Wood's New Coat

Surface preparation is an often skipped step. New wood usually arrives with a sheen, while older wood that has been exposed to sunlight will likely have an ultrathin layer of chalking — thanks to those infamous ultraviolet rays. In both situations, the surface will resist adhesion of paint or stain. So for dry non-pressure-treated wood, lightly sand all surfaces in the direction of the grain, then remove the sawdust (preferably by vacuuming). The softer, preferred decking species (cedar et al.) are easily gouged, so use a gentle hand with them. Never sand pressure-treated wood, or any wood that has been chemically treated — the dust is toxic. Wood that is assembled "wet," such as pressure-treated wood, is best left to dry unfinished for the season before painting or staining. If you're refinishing an older dock, consider using a high-pressure spray of water (well away from the lake, of course) instead of sanding.

For maximum protection, apply one coat to all surfaces after the wood is cut to length but prior to assembling the dock, covering all six sides of each piece of lumber (a primer or thinned coat is often recommended for the first coat; read the label). Apply subsequent coats after the dock is assembled. (If this is too inconvenient, do it all after the dock is assembled.) In most cases it's best to allow 24 hours between coats.

When applying a coating to a decking board that has not had its corners routed, very little of the coating adheres to the sharply angled corners. On a routed edge — with its larger arc and greater area — chances are good that the covering film will be as thick on the curve as that on the horizontal surface of the board. Admittedly, all this routing is a lot of extra work, one reason why I don't do any of it — routing or staining — and instead simply let the wood go naturally gray.

But should you still be keen to paint, end grain, by its nature, soaks up liquids, so saturate it repeatedly, letting the paint or stain soak in. This will discourage water from attempting the same trick.

Metal Coatings

One quick word on painting metal: If you don't like the look of galvanized metal, it can be painted, but the surface must be completely degreased and treated with an "etching" primer prior to painting for the paint to develop a long-term bond with the surface. Another option, although not as good, is to leave the galvanized surface to weather for a year prior to painting. Even then a primer coat may be necessary (read the paint can label).

Working with Plastic

Most types of plastic decking demand a different frame design than wood decking, with shorter spans between members. Floating docks may require adjustments to flotation to offset any weight differences that may result from this redesign. Your supplier should be able to provide you with details of framing construction and flotation (if not, change suppliers). Avoid directly polluting your work area by designing the dock around standard lengths of decking — or better still, use a plastic-decked kit, precut and predrilled. The kit makers can then return their scraps to the decking manufacturer for recycling, at least theoretically . . .

Dimensional-stock plastic "lumber" (such as recycled PE, Trex, or ChoiceDek) is installed in much the same manner as wood decking. It can be crosscut, ripped, and routed using standard building tools, although plastic "lumber" is more inclined to split or chip during fastening than even pressure-treated wood. Predrilling the ends of the decking will lessen this tendency, but wasn't this plastic alternative supposed to save work?

Plastic decking that has been extruded into a W or other nonsolid rectangular shape must be installed according to the manufacturer's instructions. Typically, the "feet" of the extruded shape snap into special PVC or aluminum clips screwed to the stringers (usually wood) below, so even badly installed fasteners can't stick out to poke toes and such. PVC caps finish off the plank ends, keeping things tidy.

Such open-sided extrusions lack the versatility of wood or plastic "lumber" because shaping or ripping seriously weakens them.

The Bauhaus Composite Decking System falls somewhere between PVC extrusions and PE-based planks. In common with other wood-and-plastic composites, it can be routed, cut, shaped, sanded, and stained (although, left unstained, it too will turn a natural gray — like wood), but it must be installed using T-shaped clips supplied by the manufacturer (although, in a pinch, it might be possible to make your own clips). Lengths of U-shaped channel are available to finish off the open ends of the extrusions (the addition of these channels being primarily cosmetic). In common with the decking, these channels are an extruded NexWood, and can also be used for runners on Bauhaus-system removable decking panels.

Working with Concrete

Concrete can be mixed by hand, in a portable cement mixer, or delivered to the site premixed and ready to pour. For smaller jobs (such as setting anchor bolts in rock crevices) hand mixing is the least expensive route. I mix small batches in my wheelbarrow — although a clean piece of plywood will also work — using a muscle-powered hoe and square-end shovel.

For medium-sized projects (such as the two 12-inch-diameter x 6-foot-high columns supporting the deck where our dog and cat gather sun-rays), I use my portable cement mixer. In many situations, the mixer can be placed right next to the job, allowing you to mix and pour without lugging the concrete around.

Fortunately for the parsimonious with strong backs, both hand mixing and mixer mixing are do-it-yourself-type jobs: The necessary tools are inexpensive to rent if necessary (I bought mine at garage sales).

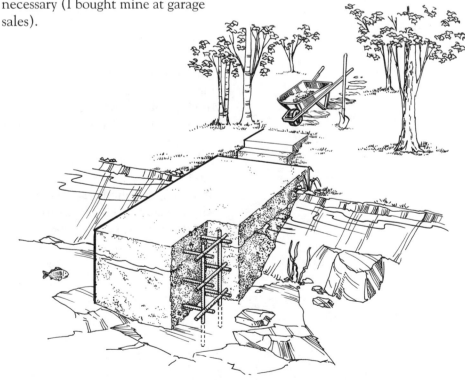

Concrete docks are not do-it-yourself projects.

Keep On Truckin'

Big projects (such as a concrete pier or deck) demand that you order your concrete delivered to the site ready mixed. Forms hold the concrete in place until it sets. If the forms fail, the concrete spills out, sets, and leaves a mess rivaling a teenager's bedroom, only with no hope of ever cleaning it up. For this reason alone (never mind slugging and pushing tons of wet concrete into place), big concrete projects are best left to contractors specializing in concrete and with plenty of experience erecting forms at waterfront locations. It's this added cost of labor that makes the installed price of a concrete pier greater than most other types of docks.

Steel reinforcement should be placed before the concrete is poured (not tossed in afterward and sort of pushed into place with a rake or shovel). Secure it in place well, so it will remain embedded within the concrete during the pour. Reinforcement that rests on the bottom or sides loses most of its effectiveness.

For small jobs, concrete can be purchased with the dry ingredients premixed, which takes much of the guesswork out of it. For the medium jobs, you can save money by buying the ingredients separately. Ask your supplier for advice on mix ratios. If he/she doesn't know, a rough guide is 1 bag of cement to 2 cubic feet of sand, 3 cubic feet of gravel, and about 5 U.S. gallons (20 L) of water. Mix the dry ingredients dry, then add the water slowly — especially as the mixing progresses — mixing until the concrete is workable.

Impressions from the end of your shovel should neither disappear immediately (too sloppy) nor remain firm and unchanged (too stiff).

A frequent bugaboo for do-it-yourself concrete enthusiasts is connections. When attaching cleats, ramp hinges, or whatever to concrete, use only dedicated concrete anchor bolts, preferably hot-dip galavanized (although anchor bolts with this coating can be hard to find — try your local dock builder). Embed the L- or T-shaped arm of the anchor bolt into the concrete to a depth of at least 6 inches. If you have any concerns about your particular application, talk to your local dock builder or concrete contractor.

A Cure for Concrete

Cement cures by chemical reaction with water, not by drying, so the concrete must be kept damp for 5 to 7 days to achieve its maximum strength. Do this by covering the concrete with plastic (to keep the water in), or periodically sprinkling it with water, or some combination. Cement should also not be exposed to freezing temperatures until fully cured; if the water freezes within the concrete before the cement cures, the cement will crack and spall.

For any outside concrete project exposed to traffic, a nonslip surface is essential. The usual practice is to gently slide a stiff push broom over the finished surface just before it begins to set, although any texture will usually work. Family initials and pour date are obvious musts.

A skilled dock builder should be able to assemble any one of the sample docks in chapter 18 in about a day or two. A typical do-it-yourselfer, whose ability to make this month's mortgage payment is unrelated to the expedient completion of the dock, could take all summer, maybe longer allowing time for swimming, fishing, and similar pleasures. Also (speaking from personal experience), as one ages both belt size and the time it takes to finish a job increase. These days, I take my best estimate of time and multiply by three. If time and money are both important, a good compromise can be to purchase a dock kit (see chapter 11).

To calculate the material cost of a dock you need a list of the necessary materials, the "Bill of Materials." It doesn't have to be fancy but should include everything needed to put the dock together (see chapter 18 for examples of format and things to include). Pricing each piece required, multiplying by the quantity required, and then adding the whole shebang up will give you a good estimate of the total cost. I say "estimate" because, in common with grocery lists, there's usually something forgotten or an impromptu purchase or design change made. Given the list, most dock materials suppliers will do the pricing for you — just be very specific about what you want (type and quality), and ask that any substitutions be clearly noted on the list.

Determining the type and number of frame members required is reasonably straightforward (just count 'em), as is the dock hardware (four corners — four corner brackets, two stringers — four stringer brackets, one for each end, and so forth). For decking, there's an easier way than counting the pieces while allowing for the correct gaps.

Deck reckoning

- For nominal 6-inch-wide boards, you will need approximately 2.2 boards for every foot of dock length. So for a typical 6- x 20-foot dock, multiply 2.2 times 20 and you get 44 6-inch-wide deck boards.

- For nominal 4-inch-wide boards, you will need approximately 3.4 boards for every foot of dock length. So that ubiquitous 6- x 20-foot dock would then need approximately 68 4-inch-wide deck boards (3.4 times 20).

- If alternating between 4- and 6-inch-wide stock (see chapter 10), multiply dock length by 1.5 to determine how many of each size you will need. (Approximately 30 of each for the above 6- x 20-foot dock.)

- If angles are part of your dock, figure out the square footage (width times length for rectangular docks, width times length divided by 2 for right-angled triangles) for each section. Then multiply square footage by the appropriate decking factor (2.2 for 6-inch boards, etc.). This gives you linear feet of the decking — in other words, the total length of all decking if the boards were placed end to end in a straight line.

Working with angles creates considerably more waste than with a good old rectangle. For example, on a 6-foot-wide dock with 45-degree decking, the longest boards will be just shy of 9 feet (square of the hypotenuse equals the sum of the square of the other two sides and all that math). While 10-foot lengths of decking are generally available (wasting only about a foot per board), 18-footers would waste even less, but are extremely hard to find, particularly in reasonable quality. Either way there's going to be some leftovers, so budget on about 10 percent of your expensive decking ending up as building blocks for the kids or kindling for the fireplace.

The number of fasteners you'll need is tough to nail down. There aren't any hard and fast rules (or even soft and slow ones), so buy lots. Or count each and every one on your plans, then add a bunch to compensate for the lost, bent, or deformed. You'll invariably have too many or not enough.

beauty by design

Good design always works in harmony with its environment. Buildings, vehicles, roadways, or docks, it doesn't matter what we're discussing, if it slaps your aesthetic senses in the face it's not good design — it's a monument, or "art." Take your design cues from your surroundings and it's tough to go wrong.

That said, the government may regulate the size and shape of your project. Some jurisdictions even regulate color. And while a few demand that all docks have reflectors, others encourage the use of nonreflective materials. So as always, check with your local dock police before letting your creative urges run free.

The interesting shape of this dock evolved from three needs — to work with and cover an existing crib dock, to have room to park a Hobie Cat, and to have plenty of space for lounging on the deck. The shape that results is unusual, appealing, and functional.

Design Options for Decking

For maximum strength, whether using wood or plastic, arrange the decking so it crosses the principal framing members at a 45- to 90-degree angle. Perpendicular decking creates less waste but angled decking creates more visual interest.

Generally, 6-inch-wide planks look tidier than 4-inch, although alternating between 6 and 4 can create an interesting (and easy) variation.

Decking also can run lengthwise, rather than the usual shorter route across the deck. The design of the dock's frame must be modified to support longitudinal decking, but before taking that step make sure you have a source of good, long boards. They are usually harder to obtain than good, short boards.

Trim

One of the axioms of selling bad design is to load it up with trim. Car looks ugly? Add chrome. Clothes look ugly? Add lace or a fancy logo. Folks just seem to love the trimmings.

Yet trim can be done tastefully. Perhaps the biggest drawback to trim on a dock (or any outdoor object, for that matter) is its potential to trap water, creating that ever-unpopular place for rot and corrosion to begin. The solution from the standpoint of taste, longevity, and cost is to keep it simple. Less is better.

▲ The decking on this dock has been installed in three different directions; this not only creates visual interest, but it also defines activity areas. As a bonus, the angled decking covering the corner bracing helps to direct traffic.

▲ The trim on the main deck could have been deleted without detracting from the looks of the dock, but as a single strip, it's not overdone. The white dock bumper on the pipe dock finishes off the dock's edge while also providing some protection from rude boaters.

The clever use of a skirt on this pipe dock partially hides the framework while still allowing for crucial below-deck ventilation. The dock seems to hug the water closer than it actually does, creating a very clean, unobtrusive appearance.

The Profile

How does the dock look from a neighbor's-eye view? Certainly the opinion of the world at large shouldn't dictate your design decisions, but this is the view presented when approaching from the water, and it's always nice to come home to beauty.

Exposed undercarriages minimize a dock's impact on the environment and allow the ventilation that deters rot. Unfortunately, the naked dock doesn't always look so good. Which is why some dock builders use skirts (see chapter 9). But never fully enclose a dock's framing. Air and water need to flow underneath.

The higher the freeboard, the more exposed the dock. The lower the freeboard, the more stable the dock. Let the dock hug the water if you can.

The deck is the most visible part of a dock and therefore has the strongest influence on the aesthetics of a dock. But an ugly frame or undercarriage can undermine a dock's beauty no matter how attractive the deck.

The profile of this lift-pipe dock works well in the lowered position (the exposed tower folds down into dock, out of sight when not in use).

When raised, a lift-pipe dock can be a bit of an eyesore. In this case, the dock is situated clear of the main shoreline, the gabions a poor choice for waterfront construction.

Shape

Shape must suit the situation (see chapter 2). L-shapes, U-shapes, and T-shapes all offer many practical advantages over the traditional rectangle, and usually look better too.

A dock doesn't have to be big, expensive, or complicated to benefit from going beyond the basic rectangle. Most shapes work equally well with modest needs and budges as they do for more grandiose plans. But remember, if all you need — or want — is a simple rectangle, then encourage your neighbors to construct the other shapes. That way you still get to look at the fancy stuff without going to the bother or expense of building it.

▲
This is a great example of a simple T-shape dock. It's small yet still gives enough room to moor the family's sailing dinghy and provide a dedicated swim area. When the dock's not in use, the canoe can be parked right on the deck.

▲
Here, we see how a dock shape can define areas of use. The wider arm of the U on the right yields ample room for testing those inviting extra-large lounge chairs, the canopy protects the boat and helps segregate the boating area, and the narrower arm on the left, with the swim ladder, lines up with the diving tower equipped swim raft. This keeps the splashing and commotion of swimming well away from the finer art of dockside snoozing, or perhaps fishing (assuming there's a difference).

The Challenging Shoreline

A shoreline that doesn't lend itself to easy dock installation can bring out the best in a creative dock builder, the more apparently impossible the shoreline, often the more clever and visually stunning the solution. The trick is to work with what you have, rather than to try to rearrange nature by attempting to impose some one-plan-fits-all on your waterfront. Good design is not only less costly to build than the knee-jerk option of explosives and earthmovers but also much less disruptive to the environment.

▲
A narrow ledge in a near-vertical rock face at the edge of deep water provided enough room for stairs to run parallel to the rock down to a small landing. Both the stairs and landing are pinned to the rock. The ram leads from the landing to a much larger floating dock. With minimal disruption to the shoreline, these stairs and large dock have created both water access and a usable waterfront area where neither existed before.

▲
This dock has been pinned to onshore rock and cantilevered out over the water, the decking cut around trees and rock formations. This inclusion of existing shore features not only results in a visually dramatic dock, linking it to both land and — by keeping freeboard low — to the water, the intrusion on nature is also obviously minimal. At the water's end, the exposed sides of the dock mirror the angles of the rock while providing three separate mooring or activity areas.

alternatives to doing it all yourself

Max's First Rule of Farming It Out

It's still your dock and your solution. Examine the wares of the pros and listen to their advice — their years of experience may suggest a different approach to your shoreline. But never let them cajole you into accepting a solution that may only be the most convenient or expedient route for them. Remember, up until you have actually made the purchase it's still your money.

A prime motivator for putting anything together yourself is cost — rumor has it you can save money (don't keep the receipts). Yet if cost is your only reason to break out the hammers, there are contractors all across North America who will gladly slap together a shoreline embarrassment for possibly even less than you and your brother-in-law Ned could, and almost certainly much quicker.

This only proves that almost anyone can build a dock. It's also true that few can match the efforts of a master dock builder. Building a top-notch dock is hard work — it takes patience, skill, and time. Building a bad dock is as easy as falling off a log, or perhaps the dock once it's completed. So if you're short on patience or time, or even the confidence to build from scratch, you still have two options for great docking: compromise your do-it-yourself aspirations and build from a kit, or hire a professional to build your dreams.

Show Us Your Kits

Kits are available direct from manufacturers and from dealers. A well-thought-out dock kit customarily includes hardware, plans, and a bill of materials to build the dock using the flotation device or pipe legs in the kit. Some kits even include all the framing and decking materials.

Prices vary according to the number of variations on the market and amount of stuff contained in the kit. Cheapest is the minimalist kit advertised year-round as a preseason special at Discount Max's Dock Supply Warehouse — bring your own plans, wood, and accident insurance. A much better source for kits is your local dock builder.

While kits are available for both floating and pipe docks, the quality metal pipe-dock kit offers the most

distinct advantage. True, most dedicated hobby hammerers can build a very good wooden pipe dock (see chapter 18 for plans), but metal pipe docks are a different story. The factory has access to good materials and hardware, welding jigs and rigs, and a trained labor force. You are unlikely to ever build anything as strong or that works as well. But unlike the professionally built turnkey pipe dock, a good kit requires enough figuring and fiddling to satisfy most of us bent on building something ourselves. And if you build the dock yourself, chances are you will know how to repair it and remove whatever needs to be removed at season's end.

Kit-Astrophies

Some kits are assembled to undersell the competition with little or no thought given to good design. These low-cost wonders often have cheap hardware (or none at all) and/or short dock sections. You can get around the short-section dilemma by buying at least two kits and the hardware to connect them (see chapter 8). But be forewarned that floating-dock plans from some materials manufacturers fail to meet even the lowest standards for stable and long-lasting docks.

No question, a kit dock can be easier to build than one built from scratch, but it's worth building only if the kit is a good one. Substandard kits risk more aggravation than the do-it-yourself route. And, true to life, the better the kit, the more it will cost.

The Buy-It-Yourself Option

Unfortunately, buying a turnkey dock is not without its own pitfalls. First, you have to find a reputable dock builder. Traditionally, membership in a trade association has been seen as an indication of professional competence. Unfortunately there aren't any associations of residential dock builders that I know of. Besides, sometimes affiliation with an association merely provides an honorable shield for shysters to hide behind. So how can you tell the good from the bad?

Educate yourself. Read books like this one before contacting any dock builder. Then ask. The best reference for any dock builder is a satisfied customer, and preferably not one whom the builder suggested. Armed with your knowledge of dock building, judge whether the "satisfied customer" is a good critic. (An ignorant reference is no better than an ignorant builder.)

Sail-by-Night Contractors

A professional dock builder's business, or at least the majority of it, should be building docks. Be extremely wary of any house builder or "Horatio the Handyman" who claims to be able to "slap together a dock" between "real" jobs or baseball games. If you've read every chapter in this book so far, then you already know more about building docks than any tradesperson who builds docks on assumptions.

When examining the differences between dock builders and their wares, compare the cost in dollars per square foot, for not all dock builders build them the same size. Also know exactly what goes into each dock. Is it western red cedar or the less expensive eastern white, or the even cheaper pressure-treated stuff? Is the hardware galvanized? (There is hardware, isn't there?) Are nails or screws used as fasteners? Chapters 7, 8, and 9 tell what should be in a quality dock and where compromises can be made. Quality costs money because it takes more time, uses better materials, and is backed by experience.

Faster than the Speed of Hearing

And finally, listen. After many years of dealing with retailers and tradespeople, including a few with ethics that would embarrass the devil, I have developed this simple rule for character judgments: Never deal with anyone who talks faster than you can think. It's a rule that only fails me when I ignore it.

Kit: Before

Kit: After

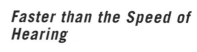

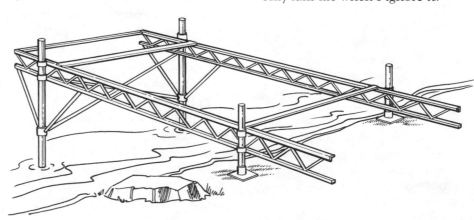

If the thought of building a dock from scratch terrifies you, take comfort in the knowledge that there are kits available that make dock building easy for everyone.

Your Dock Meets Planet Earth

Whether you're doing-it-yourself or buying-it-yourself, any dock must tie the knot with planet earth. This conjugal link, the dock's mooring system, is the crucial connection between dock and earth, the one where all external pressures eventually collide. Section 4 guides you through the process of marrying a dock to earth, while pointing out some of the potential pitfalls.

As always, your solution will depend largely on what nature provided you with for a waterfront. Chapter 12 dives right into the diverse and occasionally murky depths of anchoring systems for your dock, be it to submerged lands, directly to the shoreline, or, more likely, a partnership between the two. This chapter is a must for floating-dock devotees. Pipe-dock fans should also give it a read if harsh conditions or exposure demand that your dock's connection to land be more than just gravity dependent.

You can't get anywhere these days without good connections. Chapter 13 looks at good shore connections for all types of docks, and includes the unabridged story about ramps.

Because a dock usually relies on links to both dry land and the submerged variety in order to maintain its relative place in the world, both chapters 12 and 13 are required reading if you're keen to have your dock stay where you put it.

Chapter 14 throws cold water on the whole project by revealing how winter and foul weather can so easily undo everything done so far, with suggestions and a few tricks from the pros on how to lessen the odds of that happening. Even if the wicked ways of winter are not a concern at your shoreline, you will still benefit from knowing the ins and outs of dock installation and removal should your dock ever need to be removed to dry land for repairs, or to seek refuge from yet another "storm of the century."

mooring your dock

Mooring a dock is perhaps the most overlooked aspect of dock building, and not just by those of us who swing to the beat of our own hammers. Typical methods of mooring include anchors, spuds, mooring piles, cables, and stand-off arms, or some combination thereof. In common with just about everything associated with your shoreline, the method of choice will be a compromise between opposing criteria, such as site exposure, composition and depth of the submerged lands, the size and construction of the dock, the vessel tied up to it, the number of people frequenting the dock, and the remains of your bank account after building your dream dock. Most flotation and dock manufacturers offer mooring advice to their customers, most of which works well, but make sure the manufacturer is familiar with your local conditions before proceeding with any "one mooring system suits all" solution.

Whatever system, or combination of systems, you choose, its strength must be more than capable of handling the expected load. This is where the do-it-yourselfer (and professional, for that matter) can get confused, for there are no easy, guaranteed rules for calculating the loads. And of course, the vanity of humanity resists sinking money into stuff that can't be seen. Yet, like the foundation of a house, the integrity and longevity of everything above depends on what's hidden below.

Minimal anchorage will hold a dock in place most of the time, but one good storm will prove the shortsightedness of that reasoning. So don't view mooring systems simply as a means of hitching your dock to planet earth; think of them also as inexpensive storm insurance.

Anchors

Anchors are the most common floating-dock mooring device. They also can be used to help keep a pipe dock from being moved about in a storm. Anchors are low budget and low maintenance, making them well suited to the do-it-yourself crowd — a true down-to-earth solution.

As a general rule, budget for an anchor weight at least twice the weight of the dock. Don't scrimp, because an anchor loses a third of its weight in the water (see chapter 3). And don't use old engine parts or other carcinogen-coated rejects.

The most common dock anchor is a blob of concrete — not as attractive as the traditional ship's anchor, but it's easy to make and provides yeoman service mooring a dock. Although some dock builders use anchors as big as a foot thick and 3 to 6 feet square, at each corner of the dock, ganging groups of smaller anchors makes more sense for the do-it-yourselfer who cherishes his or her back. Groups of smaller anchors are easier to move and generally grip the bottom better, particularly rocky bottoms.

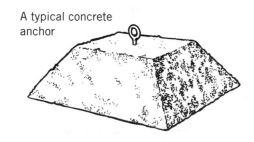

A typical concrete anchor

Anchor Placement for Floating Docks

At the end of the dock farthest from shore, drop two anchors (or groups of anchors if ganging them together) approximately below the two end corners of the dock. Chain the left corner of the dock to the

In the esoteric world of boating, an anchor line is known as a *rode,* and the length of the rode as its *scope.* The longer the scope, the greater the shock-absorbing effect and therefore the less strain on anchor connections and the boat. So when anchoring a boat, the accepted practice is to use plenty of scope, allowing the rode to droop down to submerged lands in a long, lazy curve. The rode then meets the anchor at the lowest possible angle, pulling on the anchor horizontally (mostly), which tends to drag the anchor rather than lift it.

But a slack rode lets a boat drift about in the waves, a situation that is intolerable with a dock. Slack in the chains of a dock also increases the odds of a boat or swimmer bashing into those chains. So for docks, aside from the one exception of the storm anchor (see Curved rode ahead), the path of an anchor chain should follow a straight rode. To cope with adverse conditions, increase anchor weight rather than scope, the heavy weight of each anchor assuming responsibility for keeping it firmly planted on submerged lands and the dock securely in place.

right anchor and the right corner of the dock to the left anchor with ⅜-inch (minimum) galvanized chain running under the dock at approximately a 45-degree angle. This method of chaining is known as *cross-chaining.* The shore end of the dock may also be held in place using a similar anchoring system rather than relying on the ramp or one of the alternative systems discussed below. (Anchors here help relieve stress that would otherwise be transferred to shore via the hinges.)

Curved rode ahead

Even when rodes are straight and taut, because anchor chains will always allow for some movement (a desirable thing with floating docks), strong prevailing winds can twist a floating dock to one side. Then, what is known as a *long* or *storm anchor* may solve the problem. This is the sole exception to the taut-rode rule. A storm anchor for a dock consists of a long length of chain run out from the corner facing into the prevailing wind. The scope of this chain should be about three times the depth of the water at the front

of the dock. Use a heavy chain (½-inch minimum), allowing its weight to hang straight down from the corner and then out along submerged lands in the direction of the prevailing wind. Attach a heavy anchor at the end. The chain itself could weigh 150 pounds or more, and will usually snag on rocks or dead trees, or bury itself in the mud or sand.

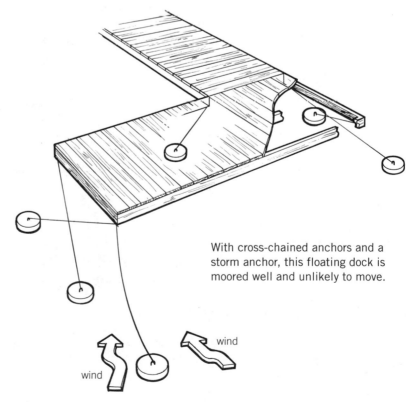

With cross-chained anchors and a storm anchor, this floating dock is moored well and unlikely to move.

wind

wind

The dock's primary anchoring still lies beneath the dock out of harm's way, its lines taut, so the storm anchor experiences very little pull. What you get is a shock absorber, a supplementary anchoring system that helps to absorb the worst of wave and wind action, lessening the strain on the dock's primary anchors.

As water levels fluctuate, scope will vary. So to keep the primary chains taut, periodic adjustments are required (another good reason for using proper dock hardware with built-in chain brackets). Obviously, this makes anchors an impractical choice for mooring docks in tidal situations (spuds, mooring piles, tension cables, and stand-off arms all are better choices — see below).

Anchor Placement for Pipe Docks

Because the legs of pipe docks moor the dock to submerged lands, anchors are needed only when a pipe dock is exposed to wind and waves severe enough to move the entire dock. Usually, two anchors at the dock end farthest from shore will suffice. Unlike a floating dock,

here we want no movement at all. So instead of chains, use four cables to link the dock to the anchors, two crisscrossed at the end (as with the chains for floating docks) and two running straight up from each anchor to the dock's frame. Each cable should have a turnbuckle, tightened just enough to remove any slack in the cable. This layout of the four cables provides excellent triangulation, again resisting movement and flexing.

Sometimes anchors are also needed at the shore end of a pipe dock, but remember that all the anchors in the world will not compensate for a dock that is of the wrong type or inadequate for conditions at your shoreline.

Do-It-Yourself Anchors

Making your own anchors is not difficult, but please, no 5-gallon pails full of cement. Pails lack the required surface area and love to rock and roll, and consequently won't stay in place.

The problem with conventional concrete anchors — the kind traditionally made in forms slapped together out of bits of scrap 2 x 6s and

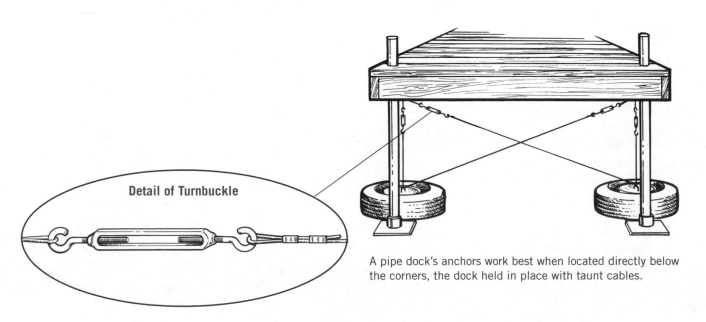

Detail of Turnbuckle

A pipe dock's anchors work best when located directly below the corners, the dock held in place with taunt cables.

the like — is that they are heavy to lug into place and a bit of a pain to make. Fortunately, there's a cheap and easy alternative — the concrete-filled recycled car tire. This is likely one of the most environmentally safe ways to dispose of old tires, since both tires and concrete remain very stable when totally immersed in water. And since tire shops often have to pay to have old tires taken away, most will be keen to give you all that you need, in 14- or 15-inch sizes.

To make a tire anchor, lay the donated tire on a flat surface (a polyethylene ground sheet leaves less mess to clean up) and fill the tire with concrete, using premixed, bagged concrete if you don't feel like mixing up your own (see chapter 9). While the concrete is still wet and somewhat sloppy, set a metal hook into the mix for later attachment of the anchor chains or cables. Either a heavy-duty, 3- to 4-inch-wide U-bolt or a 3- to 4-inch loop of chain works well. In either case anchor the hook well in the concrete — use nuts and a brace on the bottom of the U, or in the case of the chain loop, run a 6-inch-long piece of rebar or galvanized nail through the two end links, sunk into the concrete. Or for about ten bucks you can get a nifty extra-large eye hook and complete instructions (suggested tire sizes, concrete quantities, etc.) from Docks and Decks Unlimited (see Sources). Just ask for the "Re-Tire Dock Anchor."

A typical 14-inch car-tire anchor weighs just over 200 pounds (tire and three 66-pound bags of premix), and the 15-inch weighs in at about 275 pounds (tire and four bags of premix). While that may be a lot to lift, the real beauty of this anchor is that you don't lift it, you roll it. To set this overweight tire upright, slide

a long metal bar or pipe through the anchor's hook, then lift one end of the lever — using your leg muscles, not your back. (Note that a simple length of chain set into the concrete would secure an anchor chain or cable but would not accommodate the bar or pipe to lever the anchor upright.)

Once upright, with one person on each side for balance, carefully roll the tire out to the end of the dock and attach the anchor chain (or cable). Tie a long rope to the other end of the chain. Angle the tire slightly so it will land hook-side up, make sure your feet won't get entangled in the chain or rope, and then give it a roll, sending it to the bottom. This makes a dandy splash, so issue warnings as you see fit.

Sometimes anchors for pipe docks require a less haphazard approach to positioning. This requires getting into the water after the launch. Using the same lever used to get the tire upright, maneuver the anchor into position directly below dock's end.

You may need to gang several tire anchors together at each corner of the dock to make up the required weight. You can probably get by with two per corner for the floating docks in chapter 18 for average use, but add another — perhaps only at the corners farthest from shore — if your waterfront is exposed or subject to large wakes.

Whichever type of anchoring you have a hankering for, remember to secure the anchor chain to the anchor and tie a rope to the end of the chain before you chuck the anchor off the end of the dock. (Tie the other end of the rope to the dock.) Use the rope to pull the chain up to the dock's chain brackets. And keep pets and people away from the chain and rope at launch time.

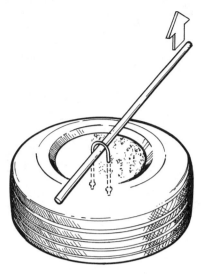

An anchor made from concrete and a recycled tire is inexpensive and just as effective as conventional concrete anchors. Tire anchors are also easy to move: Tip the tire up on edge, and roll it to the end of the dock.

Smooth Solution

Solid, smooth rock offers little grip for anchors. In this case, rock pins bolted and/or glued in place can be a good way to secure anchor chains to submerged lands. Rock pins are also occasionally used to anchor down pipe docks sitting on rock when wind and waves are a problem. However, drilling holes in submerged rock is a task best delegated. Call the pros.

Spuds on the Side

Spuds are the offspring of a marriage between pipe legs and mooring piles. They anchor floating docks in position. Typically 2- to 3-inch-diameter pipe, spuds are driven just deep enough into soft submerged lands to get a foothold, the driving tools of choice being a sledge hammer and muscle. In common with mooring piles, but in contrast to pipe legs, spuds aren't responsible for positioning a dock vertically, only laterally. In the usual arrangement, the spud passes through a *spud bracket* bolted to the side of a floating-dock section. This bracket or holder is very similar in design to pipe-leg brackets with one important difference: The sleeve is not locked

to the spud with cinch bolts or set pins the way a pipe-leg bracket is locked to a pipe leg. Instead, the bracket is free to slide up and down on the spud. This allows the floating dock to move up and down in response to changing water levels.

Spuds are best suited to waterfronts with frequent but small fluctuations in water level, with depths not more than about 4 feet, and submerged lands consisting primarily of sand or mud.

Spuds also can moor a dock at land's end, or secure a dry landing platform or mounting board (see chapter 13). Spuds are sometimes glued into holes drilled in solid rock.

Mooring Piles

The installation of piles is not a do-it-yourself job, but the dock attached to the piles can be. (See chapter 5, The Permanent Pile Dock, for the scoop on pile types, application, and installation.) When piles are used to support a permanent pile dock, they are secured solidly to the frame. When used to moor floating docks, the piles pass through pile brackets (or holders) that hold the dock in place laterally but not vertically, just like spud brackets. This allows a floating dock to rise and fall freely with water levels. Piles are ideally suited to mooring floating docks in tidal waters or in areas where seiche is experienced. Chains and anchors are usually a better choice where the movement of ice is a problem (see chapter 14) and water levels are relatively stable.

The Ins and Outs of Pile Holders

Pile brackets are available for mounting either inside or outside a dock's frame. Outside versions are easier to install — just bolt them on

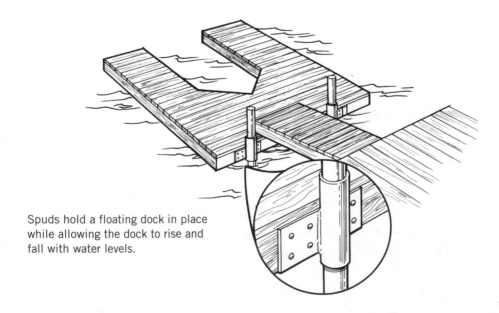

Spuds hold a floating dock in place while allowing the dock to rise and fall with water levels.

— but tend to bruise boats and swimmers. Those that mount inside the frame require more elaborate framing but don't put boats and bodies at the same risk, and the dock looks better too. Outside versions are usually a loop of chain or metal tubing large enough to accommodate the pile, sometimes with a roller on the deck side of the bracket, or four rollers contained within a square metal frame. Usually, inside versions are similar to the four-roller outside versions but mount inside the perimeter of the deck.

For heavy-duty use such as at marinas or with concrete floating sections, polyurethane rollers are often chosen. Rubber rollers are usually adequate for normal use and are the most popular choice for residential docking. Roller brackets cause considerably less wear on docks and piles than brackets without rollers. Mooring piles nevertheless require periodic replacement because of wear, rot, and a tendency to lift.

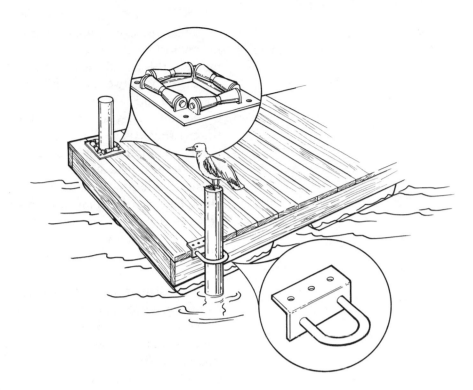

An inside pile holder consumes deck space but doesn't interfere with boat docking. An outside pile holder leaves the deck free but can obstruct boats or even damage hulls.

Tension Cables

Cables can be used in conjunction with anchors to moor a floating dock — the cables handling land-end duties — or as an alternative to anchors, or to increase a ramp's leverage on a floating section. Typically, a pair of cables extends from the dock to terra firma or sometimes from the dock to the ramp. The cables are kept under tension using adjustable turnbuckles.

Most often, cables are installed at an angle to the shore and often crisscrossed underneath the ramp, out of sight and out of the way. In this position they prevent lateral movement while also pulling the dock in toward shore, the ramp or stand-off arms keeping the dock from beaching. Cables do not restrict vertical movement.

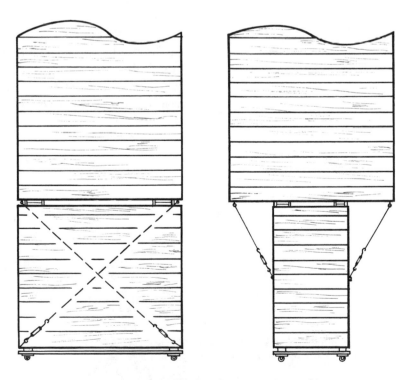

Tension cables can be used under a ramp to provide lateral support for a dock, or outside a narrow ramp to boost the strength of the dock-to-ramp connection.

Cables also can be used to connect a dock section to a narrower ramp. In this case the cables run from the dock's two shore-end corners to midway along the sides of the ramp. They transfer much of the twisting load to the ramp's frame, sparing the ramp's hinges. Because the hinges are closer together on a narrower ramp, this arrangement makes a much stronger and longer-lasting dock-to-ramp connection than hinges alone. However, the exposed cables restrict water access at that point.

The design, installation, and correct tension adjustments of cables are beyond most dock-it-yourself builders, and some professionals for that matter. If your local dock builder has a good record of using tension cables for mooring, that is your best source for site-specific information and supplies.

Stand-Off Arms

My first encounter with stand-off arms occurred when my once-true-love used them to defend her nice-girl status. I have since found that stand-off arms work equally well to prevent docks from making unwanted contact with shorelines.

Stand-off arms on docks are solid arms, usually metal and adjustable for length, that hold the dock away from shore. The arm is typically hinged at both ends to allow for vertical movement, so a floating dock can rise and fall with water levels. Stand-offs work best when the dock's width — that is, its dimension parallel to the shoreline — is at least as great as its length. The wider the dock in relation to its length, the less stress on the stand-offs and their connections. This is particularly important in areas of extreme exposure or seasonal ice with a bully attitude.

Stand-offs are traditionally used to moor a floating dock running parallel to shore. Mounting points must be solid, such as rock pins into bedrock or poured concrete on the land end, bolts and proper dock hardware designed to distribute the load on the dock end. Stand-offs can be installed by do-it-yourselfers, but like cables should be bought from a knowledgeable dock builder aware of the conditions of use and installation.

Keeping these dock-mooring methods in mind, we now turn our attention to ramps, your dock's traffic connection to shore.

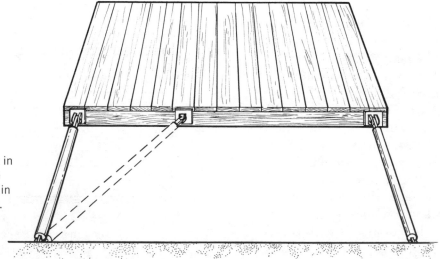

Stand-off arms hold a floating dock in place laterally, close to shore, while still allowing for vertical movement in response to fluctuating water levels.

providing shore access to your dock

A dock without shore access is not a dock at all, it's a raft or stand-alone mooring wharf. Coincidentally, much of what has been discussed so far could apply to either of those devices. However, in this chapter that situation ends as we explore the crucial link between your dock and your shoreline.

Ramps are the preferred link between residential docks and the shoreline because they're easier to use than steps and because they easily accommodate fluctuating water levels. But a ramp is not always necessary. If water levels are fairly stable or the dock remains at the same height regardless of water level then the dock can simply abut the shoreline. And even floating docks can form a rampless connection when installed parallel to the shore (perhaps held in place with spuds or stand-off arms) or directly hinged to a crib or bulkhead.

When attached to a permanent dock, a ramp usually becomes an integral part of the whole structure. But if the dock is mobile, such as a pipe dock or floating dock, a ramp must allow independent vertical movement at both ends in response to changes in water level, surface conditions, or Flotilla-the-Hun-style boat-parking techniques. The trick for any such connection to dock or land is to allow vertical movement while still restricting lateral movement of the dock. A nonpermanent ramp also should be quick and easy to disconnect to accommodate seasonal maintenance. Well-designed dock hinges accomplish all this and more (see chapter 8). In fact, ramp construction remains quite simple until we get to choosing the best method to connect ramp to shore. We may have already decided on hinges, but hinged to what? Often, this is the most challenging aspect of dock building, and the most site specific.

But let's set aside connections for the moment and deal with what makes a good ramp good.

Ramp Rules

While ramp angles on permanent docks remain constant — and on pipe docks vary only at the owner's discretion — the angle of a ramp attached to floating dock will vary with daily tides or seasonal fluctuations in water levels. As the water level drops, the angle of a ramp connected to a floating dock increases, and as the water rises, the angle diminishes. Judging by some of the frightfully steep ramps adorning some shorelines, a few folks seem to have missed this axiom of angles.

The Angle on Ramps

Any ramp at an angle steeper than 30 degrees from horizontal is a challenge to go up or down, and for some folks any angle greater than 20 degrees can seem intimidating and uncomfortable. For the handicapped, ramp angles should never exceed 8 degrees from horizontal (and even that can be unnerving if you happen to be the one in the wheelchair).

To maintain an angle of no more than 30 degrees, the length of the ramp should be at least double the height of the ramp at the lowest water level. For example, if the difference between the water at its highest and lowest levels is 4 feet, then you would need at least an 8-foot-long ramp. A 3-foot difference would call for a 6-foot ramp, and so on.

Where access for the handicapped is part of the plan (restricting the ramp angle to 8 degrees), the length of the ramp should be at least 7¼ times the maximum ramp height for the season. So a 4-foot

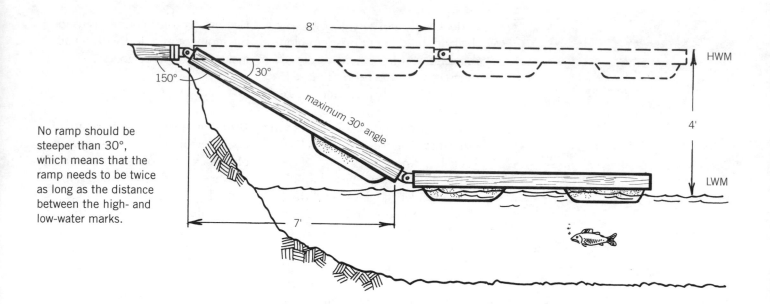

No ramp should be steeper than 30°, which means that the ramp needs to be twice as long as the distance between the high- and low-water marks.

maximum ramp height would require at least a 30-foot ramp. (In many areas this is the maximum length allowed without an intermediate landing.)

Since a longer ramp is also heavier, the dock (or the end of the ramp) may require more flotation to offset the additional weight. This extra flotation should be near the juncture of ramp and dock.

Disappearing Length

As a ramp tilts downward in response to decreasing water levels, it doesn't extend as far from shore. This shortening is just over 13 percent at the maximum 30-degree angle. So a 10-foot ramp would only extend 8 feet 8 inches from shore when sloped at 30 degrees. When working out the ramp length you need, keep in mind that this shortening effect will pull the dock back toward shore. This in turn could leave the dock in less than the 3-foot minimum water depth for floating docks.

In areas where water levels vary greatly, install the ramp so it's level or nearly so at the high-water mark. If you can't manage this, or the change in water level is so great

that the ramp becomes impossibly steep, you can consider a longer ramp, lengthening the existing ramp with an additional section, raising the dock mounting point by installing bolt-on steps, or (for seasonal changes) lowering the shoreline mounting point as the water level drops.

In Traction

Even moderately angled ramps can become slippery when wet, especially if you use cedar decking. One inexpensive way to increase traction is to attach 1 x 2 slats across the width of the ramp at 1- to 2-foot intervals. This gives a "textured" foothold. For the same reason, metal ramps should always have a perforated or expanded metal floor to afford some grip. Another solution is the plastic "traction" mats currently on the market, Dock Edge's Aquamat for example. Aquamat is a series of small, connected UV-stabilized PVC squares, a product originally designed to provide traction on boat decks. Each package covers about 6 square feet, and like other PVC dock accessories it's not inexpensive, particularly when you add the required edging to prevent tripping over its edge. And while it's supposed to grip to wood without any fasteners, it does tend to creep, slowly sliding down the ramp over time. So fasteners are necessary. Aquamat does, however, provide excellent traction.

Steeper ramps can be made less intimidating by restricting widths to 4 feet and adding railings to both sides (the narrower width allows nervous users to hold on to both sides). Often a single railing is all it takes. A single railing leaves an open side, making it easier to move large objects like canoes, outboard motors, deck chairs, and mega picnic baskets.

This may require a beefed-up dock-mooring system in order to keep the dock from wandering. Also, roller ramps can consume a fair bit of deck area, leaving less room for deck chairs, sunbathing zones, and other priorities of leisure. And as a final consideration, a ramp resting on the dock creates a step, and therefore presents a hazard. Any exterior step should be at least 5 inches high, preferably 6 to 8 inches, if the eyes are to easily perceive it as a change in elevation. If you can't avoid a step smaller than 5 inches in height, extend the last decking board on the roller ramp to meet the dock, hinging it so it can respond to changes in ramp angle.

Ramps on a Roll

Another way to reduce ramp angles is to use a roller dock ramp. Here the dock end of the ramp rests on top of the dock — the ramp moves along the dock on small wheels or rollers as the dock rises and falls in response to changing water levels. The ramp angle is less than it would be if the ramp were hinged directly to the land end of the dock. Unlike hinges, however, some roller-ramp designs permit side-to-side movement of the dock.

Two-foot-long slats attached to the ramp at regular intervals provide traction in wet weather.

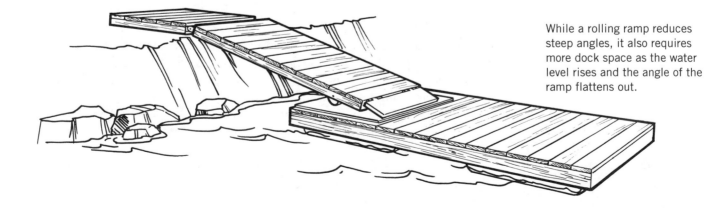

While a rolling ramp reduces steep angles, it also requires more dock space as the water level rises and the angle of the ramp flattens out.

Stair Ramp

A stair ramp is not really a ramp at all but a staircase that changes angle as the water level changes. The steps automatically adjust to remain level as the angle of the staircase changes from 0 to 45 degrees. This is not do-it-yourself technology, nor is it inexpensive, but it can provide reasonable access where other solutions are impossible. Stair ramps are most common where tidal changes in water level are great.

Ramp Size

The ideal width for a ramp is controversial. A 2-foot-wide ramp is like a gangplank — it needs railings on both sides. Generally, a ramp the same width as the dock (in other words, 6 feet wide for a 6-foot-wide floating dock) makes for a safer, friendlier entrance. You can transport a canoe over it, an outboard motor, chairs, lunch; you can even walk past someone doing the same thing, with less fear of falling into the drink. Ramps and docks of the same width avoid the kind of congestion that occurs when road construction closes three out of four lanes of a highway. A wider ramp also provides a stronger physical link to land. Floating docks especially exert a great deal of lateral stress on a ramp. Wide ramps are better able to resist these lateral forces without overstressing the hinges.

On the other hand, wide ramps are heavier, requiring more flotation at the ramp end of a floating dock as mentioned above, and are certainly more difficult to install and remove. They also cost more and have a greater environmental impact on the shoreline and aquatic life. And of course the whole debate could be for naught since your local dock police may dictate ramp width, and even the necessity and size of ramp railings.

The Ramp Connections

Of the two points of connection, dock to ramp and ramp to shore, the easier by far is the dock-to-ramp connection. In most cases, it's simply a matter of installing a good set of hinges (see chapters 8 and 9), with options as noted above. But at the shore end, installing a dock's ramp suddenly becomes more complex.

The shore connection must be strong enough to keep the dock in place come storm or high water — hurricanes and similar tantrums excepted. Also, the placement of the shore anchor usually determines the angle of the dock to the shoreline. In some situations, the connection itself must be portable so the dock can be moved with seasonal changes in water level. And just to complicate matters further, everybody's shoreline is different.

The solution to your shoreline connection may involve hinging your ramp to a stationary fixture like a crib, bulkhead, bedrock, or other theoretically immobile structure, or perhaps to a temporary landing platform.

For those without an existing crib or bulkhead to attach a dock to, the easiest and often best solution is to connect directly to good old planet earth. From the narrow perspective of a dock-to-shore connection, the planet's shorelines can be divided into two types — soft and hard.

The shore-connection systems of choice for do-it-yourself dock builders are mounting boards and landing platforms. A *mounting board* is similar to what the building trade calls a double header — two pieces of 2-inch-thick dimensional stock fastened together to approximate one 4-inch-thick stock. The mounting board should be at least as high as the ramp's end header and as long as the ramp's width. A hinge bracket is bolted to each end of the mounting board on the ramp side, the bolts running through the header to either a pipe-leg bracket or spud bracket on the other side. Pipes or spuds then secure the mounting board to land.

A *landing platform* is basically a dry-docked section of ramp, using the same construction techniques and hardware as the ramp. The platform should be the width of the ramp and at least 3 feet long. Hinges are attached just as they are to a mounting board (or ramp). Because the platform has four corners, four pipes or spuds are adequate for securing the platform to land.

A mounting board is less work (and less costly) to build and install, but the landing platform often looks tidier while providing a drier path to the dock if waters occasionally wash up onto shore or the shoreline become soggy or damp. Chapter 18 has plans for both.

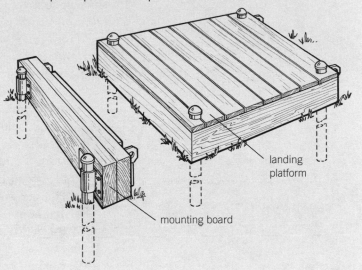

landing platform

mounting board

Soft Solutions

The majority of the continent's shorelines are soft, consisting of sand, clay, mud, loose sediment, or gravel and loose stone. In these situations, mounting boards and landing platforms (see The Mounting Point) are usually held in place with spuds or pipes pounded, pushed, or sometimes just dropped into place for a healthy hold on the world. Another system that works well on soft terrestrial bottoms, especially sand, is the *auger*. The auger attaches to the bottom of a pipe leg, the auger-tipped end burrowing into earth as the pipe is turned, typically with a wrench-driven bolt at the top end. Reversing the direction of rotation removes the pipe. The pipe is secured to the dock, mounting board, or landing platform with cinch bolts using a pipe-leg bracket or variation thereof.

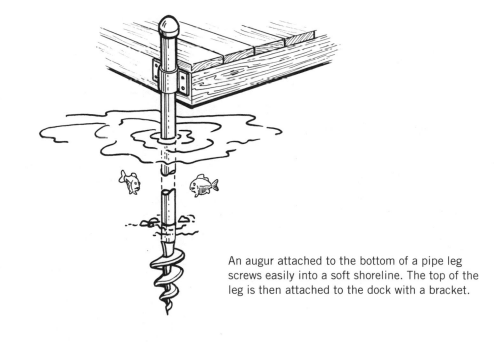

An augur attached to the bottom of a pipe leg screws easily into a soft shoreline. The top of the leg is then attached to the dock with a bracket.

Hard Solutions

Connecting to rock is more difficult than connecting to a soft shoreline, but the connection can be as solid as a rock. Unfortunately, not all rock is all that solid. For instance limestone, sandstone, and shale are porous and layered. They often pull apart with a bit of leverage. However, granite is extremely hard and stable. Hard or not-so-hard, a hole must be drilled into the rock to hold pipes, spuds, or bolts (a heavy-duty hammer-drill with an appropriate carbide core bit may work for softer rock; a jackhammer is a must for the really hard stuff). Generally, rock drilling rates high on the "jobs to avoid" list.

The hardness of the rock also affects the depth of the hole — the harder the rock, the greater the potential holding power, and the less we need to penetrate the earth. Depending on the size of the dock and its load, softer rock such as limestone may need 2- to 3-foot-deep holes to hold a mounting board's spuds; granite might get away with 6 inches.

Stick with it

There are two tried and true methods of attaching a connector to rock — adhesives and friction fasteners. Several suitable adhesives (Rockite and Flow-Stone are two) are available to bond metal to rock — and to several other things including your fingers if you're not careful. (If you're the type who refuses to read instructions before using things, have someone else read them to you; they *are* important.) Rock adhesives usually require a hole in the rock slightly larger than the object being stuck into it. For instance, drill a 2-inch hole for a 1½-inch pipe, then blow out the dust (being careful not to

breathe the dust or to let it get into your eyes). Mix the adhesive, and either fill the hole with it or apply it to the surfaces of the rock and pipe (read the instructions), then place the pipe in the hole, plumb it, and wait for the adhesive to set (typically about 10 minutes).

Get a grip

A *friction fastener* grips the rock by pushing outward against it. The most common of such connectors for dock use is the expandable rock pin (also referred to as a rock bolt). Unlike pipes or pins that are glued in place, the rock pin fits tightly into a predrilled hole. Depending on the design, the pin then expands against the rock as an integral bolt is screwed into the pin, or expands as the pin is tapped with a set punch. For added strength (and/or peace of mind), pins are sometimes used in conjunction with adhesives. Expandable rock pins work extremely well for bolting stuff to granite, but lack sufficient depth for use on soft rock. When the shape of the shoreline is suitable some dock builders rock-bolt hinges directly to the rock, eliminating the mounting board or landing platform.

Protruding rock pins can burden an attractive granite shoreline with the look of acne, and poke unsuspecting toes. To eliminate both concerns cover multiple pins with a suitable wood 6 x 6 placed horizontally over the pins and bolted to them, and then cover that over with decking to match the dock.

You'll find rock pins and rock adhesives at places that rent rock drills.

There's always a hitch

A nifty alternative to the rock pin is the 2⁵⁄₁₆-inch trailer-hitch ball. The threaded end of the trailer ball is embedded (using a suitable adhesive) into a hole drilled into the bedrock. A trailer hitch is then mounted with suitable framing to a ramp. With the ramp hinged at the dock and the trailer hitch securing the ramp to the shore, the system allows for sufficient vertical movement where water levels don't fluctuate much. Come winter, the ramp can be unhooked easily from terra firma and folded up onto the dock.

Do-It-Yourself Rock

You can also create your own piece of hard planet suitable for attaching a ramp using the magic of concrete. You can pour the concrete into tube-forms, or build forms to pour a concrete landing platform (sometimes even the surrounding soil can be used as a form). Special galvanized T-bolts are set into the wet concrete so hinges can be bolted in place once the concrete has dried and cured. (See chapters 7 and 9 for more on concrete.)

Portable Points

A possible remedy to seasonally receding waters leaving a dock sitting high and dry is to move the mounting point farther out. If your terrain is soft, this can be as simple as pulling up stakes and relocating the mounting board or landing platform farther out (a good application for augered pipe on sandy, submerged land). The usual dock builder's trick for rocky sites is a series of mounting points appropriately spaced for relocating the ramp as the water recedes.

The connection to shore, and your dock's mooring system, are closely related and sometimes even the same. Choosing a compatible pair will ensure ease of use and maintenance. This is particularly true for docks exposed to the harshness of winter. Chapter 14 exposes the nastiness of winter in a chilling account of what your dock could encounter, and how to lessen the odds of your dock's untimely demise at the cold hands of nature.

your dock and winter

In most of North America, ice is the most obvious winter foe of residential docks. However, nature wields a great deal more. High winds, huge waves, tropical storms — there's an inexhaustible stash of ammunition nature can use to remind us who's really in charge. So while the focus of this chapter is on the damage ice can do and how to prevent it, you may be wise to take precautions against nature's annual mood swings even if ice only appears at your shoreline in drinks.

Ice Capades

Generally, ice causes the most trouble for docks when it's breaking up in the spring. When ice begins to melt, it starts to shift. Runoff from melting snow lying on the ice and the surrounding area flows under the ice and jacks it up, and then the ice moves. Water levels can also drop under the ice, leaving it clinging to docks and shorelines. Shifting or heaving ice can topple cribs and smash floating docks against the shore, or trap and crush them between packs of moving ice. And if a wind begins to blow when the ice is floating free — and not attached to the dock — the ice can pound against the dock with the

power of a jackhammer. All this unruly behavior can cause some serious damage in a few short hours.

A well-built dock surrounded by open water or sitting above the ice can cope with a surprising amount of this abuse. But ice attached to the dock can twist and pull at the dock in different directions. Anything left attached to the dock that offers ice (or even heavy-duty waves) a better grip increases the odds of damage. Dock ladders and recycled-tire bumpers are two of the worst culprits. And once the twisting process begins, there's really nothing you can do but sit back and try to enjoy the show.

Pack Ice

Then there's pack ice. This quirk of nature is especially lethal and can crush any structure humanity ever put in its way. Even concrete and metal docks have been pushed back up onto shore by pack ice.

Technically speaking, *pack ice* consists of variously sized pieces of frozen salt water that drift about freely in ocean currents and winds. You wouldn't think it would be much of a problem for those of us situated between polar circles. However, come spring the ice at

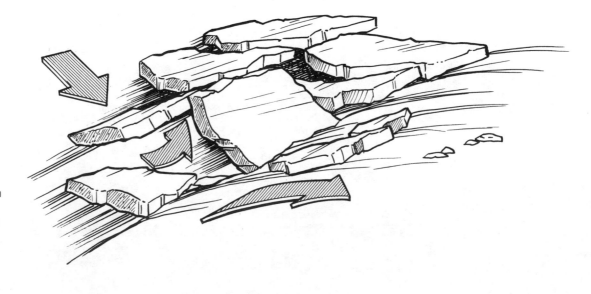

In spring, runoff from melting snow seeps under the ice through cracks, which can jack up the ice. The ice then breaks into pieces and begins to move, usually toward your dock.

many waterfronts — freshwater or saltwater — mimics the behavior of pack ice, piling up on shorelines like cordwood, driven there by winds and currents. So we call it all pack ice. Nobody seems to worry about the lack of penguins and walruses.

Seiche Who?

When the water in a lake or bay oscillates from shore to shore it is called a *seiche*. As the water level drops on one side of a lake — sometimes by as much as a few meters in a few hours — the opposite side rises correspondingly. The water flows back and forth between shores until the energy is spent. If you've ever jumped into an unbaffled water bed, you're already familiar with the sensation. In the case of lakes, the suspected cause of this poorly understood quirk of nature is a change in atmospheric pressure combined with strong winds.

When seiches take place under a frozen lake, rising water lifts the ice, along with everything attached to the ice including cribs and piles, and then drags or dumps the lot back down as the water recedes, the process continuing until the seiches cease.

Although seiches are rare in North America, it's not uncommon for them to slosh about in San Francisco Bay, where seismic activity is thought to play a role; Lake Superior, where it causes the most disruption; and, to a lesser extent, the other Great Lakes.

Battle-Proven Solutions

Anything left in ice is subject to damage. Although permanent docks are designed to stay put all winter, nature doesn't always honor that intention. For instance, at Deadmans Cove in the north of Newfound-

land, winter ice floes and icebergs regularly destroyed the town's commercial pier, taking it all out to sea. Eventually the locals took to dismantling the whole shebang each fall and rebuilding it in the spring, taking their cue from the old adage, "He who runs away lives to fight another day." So in some situations the best solution (and maybe the only one) is to remove your dock from the water for winter.

Of course, if the ice at your shoreline does a leisurely meltdown, or the water at your site never freezes, it's quite possible, preferable even, for a well-built dock to remain in the water year-round. Every time a dock is moved, there is potential for damage. The factors determining whether to remove it or leave it in are dock type, size of the body of water, the shoreline's exposure to weather, the local history of ice behavior (ask the neighbors if you're new to the area), and, perhaps most important, your willingness to gamble. Nature offers no guarantee of consistency.

And, as always, the dock police may make the decision for you; some jurisdictions insist that docks be removed for winter. If in doubt, check with the appropriate local authorities.

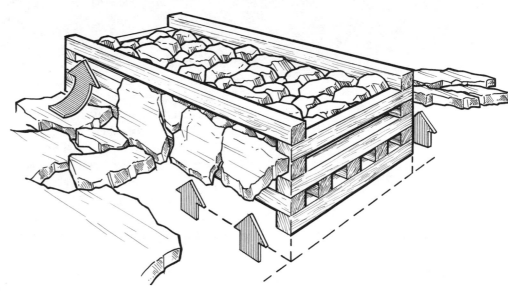

Ice grips the dock, lifting the dock as the water rises, then breaks up as the water level drops, letting the dock fall. If the dock has been well constructed, chances are reasonable it will survive this abuse. But nature offers no guarantees.

Docks of No Retreat

Any dock permanently secured to submerged lands in an area prone to freeze-up risks being lifted, twisted, and pulled about by ill-mannered ice. Because of its sheer mass, the concrete pier is not as susceptible to being shoved around by nature, but neither is it immune. If a crib has been constructed properly (see chapters 5 and 18), when lifted it *usually* will lower back down without incident as the water level drops or the ice melts.

All Rise, Winter Is Now in Session

The piles that support permanent pile docks tend to rise up out of their holes even without the assistance of ice. In most cases this is merely a minor irritant, the piles being periodically "reset" (see chapter 5). Generally, things only get out of hand (or out of hole) when ice conditions frequently raise and lower the pile, as in the case of seiche. The ice grabs on to a pile, the water below the ice rises, and the pile lifts, sucking silt into the hole as it rises. When water levels drop and the ice lowers, the pile can no longer fall to its original depth, the silt having partially plugged up the hole. As this process, called *jacking*, is repeated over the coarse of one or more seasons, a pile can actually be jacked right out of its hole. And, thanks to the vagaries of nature, a dock's piles rarely rise equally. This improv rearrangement of heights often distorts the dock's platform into shapes reminiscent of twisted licorice. The softer the submerged land, the more likely soil will be sucked into the void left by the rising pile. However, even piles driven into limestone or shale can experience jacking, although normally not to the same extent.

To prevent jacking, sometimes piles driven or socketed into hard submerged lands (such as limestone or granite) are pegged to the rock. Concrete decking also can successfully weight down the piles. However, ice has been known to snap piles that refuse to budge. And piles that resist the movement of ice are more likely to suffer from surface abrasion. Wood piles in particular are in danger of excessive wear at the waterline, the slow gnawing of the ice gouging the wood and weakening the pile.

Rather than directly confront ice (a risky venture at best), some dock builders have used tapered steel pilings painted black and narrowing toward the top in an attempt to discourage the ice from getting a firm grip on the pile.

One innovative solution to jacking is the *sleeved pile*. A steel-pipe pile is driven into the submerged land, ending about 5 feet below the low-water level. Another steel pipe, an inch or so greater in diameter, is cut in half (at the 4-foot mark for an 8-foot-long pipe, for example), a bearing plate inserted, and the pipe welded back together. This larger-diameter pipe is then slipped over the driven section, the bearing plate resting on the driven pile, and the dock attached to the sleeve's upper end. When the ice grips the outer sleeve and causes it to rise, the sleeve slides up along the driven section, which remains securely planted into the good old submerged terra firma. When the ice melts or the water level drops, the sleeve slides back down onto the driven pile, returning to its original height. Very little if any jacking occurs, because the pile below is rarely pulled upward to allow silt to slip in below.

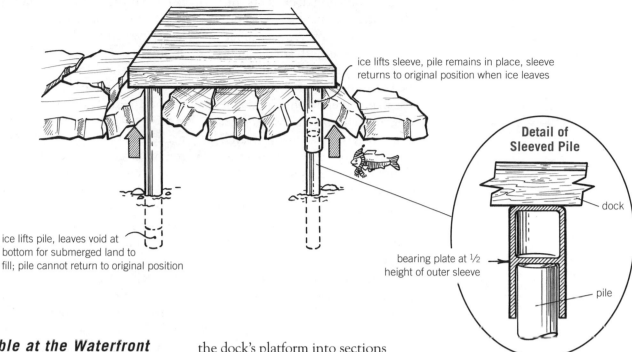

ice lifts sleeve, pile remains in place, sleeve returns to original position when ice leaves

ice lifts pile, leaves void at bottom for submerged land to fill; pile cannot return to original position

Detail of Sleeved Pile

dock

bearing plate at ½ height of outer sleeve

pile

A sleeve prevents ice from lifting a pile out of the ground. Instead, the ice forms around the sleeve, leaving the enclosed pile untouched.

Rubble at the Waterfront

A potential problem for docks designed with open spans between permanent supports (such as permanent pile docks and some crib docks) is the creation of *ice rubble*. As the ice cover rises and collapses below a dock's permanent platform, chunks of ice can break off from the main sheet of ice and stick to the pile or crib, exposing a patch of open water, which then freezes over. As the ice sheet lifts again, it pushes up against the previous ice remnants adhering to the dock's structure, breaking them free. As this process repeats, ice rubble can begin to accumulate below the dock's platform. It is possible (as some dock owners have discovered to their displeasure) for the rubble to mound up high enough to lift the platform right off its supports, even when the piles and cribs have not been disturbed.

If jacking or ice rubble is a concern at your waterfront, much of the resultant damage to a permanent pile dock can be reduced by dividing the dock's platform into sections and then hinging those sections together. They won't dance about when people pay a visit like hinged sections on a floating dock because the sections remain firmly attached to the piles or cribs. But hinges still allow independent movement of the sections if the piles rise or ice rubble pushes up from below. This arrangement could be preferable to having ice move the entire dock, risking total destruction.

To protect piles from wear and tear from unintentional boat bashings, sometimes vertical wood planks are bolted or nailed around each pile at the point of likely contact. However, these "bump 'em" planks can give ice a dandy grip on the pile and pull it out. A floating sleeve, such as a piece of PE pipe or, better still, corrugated HDPE pipe (such as Big O; see chapter 15) works much better at protecting piles, and allows for independent movement between the pile, bumper, and ice. (It also may lessen the odds of ice sticking to the pile.)

Exit Ramp for Ice

A friend's crib dock abuts the shoreline of a small bay susceptible to the buildup of spring pack ice. His solution is both simple and effective. At the end of each season he places heavy wooden beams at the exposed end of his crib, angled down at approximately 45 degrees from the crib to submerged land. When the pack ice arrives, rather than butting heads with the dock, it climbs the beams up onto shore. After the ice has melted off his bay, my friend drags the beams back up onto shore. It's a bit of a chore but his dock is still there while his neighbors' attempts at keeping a permanent dock in place have all failed.

Retreat at Your Discretion

Some floating docks can be left in the ice — assuming there is no pack ice, spring storms, fickleness on the behalf of nature, etc. More than one northern dock builder has told me that up to 90 percent of their floating docks remain in the water all year.

If the decision has been made to leave a floating dock in, the most important thing to do is to sever the link between the dock and the shore — in other words, disconnect the ramp and allow the dock to free-float. And leave plenty of slack in the chains so the dock can move if the ice wants to move it, and to account for spring water levels that might exceed the usual high-water mark. If water levels rise beyond the reach of the anchor chains, the chains could either hold the dock below the water's surface, snap a chain and possibly set the dock adrift, or break a chain holder, none of which is a good thing. If there's not enough room at your waterfront for the dock to wander with the ice and maintain a safe distance from shore, it's better to remove it or relocate it for the winter than to skip the step of slackening the anchor chains. Any dock that attempts to resist the ice, or that is allowed to come in contact with the shore, is more prone to damage than one that has the freedom to move. And good design and construction techniques dramatically increase the odds of dock survival.

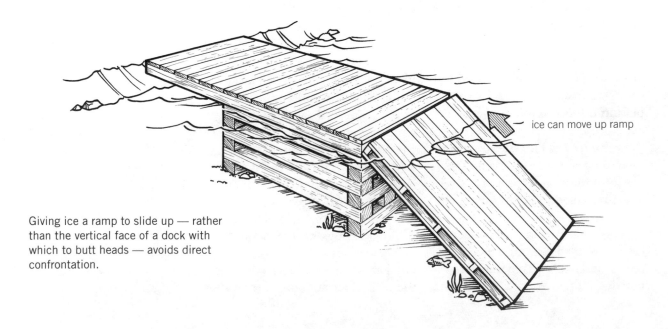

ice can move up ramp

Giving ice a ramp to slide up — rather than the vertical face of a dock with which to butt heads — avoids direct confrontation.

Sound the Retreat

No matter what precautions you take or materials you use, some sites demand that any dock you put in be removed for the winter; otherwise the ice will do it for you in the spring. This realization will likely come as a great disappointment to those who had high hopes for a low-maintenance solution to their docking problems, but life's a bit tough on us all at times.

Pipe Docks

Any standard pipe dock must be removed if the water lapping at your shoreline shows even the slightest inclination toward becoming solid. Even when the ice is sort of laid back and passive, pipe docks tend to get knocked about, shifting off their moorings. And yes, moderate amounts of ice activity can turn pipe docks into one-way accordions.

Before removing a pipe dock, mark where it lies — at both ends. For instance, if the dock runs out from a concrete bulkhead, mark where it connects to the wall with two small dots of spray paint (please, no hearts inscribed with aerosol proclamations of undying love). For bedrock, spray paint also will work, although if you've used rock pins or bolts to connect the dock to shore, you've already got the markers you need. If the dock is moored to a more typical shoreline, a couple of stakes pounded into the dirt or sand will suffice (paint the ends a bright Day-Glo to ward off traveling toes).

If you've designed your pipe dock so that the legs rest on patio stones sitting on the submerged lands, marking that end of the dock is already taken care of. The more markers you have, the easier it is to get the dock back into the same place every year.

Testing the waters

With markers in place, the simplest way to remove a standard pipe dock is to get into the water and haul it out. If the dock is designed with ease of service in mind, this is not as daunting as it might seem, but you will need the help of a friend or two. Whether the frame is wood or aluminum, removable decking greatly reduces the workload.

Remove the decking sections and float or carry them to shore. Then bring in the dock frame sections (or bring it all in at once if the dock doesn't have removable decking panels). Many folks make the mistake of disassembling everything at this point. Every year, they undo all the set screws and remove all the pipes, or legs. Not necessary. Instead, leave the pipes in the dock frames, flip the entire frame over (with removable decking already removed if applicable), the legs pointing skyward. If it's a wood frame, simply float it to shore. Getting an aluminum frame out of the water takes a little more effort because it has to be carried in. However, once on shore the lighter aluminum has an advantage over wood because both versions must be carried. In either case, this simplified method of removal beats taking the whole thing apart or trying to drag it in with the legs waterside down.

All well and dandy, but this getting-into-the-water stuff typically occurs just before or just after the annual freeze-up. I prefer to limit my exposure to frigid water to sipping from a tall glass, with cubes. For wading around in it, wet suits (the first choice) or chest waders are the answer. Chest waders are less expensive, but the value of a wet suit increases as the temperature of the water approaches freezing. Regardless of your cold-water

When installing a pipe dock, float or carry the first section out with the legs pointed up in the air, jostle it into approximately the right position, and flip it over. Then, using the markers you established last fall, position the frame exactly where you want it. Level the section, adjusting the height of each leg if you have to, and attach the ramp to the shoreline connection point if applicable. If your pipe dock uses removable decking, set the first decking panel in place. Install each subsequent section in the same manner, connecting it to the previous section.

For those lucky enough to be able to take advantage of the pipe dock on wheels, wheel the dock in and insert the sections of decking until you've reached the cranking mechanism. Then crank the wheels up and watch as the dock settles down on its legs. Install any remaining decking and the barbecue, then get out the burgers. It's all relatively quick and painless, and in most cases, dry too.

For those who dry-docked the floater for winter, float the dock out, hoist up the chains with the cable you remembered to tie to the chain ends (you did remember, right?), slip the chains into the easy-attachment corner braces, install the ramp and deck chairs, and then sit back and watch the kids scramble to be the first one into the lake this year.

fashion preference, exercise some caution to prevent tears in the fabric.

If your submerged lands are gently sloping and firm, then you may be able to take advantage of a pipe dock on wheels, eliminating the need to test cold waters (see chapter 4 for alternatives to the basic pipe dock).

Floating Docks

While floating docks sometimes can be left in the water year-round, it's always a risk. Nature is unpredictable, particularly when it's swapping winter for summer and vice versa. (Just try coaxing a meteorologist to put money on the accuracy of a weather forecast during one of nature's mood swings.) If you don't know the history of ice conditions on your bit of waterfront real estate, find out. If it gets a disaster rating, and there's no protected bay within easy floating distance, you really don't have any alternative to hauling your floater out for the winter. However, even this can be risky, because often more damage is done to floating docks by removing them than by using them.

If your floating dock is built to recommended standards, you're looking at a fair bit of weight to haul from season to season. A typical 6- x 20-foot floating dock with a wooden frame will weigh in at about 1,000 pounds, while an aluminum-frame dock of similar measurements will run about 600 pounds. If your dock is accessible enough from shore for a mobile crane to sneak in and hoist it out, and you can afford this semiannual expense, dock heft is not an issue — yet one more proof that cash is king. For those of us with docks not easily reached by a crane, or for whom cash is more an absentee ruler than king, a heavy floating

dock can be removed with the aid of an ATV, the family tractor, your neighbor's pickup (no sense putting your own through such abuse), or a few friends aided by plenty of sweat, a small collection of simple machines, and your choice of key phrases. (See Friction on the Waterfront and Popular Mechanics for hints on how to ease the pain of using muscle to move things.)

Skid row

If the flotation used under your dock is expanded foam, such as Styrofoam buoyancy billets, it's essential that some form of integral skids be permanently attached to the bottom of the dock to protect the flotation when it's removed from the water before winter comes. Dimensional lumber such as 2 x 4s or 2 x 6s serve as acceptable skids. More abrasive-resistant types of flotation, such as the foam-filled, dedicated HDPE float drum or HDPE pipe, usually don't require physical protection before the dock is dragged out of the water — the floats themselves act as skids. Still, in either case the odds of damaging a float are reduced if a couple of planks serve as mobile skid plates.

Come along

A come-along (sometimes referred to in catalogs as a ratchet-hoist puller) is a handy tool that combines several basic machines — a pulley, a winch, a ratchet mechanism, and a lever — to reduce the effort required to move a heavy weight. It's cheap to buy, portable, and versatile, and it requires no special talents to use. However, it's also a bit fiddley and probably will need to be disconnected and reconnected several times as the dock inches along to its dry-land resting place. (Other devices also work well. See Popular Mechanics for some ideas.)

There comes a time at season's end when friction rules the day. I'm not just talking about grouchy friends and family members who would rather be sailing than helping to drag in the dock they used so generously all summer. No, there is a friction even more difficult to overcome — that which exists between a beached dock and the beach beneath it.

Fortunately, friction of this type is governed by a few rules. Friction resists motion. That resistance is proportional to the weight of the object — the floating dock in this case — and to the nature of the surfaces in contact — the dock and the shoreline. Generally, the smoother the surfaces, the less friction. Also, friction between similar materials, such as wood to wood, is greater than between dissimilar materials, such as plastic to wood.

The frictional force is greater when the dock is at rest than when it's in motion, meaning that it takes a greater effort to get a dock moving than to maintain that movement (although once moving, increasing its speed doesn't decrease friction). And rolling friction is less than sliding friction. Lubricants, such as water and grease, further reduce the friction between surfaces by forming a thin layer between them. (Judiciously applied liquids can reduce the friction from those friends and relatives too.)

Small bottoms preferred

In order to get the dock moving, you have to apply a force to the dock that is equal to or greater than the frictional force. Although in theory reducing the contact area doesn't directly reduce friction, the smaller the contact area, the more control we have over the type of surfaces likely to come into contact. For instance, a flat-bottomed dock dragged up over a beach is more likely to find humps and bumps to interlock with than is a dock with two 2 x 6 skids secured lengthwise underneath and pulled over a bed of timbers or logs. Because dissimilar materials interlock with each other less than similar materials, docks with plastic floats usually will move over that log bed even more easily. Another method of achieving the same end is to attach plastic strips to the bottom of the skids. Snowmobile sliders, which are high-density plastic strips about 48 inches long by 1¼ inches wide by ¾ inch high, can be screwed into place using counter-sunk brass or stainless-steel screws. Snowmobile shops often throw out used sliders that, while worn, would in most cases serve admirably as friction reducers under your dock.

Watered-down approach

The effort required to move a dock over your shoreline can be reduced by lubricating the contacting surfaces with water. However, because the lubricant is not contained in the space between the contacting surfaces, the weight of the dock will tend to squish it out — so keep the hose or the bucket brigade running. And remember, the friction-reducing capabilities of water are not restricted to the dock and the surface below; wet shoes, for instance, will have difficulty finding traction. So place someone responsible in charge of the hose. Otherwise, threaten the hose operator with serious friction, followed by a cooling-off period in the lake, if he or she doesn't behave.

I have a come-along rated for 2 tons, which should easily handle dragging duties for most floating docks. And no, you can't borrow it — for the few bucks it's worth, you can buy your own.

But an electric winch (see Which Winch, chapter 16) with enough snuff to drag your dock out can extract megadollars out of even the tightest of wallets, so let me know if you get one in case I need to make use of it. The beauty of an electric winch is that it uses a motor instead of muscle to do the work. Models are even available with remote controls, which allows everyone to keep well back of the cable when the winch is operating. Cables and ropes break occasionally. When they do, they whip back and can really hurt (which is one reason why I bought the slightly more expensive come-along rated for 2 tons instead of its lesser 1-ton sibling). Remote controls also allow you to view the action from the safe depths of a comfy lawn chair.

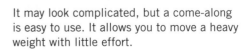

It may look complicated, but a come-along is easy to use. It allows you to move a heavy weight with little effort.

Rope to the rescue?

If your floating dock is moored using anchors and chains, rather than dropping the chains into the water (which requires you to dive into chilled waters in the spring), tie the chains up. Mooring buoys and boat fenders are often used as chain-end buoys. One dock builder I know uses new 1-gallon plastic gas cans filled with urethane foam insulation. Gas cans are red, making them easier to see, but be sure to use new containers only; even the hint of gas in a used can will deteriorate the foam, not to mention the quality of your lake. Less robust plastic bottles, such as bleach containers, aren't strong enough to cope with the weight of the chain or the abuse of ice. If you insist on using them to save a few bucks, make sure you also own a wet suit, diving tanks, and goggles so you can dive for the sunken chains in the spring.

Common practice is to attach a section of ubiquitous, yellow, polypropylene rope (because it floats) to the free end of the chain, the other tied to the buoy or some land-based mooring point. I've even advocated such practice in the past. Unfortunately, once in a while nature gets really ornery, encasing the floating rope and/or buoy in ice just before the ice shifts out to deeper water, carrying the rope, buoy, and often anchor with it. Then it's time to dig out the wet suit and goggles again.

Should you want to lessen the risk of diving in cold waters, a better solution is to use ⅛-inch steel cable, attached with a shackle to the chain, the cable then moored to some point on the shore (make a map of this location for springtime reference). Both the chain and cable sink, so the ice can't grab hold of either. (For the same reason nylon rope will also work, but there is a risk of severe ice movement cutting the nylon.) In the spring, float the dock into place and hoist the chains up with the cables, hook the chains in place, disconnect the shackles, and you're ready to sit on your dock and wait for the water to warm up enough to go swimming without the wet suit.

Popular Mechanics

While marine railways, cranes, and backhoes are undoubtedly handy devices to have around the house when it comes time to haul out a ton or two of floating dock, these machines (in common with all other machinery) are merely variations of three simple machines, appropriately known as the three primary simple machines. These are the *inclined plane,* the *pulley,* and the *lever.* Understanding how each works, and then using all or any of these readily available tools can greatly reduce the sweat and sour language often associated with dragging in a fat floater.

Each of these machines amplifies the force applied (you and your friends hauling the dock out, for instance) while increasing the distance over which that force must be exerted. The amount of amplification is known as the *mechanical advantage.* Let's examine the three machines to see how we can make them work to our advantage.

Inclined to Slope

Many waterfront residents have ready access to a natural inclined plane, the gradual slope of the shoreline up from the water. If faced with a steep rise, it may be possible to construct a more gradual inclined plane, such as a ramp, rather than lift a heavy object like a floating dock over the rise. The mechanical advantage of the inclined plane is calculated by dividing the length of the slope by the height raised.

Mathematically inclined

Let's say we have to lift a 1,000-pound dock a height of 4 feet. Ignoring losses for friction for the moment, if we were to move that dock straight up we would need 1,000 pounds of upward force (the *applied force*) over a distance of 4 feet. However, if we build an 8-foot-long ramp, the theoretical applied force required to lift the dock up 4 feet is now reduced to 500 pounds, but the force is exerted over twice the distance. The mechanical advantage is 2 (8 divided by 4). Of course, in the real world, frictional losses would reduce that advantage somewhat. The applied force needed to move the dock would be somewhere around 600 pounds of total grunt (see Friction on the Waterfront for hints on how to minimize frictional losses). But this is still too much to my way of thinking.

One method to reduce that effort even further is to lengthen the ramp, decreasing the angle of the slope, which in turn increases the mechanical advantage. Let's take another stab at moving our 1,000-pound dock, this time doubling the length of the ramp from 8 feet to 16 feet. This rewards us with a mechanical advantage of 4, reducing the applied force to move that 1,000-pound load up the 4-foot rise to a more manageable theoretical 250 pounds (1,000 divided by 4). But since friction increases as the surface we're dragging the dock over comes closer to horizontal, the applied force must increase to about of 360 pounds if the dock's going to budge.

The Bully Pulley

Obviously, lengthening the ramp is not always feasible, or even desirable, in the often confined spaces of shorelines. This is where the pulley comes in. If we attach a pulley to the dock, then run a rope through

that pulley, tie one end of the rope to the base of a stout tree, and hold the other end in our hands, we have created a simple machine. When we pull on the end of the rope in our hands, the force required to move the dock is now distributed equally between the length of rope running to our hands and the length of rope running to the tree. Discounting the frictional loss inherent in the pulley mechanism (which is small), the force required to move our dock — that 1,000 pounds reduced to 600 pounds by the 8-foot inclined plane — is now reduced to about 300 pounds, our pulley yielding a mechanical advantage of 2. (If the pulley were mounted to the tree instead of the dock there would be no mechanical advantage. The pulley would then serve merely to alter the direction of the applied force.)

Divvying up the workload

Okay, so a 300-pound force still sounds like a lot of work, but we're getting there. Suppose we add another pulley to this simple machine. The new pulley is attached to the rope we were holding just where it leaves the existing pulley — which is still attached to the dock. Next, we run a second rope through the new pulley, tying one end of it to the base of a stout tree, again clasping the unattached end in our hands. Now when we pull on that rope, the second pulley divides the 300-pound load between our two new sections of rope, meaning that

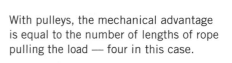

With pulleys, the mechanical advantage is equal to the number of lengths of rope pulling the load — four in this case.

a force of only 150 pounds will now move our 1,000-pound dock up the ramp (again, discounting for the small frictional losses of the pulleys). The mechanical advantage of our combined pulleys is now 4 — equal to the number of lengths of rope pulling on the dock.

Block and tackle

As we add pulleys and rope, the mechanical advantage increases and the force required to move the dock decreases. A *block and tackle* (occasionally referred to as a compound pulley) is a group of pulleys operating in unison, linked together with runs of rope, cable, or chain, the mechanical advantage equal to the number of lengths of rope.

It may seem obvious, but it's still worth noting that the strength of rope, cable, or chain depends on its thickness (diameter), condition, and type, so it's wise to purchase from a supplier who has a good knowledge of the product and access to strength charts that indicate the breaking strength of each type. Whether working with rope, cable, or chain, the working load should never exceed 10 to 20 percent of the breaking strength.

Leverage Your Purchase

The third simple machine that can help move our dock is the lever. In its most basic form, a lever consists of a rod and a pivot point, known as the *fulcrum*. The mechan-

A block and tackle is a series of pulleys and lengths of rope combined into one unit, the mechanical advantage being four in this case.

ical advantage of a lever is determined by the ratio of the lengths of lever extending to either side of the fulcrum, the two lengths known as the arms of the lever. The longer the arm destined to receive the applied force (you pushing), the greater the mechanical advantage.

A typical improvised lever might be a long pole pivoted about a log on the ground. If the short arm of the lever — that is, the length of the pole squiggled under the dock and resting on the log — were 2 feet long, and the other end were 20 feet long (yielding a mechanical advantage of 10), theoretically we would be able to lift our 1,000-pound dock by pulling down on the lever with a force of 100 pounds. Of course, the dock would never balance on the end of our pole, the far end of the dock still remaining on the ground. So we wouldn't really need all that leverage, meaning we could reduce the length of the long arm of the lever by half and still raise one end of the dock.

Why would we want to do this? To slide something underneath, perhaps, such as logs or rollers to help skid the dock over rough terrain. A lever can prod a dock along in short pushes, which is useful if the dock needs a nudge to coax it into its final winter resting place or back onto the ramp (inclined plane) after it has slid off. The lever also proves a handy device to initiate the dock's slide down the ramp for spring launch.

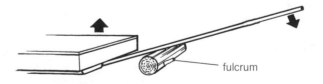

The longer the arm of the lever on the opposite side of the fulcrum to the load (the dock in this case), the greater the mechanical advantage.

When something goes into storage — be it a dock, downhill skis, or your aunt's famed peach preserves — the idea is to keep it safe and secure environment so that it will be available for future use. So if your waterfront is subject to heavy winter waves or pack ice, store your dock far enough back from the shoreline to avoid being damaged by angry outbursts of nature. It's one thing to leave the dock in the water and have nature smash the heck out of it; it's entirely another to go to all the work of dragging it up onto shore only to have nature take a good whack at it there. Besides the threat of weather, foam billets must also be protected from sun damage (UV rays) and from rodents that have learned to appreciate the value of good insulation.

Removable sections of pipe-dock or floating-dock decking should be stacked on shore, the top of the pile covered with a tarp (leaving the sides open to air) to protect them from the weather. Never use plastic to cover wood — it can leave a sheen on the surface. Stack pipe-dock frames upside down, staggering the sections enough to allow each to clear the legs of the section below. Then chain the whole shootin' match up to something solid, like a stout tree or large Doberman.

A floating dock doesn't have to be left in front of your own shoreline, if that's where the ice buildup is most severe. One alternative to dry docking is to untie the dock from its moorings and float it to a safer place, securing it to a tree or whatever else makes for a handy hitching post. In some areas I have visited, it's not unusual to find an isolated bay with a dozen or so docks hibernating in the ice. Everybody just pulls them in and leaves them there. Tied to shore, it might be wise to put your name and address on it as well. And a chain and padlock wouldn't hurt, for any season or location.

If you relocate your dock for the winter, be sure to choose a spot that is out of the way of traffic. If a dock impedes navigation, whether the water be frozen or otherwise, you could be charged. You also could be liable if a snowmobiler were to splat against the side of your floater. So keep the dock out of the way, yet conspicuous.

Machines in Reverse

Simple machines can also be used in reverse — the inclined plane and pulley easing the descent of the dock, for instance. And a large force applied to the short arm of a lever (the weight of the dock, for instance) can catapult a small object at the end of the long arm (you, for instance) into unplanned flight. Just because these machines may be officially labeled as "simple" doesn't necessarily reduce the risk of use (or misuse).

Going Straight

All simple machines lose efficiency when the direction of the applied force is not in line with the direction we want to move the load. Ideally, the applied force should be directly in front of the dock, the ropes and cables running parallel to the angle of the inclined plane. However, if life were ideal we wouldn't need to remove the dock in the first place. So because of terrain or the location of available trees to tie onto, the ropes and cables will often be at an angle to the proposed course of the dock. As that angle increases, so too does the force required to move the dock. So to minimize effort, aim for the straight and narrow — advice I admit to having a lifetime of difficulty attempting to follow.

Bubblers and Marine Agitators

Bubblers and marine agitators can help keep the ice at bay (or in somebody else's bay, anyway) by maintaining a buffer zone of open water between the ice and your dock. Both are designed to discourage ice from attaching to the dock, the bubbler by using air to disrupt the formation of ice, while the marine agitator relies on the constant circulation of warmer water. However, both have stirred up as much confusion as they have water.

Forever Blowing Bubbles

A *bubbler* consists of an air compressor connected to small-diameter tubes through which the air is pumped. Bubblers are not normally purchased "off the shelf" as agitators are, but rather are assembled to suit each particular site. The tubes usually are made of copper or rigid plastic (such as ABS or CPVC, although flexible, vinyl garden-type hose is sometimes used), and are positioned to encircle the dock, cribwork, boathouse, or boat. The sections in contact with the water are perforated, allowing air to bubble out through the water. The resultant agitation and circulation of surface water discourages ice from forming. Manufacturers usually suggest that the holes be drilled in the underside of the pipe, rather than in the top or on one side, the theory being that this splits the bubbles in two (since the air tends to rise on both sides of the pipe), thus increasing the bubbler's effectiveness. And because the holes point down rather than up, it also lessens the odds of those holes silting up when the bubbler is not in use.

Depending on design, a bubbler may not be able to open the water once it has frozen, in which case it should be turned on before ice has formed. For the same reason, a bubbler may not be able to cope if there's a power outage that lasts long enough to allow ice to form and thicken. On the plus side, the bubbler has very little impact on lakes or rivers, keeping only the immediate area around the dock open, and bubblers have little or no effect on submerged lands. This minimizes the potential dangers to both humans and aquatic life. Bubblers also require less water to operate in than agitators (about 3 feet minimum), although, in common with the agitator, the deeper the water (and therefore bubbler), generally the wider the opening in the ice. Two potential drawbacks to blowing bubbles are that the air pump can be very noisy, and the average bubbler costs about twice as much as a comparable agitator.

Paid Agitator

As the name implies, *marine agitators* work by agitating the water, drawing the warmer subsurface water to the surface while keeping the surface in a constant state of agitation.

An agitator is essentially a submersible electric motor operating a propeller, both of which are mounted in an open-ended cylinder. When the agitator's propeller is spinning, water is continuously drawn up from the bottom and through the cylinder, and then forced up to the surface. By keeping the water moving faster than about 1½ feet per second (which is about as slow as a grocery-store checkout on a Saturday afternoon) the

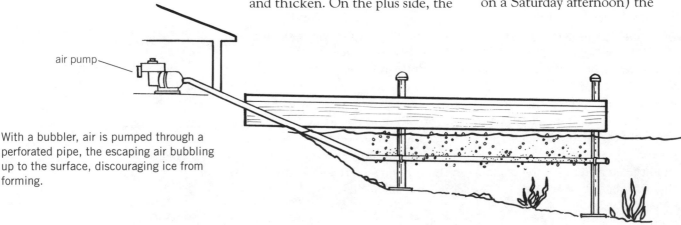

air pump

With a bubbler, air is pumped through a perforated pipe, the escaping air bubbling up to the surface, discouraging ice from forming.

agitator discourages ice crystals from forming a solid ice cover.

What happens during a power outage? At minus 20°F (about minus 30°C), not much more than 4 inches of ice will form during a 24-hour period. Therefore, if the unit is mounted about 3 feet below the surface (and you should have at least that much between the agitator and submerged lands), an owner should have a few days grace before the ice reaches down to the agitator and freezes the propeller in place. Unlike some bubblers, as long as the propeller is free to move an agitator will soon reopen the area above it.

The size of the open area is dictated by the design of the agitator, the horsepower of the motor, and the positioning of the agitator relative to the dock and water's surface. The challenge in operating an agitator is not in making the hole big enough, but in minimizing the agitator's effect. Agitators are available from about ⅓ hp to 1½ hp, the more powerful units being designed to operate in sewage lagoons. For more conventional applications, the less horsepower the better. It doesn't take much power for a marine agitator to keep the water circulating and in a state of continuous agitation (think of it as a teenager/parent relationship), and therefore the surface open around your dock. As a bonus, a smaller agitator also costs less to purchase and operate.

Area of Influence

While the effects of a bubbler usually don't extend much beyond the dock, an agitator that's too big or poorly situated can easily open up a dangerously large area of ice. During mild spells, open areas created by agitators can stretch out to include neighbors' docks, creating a

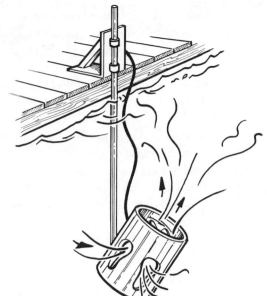

Agitators draw warmer water up from the bottom, forcing it to the surface, the temperature and movement of the water discouraging ice from forming.

hazard for anyone who walks, skis, or snowmobiles across the ice, not to mention wandering animals. And unlike the bubbler, an agitator stirs up currents below the ice, which can create dangerously thin ice for a considerable distance around the visible section of open water. If that thin ice is covered with snow, it can be especially deceptive.

Any open area of thin ice or open water you create, by any means, must be fenced off. Bright orange plastic snow fencing works well for this task, and install at least one flashing warning light of the color associated with snow hazards in your area (blue in most jurisdictions). Also, post signs warning of open water.

Opening up a can of legalities

Isn't this overkill for a bit of open water? Absolutely not. The potential for harm to animals and humans aside, it's likely the creator of the hazard would be liable for any mishaps. There also are laws in most jurisdictions governing the creation of such hazards. For instance, under Section 263 of the criminal code of Canada, "Every one who makes or causes to be made an opening in ice that is open to or frequented by the public is under legal duty to guard it in a manner that is adequate to prevent persons from falling in by accident and is adequate to warn them that the opening exists." Anyone who fails to do so could be fined, imprisoned, even charged with manslaughter should a drowning occur. Legal precedents indicate that the law also would likely be interpreted as referring to the area of thin ice surrounding the actual opening created by a marine agitator. Fortunately, snow fencing, lights, and signs are cheaper than lawyers and out-of-court settlements.

A kinder, gentler agitation

There are some simple ways to minimize the negative effects of a marine agitator. Like the dock itself, each installation is different, so before you buy, call the manufacturer for advice about size and mounting. The size of the hole in the ice can be controlled with a timer and/or a thermostat. Install either (or both) in a sheltered area, mounted on a post, and keep them protected from the wind, rain, and snow. Set a thermostat to turn on when the temperature drops below freezing. If positioned so that the sun's rays can reach it, the thermostat will shut off when the sun shines on it, restricting operation primarily to nights and cold, cloudy days. An agitator controlled by a photo-cell also works more efficiently, the unit being switched on at night, running for only about 12 to 14 hours each day. Regardless of which method you use to reduce the operating time of an agitator, you always save on electrical operating costs.

Speaking of reducing operating time, a marine agitator doesn't have to operate all winter in order to protect your dock during ice breakup. You can install it about 4 to 5 feet below the surface in late fall before the ice forms, and then switch it on around the middle of February. Because it takes about a week for an agitator to melt through 2 feet of ice, this usually allows plenty of time for it to create that protective corridor of open water around the dock. However, there are no guarantees when it comes to nature's capricious behavior, the proverbial January thaw (which can arrive in any month) being a fine example. Those with unattended seasonal homes may not want to risk their dock in exchange for the savings of a sedentary agitator.

Bubblers and agitators are useless against pack ice. The only solution to a pack-ice problem is moving the dock out of harm's way.

Environmental agitator

Ecologists have expressed some concerns about the long-term use of agitators. The resulting disruption to submerged lands and water temperatures has not been studied sufficiently to determine the effect on fish habitat and reproduction, but the opinion has been expressed, and it seems likely, that it will have a negative impact.

Your waterfront is also a battlefront. On one side is land, submerged or otherwise, defending the status quo. On the other side are the combined forces of air and water continuously attacking land's resolve. Caught in the middle of this dispute is your dock and its link to the shoreline. Thus far we have largely dealt with increasing the odds of your dock surviving this ruckus. In the next section, we look at giving your boat some of the same advantages.

section 5

Your Dock and Your Watercraft

No dock exists for its own sake. Some inevitably are built to serve primarily as fashion statements — we are, after all, still dealing with humanity here — and docks also can be great places from which to go swimming, cast a fishing rod, and/or merely lounge about on a sunny afternoon (or any other time a lounge might take your fancy). Yet certainly the principal function of the species residential dock, and the reason so many are attached to the waterfronts of North America, is to accommodate the parking of watercraft. A residential dock is not just the interface between land and water, but also between people and watercraft. This is the focus of section 5 — how to make your dock, and shoreline for that matter, more boat friendly.

Chapter 15, recommended reading for millions of boaters everywhere, examines the many ways to minimize the hassles of mooring a boat to your dock. And should the best solution to mooring a boat at your shoreline be to remove it from the water entirely, chapter 16 provides the necessary data on drip-dry docking.

mooring your boat

Although mooring a boat in the water is essentially a marriage between dock and boat, this chapter concentrates on the dock half of that relationship. The boat's side of the story has been dealt with many times before, in many journals, so we'll just touch on it from time to time.

Much of the wear and tear that a boat endures comes from dockside abuse. Bounced off the dock (or other boats) by wind, waves, and humans, the family showboat soon can look like a refugee from Sam's Sampan Salvage. And every time the boat hits the dock, the dock also suffers.

Not surprisingly, the main bane to safe and happy mooring is the same for both boats and docks — exposure. If the water at your shoreline gets nasty quickly, or varies greatly in depth — whether day to day or season to season — your boat is vulnerable to nature's mean streak. And fellow boaters can (usually unwittingly) batter a shoreline with a barrage of wakes.

The weight, size, and shape of your boat will determine the amount of force these elements can exert on the dock. For example, a light pontoon boat with side curtains presents a large surface area to the wind. So any dock with this type of boat attached to it is more susceptible to damage in a howling storm than would be the case for the same dock clutching a much lighter 14-foot utility boat, or even a much heavier and sleeker cabin cruiser.

No matter which method of mooring you choose, it will undoubtedly include rope, a rather knotted and tangled subject already well covered in several books about boating (see Sources for suggested reading). Very briefly, avoid polypropylene (that ubiquitous yellow stuff) for mooring lines. It frays, breaks down under sunlight, is slippery, and doesn't hold a knot well. By far the best material is nylon, prepackaged as a dedicated mooring line with loops to slip around cleats and whipped ends (a small-diameter cord wrapped around the end of the line to prevent unraveling). For quality, dedicated mooring lines, see your local marina rather than a general hardware store.

Bitts and Pieces

On both dock and boat, mooring lines are tied to bitts, bollards, cleats, or rings. Bitts are like pants — they come in pairs except everybody knows there's only one of them. Officially, *bitts* consist of two vertical wooden posts and, sometimes, a horizontal bar runs between them. When bitts are made of metal (usually with a Madonna-like waistline tucked in just below the top to hold the rope in place), they are known as *bollards*, although the terms and shapes are argued by experts from all factions of the boating world. Call them either name and you're sure to initiate a lively debate among keen sailors.

In regulation dress, both mooring devices are heavy-duty items designed more for mooring freighters than for runabouts. Therefore, both are more likely to turn up for duty at commercial piers and marinas than at residential docks. It's not unusual, however, to find smaller versions attached to the decks of recreational boats, particularly sailboats.

While it would help to have your Boy Scout or Girl Guide badges for knots and hitches when securing mooring lines to bitts and bollards, cleats are a simple matter. The *cleat* is a chopped and lowered T, the rope wrapping around the arms of the T, overlapping itself in the

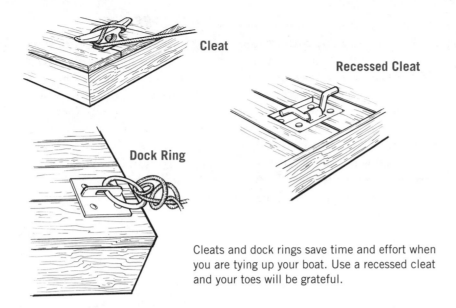

Cleat

Recessed Cleat

Dock Ring

Cleats and dock rings save time and effort when you are tying up your boat. Use a recessed cleat and your toes will be grateful.

process for a firm hold. Cleats for docks are most often cast aluminum, although they also are available in brass or bronze for those looking to unload a little excess cash. Cleats are the best conventional method to tie a boat to a dock.

Dock rings (which are like big earrings, a steel plate substituting for the earlobe) are also popular, although mainly for their price advantage. As with bitts, you need to know your knots to use rings. A variation of the conventional dock ring is the portable dock ring. While designed to slip in between the decking boards of any dock when needed, and removed when not, it's questionable how useful they are, considering that many docks lack suitable decking. Extra rope is decidedly more versatile when mooring away from home base.

Toe Crunchers

Usually your toe will find traditional cleats or rings before your eyes do. The recessed versions of both work just as well but are less likely to mash the toes. Hinged and recessed cleats and recessed rings sit

flush with the deck surface of a dock, the actual cleat or ring hiding in a shallow metal "cup" set into the decking. When needed, simply flip it up out of the "cup" and secure your mooring lines in the traditional manner. Another option is a cast-aluminum hinged cleat that folds flat. Folded, these are still slightly proud of the dock's decking but don't require routing recesses into the decking.

Any mooring device should be at least large enough to handle the diameter of your mooring lines, the mooring lines in turn at least large enough to handle the size and weight of your boat — in a storm. So buy the mooring device to suit the mooring lines, not the other way around.

The Bump and Grind Review

No matter how well the family flotilla is secured to the dock, there's still a chance nature will take a swing at it hard enough to send it ricocheting off the dock. While boat fenders are cheap insurance against damaged hulls, dock bumpers are the answer for docks.

The tug on any mooring device (such as a cleat or mooring whip), or perhaps even a dock ladder if you've got a horde of rowdy kids, should be distributed over as much as the dock's frame as possible. Any accessory attached to the dock with screws or lag bolts puts the entire load on the wood fibers immediately surrounding the fastener's threads, a very small and insubstantial area. If the cleat (or whatever) is bolted in place, the load is distributed over the adjacent area of the structure by the bolt, nut, and washer. Better still, bolt your mooring devices and dock accessories through the decking to a bracket attached to the frame — the stress is then distributed over a much larger area of the structure.

If your dock has removable decking panels (see chapters 4 and 9), don't attach mooring devices to them. Instead, bolt directly to the dock's frame, or to individual nonremovable decking boards that have been securely fastened to the frame.

The position of a mooring device should be determined by the angle of the mooring line, rather than dock aesthetics. For cleats, bitts, and the like, farther apart is better than closer together. Smaller angles pull up on the cleat, putting the stress on the fasteners. Larger angles pull in a more sideways fashion, sharing more of the stress with the dock.

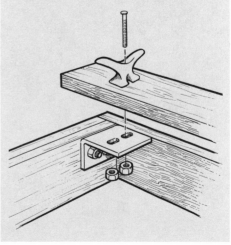

A dedicated mooring pile is one that stands out in the water all by its lonesome, its purpose not to moor a dock but to moor a boat. This frees up the dock for other activities, or perhaps other boats that come and go with greater frequency. Tying up to a dedicated mooring pile can be a bit of a hassle in areas faced with tides, seiche, or large wakes. As water levels fluctuate, the angle of the mooring line varies and therefore so too does the distance between boat and pile. A simple fix is to slide a section of corrugated HDPE pipe — also known as Big O — over the pile. The 1- to 2-foot-long section fits the pile like a loose sleeve. Because the specific gravity of HDPE is approximately 0.95 — less than water, in other words — Big O floats, so there's no need to secure it to the pile. This in turn allows it to float freely in response to fluctuating water levels, rising and falling with the water. As a bonus, the corrugations molded into the pipe work to provide a reasonable amount of grip for the mooring lines. Of course, Big O wasn't originally designed to do all this stuff, but if it works, why not? And it's cheap to boot.

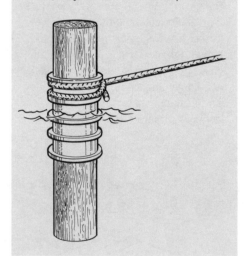

Boat fenders won't protect the dock from the park-by-ear techniques of visiting boaters, nor will fenders keep swimmers free of splinters and bruises when frolicking about the edges of the dock. Dock bumpers will at least reduce the potential for such fun-threatening injuries. Bumpers work great in conjunction with fenders. Bumpers are also a tidy way to finish the edges of docks.

Vinyl Strip Show

The majority of dock bumpers are long, molded strips of vinyl. Bumpers typically are secured to the outer perimeter of the dock using stainless-steel screws and cup washers (best choice), or galvanized roofing nails. Some bumpers are simple channels (sold cheap by the linear foot) that attach to, and protect, the sides of the dock only. An L-shaped variation (sold for about twice as much as the aforementioned cheapie) that fits over the outer edge of the deck as well offers some additional protection if a boat (or swimmer) bangs down on the dock's edge. For most styles of dock bumper, special corner pieces that wrap around the dock's corners are available. These not only dress up a dock but also add a modicum of protection.

Dock Leggings

For docks with exposed piles, pipe legs, or spuds, *fender boards* (horizontal boards in front of the piles, legs, or spuds) will provide an uninterrupted surface for boat fenders to rub against. PVC caps and shrouds that slide over pipes or spuds are not as good as dock bumpers or boat fenders, but better than nothing.

Vertically mounted bumpers (also known as vertical rub rails) are a must for any nonfloating dock exposed to fluctuating water. They provide a cushion for a boat to nudge up against regardless of what the water's doing. Install them at intervals along the dock's edge to accommodate expected boat sizes. There are bumpers designed specifically for such applications using vertical runs of high-impact PVC tubing held out from the dock by special polyurethane mounts. They're available in sizes to accommodate various sizes of boat, usually in 1¾- to 3-inch diameters. However, most standard dock bumpers work either horizontally or vertically.

If there is a possibility that shifting ice could be a seasonal visitor to your shoreline, any additions to the side of your dock — such as bumpers — could provide a handle

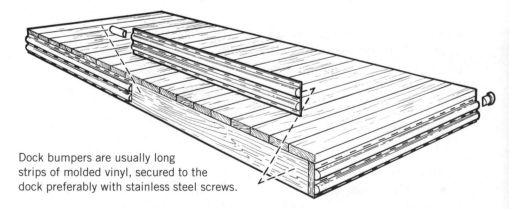

Dock bumpers are usually long strips of molded vinyl, secured to the dock preferably with stainless steel screws.

for the ice to grab on to (see chapter 14 regarding potential problems with ice). Bumpers and fender boards may have to be removed before each winter.

A Tired Solution

Contrary to tradition, tires — new, used, whitewalls, or even when draped in cast-off carpeting to protect the boat's hull from contact skid marks — do not belong on the side of docks. Besides adding a visual blight to the shoreline, dock-mounted tires can damage boats and, where tire rubs against dock, offer a grand place for rot to begin. Save your worn-out tires for anchors (see chapter 12).

Mooring Tension

The role of boat fenders and dock bumpers is to soften the blow of minor impacts between boat and dock when the boat is parked or parking. The role of a tension mooring system is to prevent after-parked impacts.

Note: The term *tension mooring system* is one coined by me to describe mooring systems that use some means of tension to hold the boat away from the dock. So unless your local marina personnel have read this book, chances are they won't know what you're talking about if you ask to see the store's selection of tension mooring systems. However, as we shall see, this shouldn't be a problem.

If you've ever had to sit between two sparring kids to keep them separated (ah, the joys of parenthood), then you've experienced the basic concept of any tension mooring system. A tension mooring system holds a boat alongside, but not in contact with, the dock. Much as you did with the kids, it separates the combatants of boat and dock, and can be very effective in situations where wakes from heavy traffic conspire to bring the boat and dock angrily together.

Bumper Wheels

To understand how a bumper wheel (or dock wheel) works, picture the steering wheel of a city bus, reduced to a 10-inch diameter and heavily padded, mounted horizontally at the corner of the dock. As a boat bumps into the edge of the wheel, the soft vinyl and turning motion absorb the energy of minor parking errors, all the while helping guide the craft into harbor. A bumper wheel will set you back about the equivalent of three to four CDs of reissued Everly Brothers tunes.

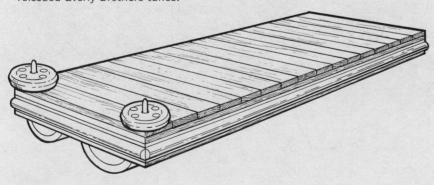

Strong-Arm Tactics

While variations abound, tension mooring systems fall into two basic categories: the rigid-arm type (which your marina will know by trade names such as Wake Watchers) and mooring whips (a term every marina should be familiar with). The rigid-arm system holds the boat out from the dock using twin metal arms (one each for bow and stern) that swing either out or down to the boat. The boat is attached to the arm with either mooring lines or springs. Using spring tension, the arms keep the boat bobbing about in the water 3 or 4 feet away from dockside. Adding fore and aft spring mooring lines (crisscrossed) is usually recommended in rough conditions or when leaving the boat unattended for long periods. To get into the boat, simply swing one arm back toward the dock and the boat will follow.

Whipped into Shape

When it comes to dockside showmanship, it's hard to beat mooring whips. A pair of fiberglass rods, typically 12 to 24 feet long, arc out from the dock at about a 30-degree angle, bending like twin fishing rods under the load of a mighty catch — the catch in this case being your boat. The ends of the whips tie up to your boat with mooring lines, each line having a friction lock to adjust the tension to suit location and boat type. Unlike a rigid-arm system, conventional mooring lines must also run between the boat and the dock. As the whips pull the boat away from the dock, bow and stern mooring lines pull it back. Fore and aft spring lines control the boat's movement along the length of the dock. This combination of lines keeps the tips and the bases of the whips in line so that the boat is constantly being pulled in a straight

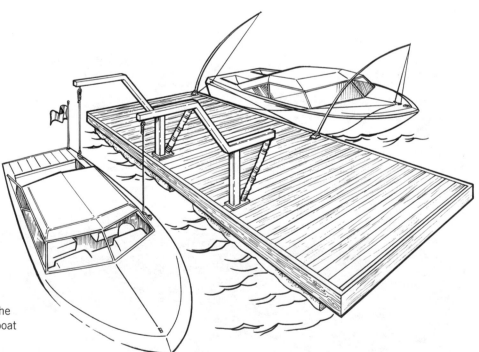

The rigid arm system (left) and mooring whips (right) both use tension to allow the boat to move a little while keeping the boat from contacting the dock.

line out from the dock. What you get is a sort of stalemated tug-of-war, the boat sitting out from the dock far enough to prevent wave action from bringing the two together. When you want to board ship, haul it in using one of the mooring lines, disconnect the whips and lines, and you're out to launch.

Caveats

The importance of correct alignment limits the versatility of all tension mooring systems. Each system is set up for one particular boat at one particular dock. If a visiting boat's cleats do not line up, the mooring system will not be as effective. Mooring whips can be mounted on the boat, allowing you to take them with you, but the odds are slim that the cleats on any dock away from home will line up with the whips on the boat. It will happen occasionally, just not to us.

And while on the subject of things slightly out of whack, don't let the kids play Tarzan on any tension mooring system. It's undeniably tempting, but it could break the system, especially whips.

Choosing a system the correct size for your boat is very important. What works for your neighbor may not work for you. And unfortu-

nately, not all marine outlets are as attuned to the peculiarities of tension mooring systems as they should be. Manufacturers' charts that relate boat length and weight to mooring-system size (some systems will handle boats up to 72,000 pounds) are a help, but it is impossible for any chart to consider unusual conditions or all the differing boat configurations. If in doubt, consult the manufacturer.

Most wet mooring situations will benefit from a tension mooring system, but it's important to stress that, contrary to some brochure hyperbole, none replaces boat fenders or dock bumpers. You still need the old standbys to protect your boat and dock from the occasional bungled parking job and to make sure your dock is accessible to visitors. Plus there's always the possibility that a tension mooring system will be overpowered by that one nasty summer storm.

While wet mooring systems will fill the bill for the majority of North America's boat-parking needs, in some situations nature proves too unpredictable to tempt with a boat left to innocently bob about in the water, much as an unsuspecting hen might cluck in front of a stealthy fox. At times like this, we must turn to chapter 16 and consider dry docking.

dry docking

Storms, wakes, waves, algae, zebra mussels, pollution — at times it seems nature's sole reason to exist is simply to wreck your boat. So the best way to keep your boat in prime condition is to not put it in water. However, what's good for the boat is obviously not always good for the boater, for a boat out of water is like a politician out of your pocket — neither functions at its best. What we need, at least for the boat, is a compromise. Such as dry docking.

Dry docking gets a boat out of the water when it's not being used. The less time in the water, the less a boat is exposed to those aquatically inclined destructive forces.

The conditions that suggest a dry solution to boat parking as opposed to leaving the family scow in the water are the same as for wet mooring solutions or dock building — it's only the severity that differs. Exposure, wind, wakes, the topography of submerged lands and uplands and the composition of both, boat size and shape, wallet size and shape — all must be assessed to determine if a dry-docking system is needed and, if so, which one will work best for you.

For example, there is a shoreline on a lake just a float down the river from me that is wonderfully sandy on both sides of the shore and relatively shallow for a good distance out — an ideal spot for windsurfing and general frolicking about in the waves, as most of the local townsfolk will attest. Yet, with an open exposure that can turn calm water into rolling whitecaps in a matter of minutes, the only way to ensure safe parking along the shoreline is get your boat out of the water.

This brings up a crucial point: Alternatives to the traditional wet dock must be both easy to use and reliable. With a storm brewing on the horizon, you may not have the luxury of time. Even without the

urgency of emergencies, fussy mechanisms and procedures are irksome to use, increasing the likelihood that they will not get used, which defeats the whole reason for owning them. Boat trailers, for instance, while great for transporting the yacht hither and thither, are about as convenient for regular parking as downtown Megalopolis during rush hour. Fortunately, there are several good dry-docking systems that work well.

Regardless of type, dry-docking systems should be installed so that the boat is parked well out of the water, even in the event of a sudden storm tossing up high waves. To allow for draining, the system must park the boat so that the bow end is higher than the stern. And don't forget to pull out any stern drain plugs — the weight of a water-filled boat will collapse many dry-docking systems. (And, conversely, remember to reinstall the plugs when you launch the boat again.)

Generally, the smaller your watercraft, the more choice you have when it comes to dry docking. It's simply a matter of weight; less boat equals less weight equals more choices. For instance, while some small boats can be hoisted out of the water using only the force of muscle, this isn't even a consideration if your boat leans more toward cabin cruiser than canoe. So let's begin one step up from muscle-only methods as we haul ourselves along to the heavyweights of dry docking.

Portable Dry Docking

Stony shorelines are a pain to walk on even without struggling to muscle a sailing dinghy or skiff onto shore. And the wheels of boat trailers just disappear into the stones, so that rules that out. One solution to the problem may be portable skid tracks (such as the Beach Hauler).

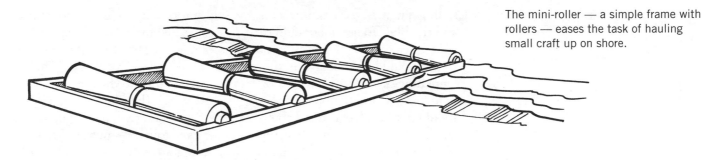

The mini-roller — a simple frame with rollers — eases the task of hauling small craft up on shore.

Typically, a flexible ladder is laid out on the beach, the rungs of the ladder made from steel tubes sleeved in a high-density plastic tube (usually HDPE), held in place by a frame of detachable steel rods. Coaxed into motion by human energy, the boat slides over the slippery tubes. For the skid track to function, the beach must be relatively level, which rules it out for shorelines with lumpy terrain. Some portable skid tracks are small enough to fit into a carrying bag and can be set up in less than half an hour, but these are inadequate for boats much heavier than portage-friendly canoes.

For slightly larger boats weighing up to 500 pounds, which includes most utility boats up to about 16 feet in length, some personal watercraft, and many small sailing dinghies — check with the boat's manufacturer — one answer to beaching your boat may be a device called the mini roller, manufactured by Naylor Systems. Picture a small boat trailer without wheels, only with no winching mechanism, and you're not far off the basic concept. Bringing a boat in, you pull it up as you would when dragging a boat up on shore, only now the hull is gliding over six 12-inch keel rollers. To keep it from rolling away, let the bow rest on the shore with the stern 6 to 8 feet from the waterline. To launch the craft, lift the bow and the boat slides back down into the water.

At 10 feet in length and about 50 pounds in weight, the mini roller itself is light enough to easily move farther out as the water recedes during the season, keeping your dry parking spot accessible. On solid-rock shores subject to waves, Naylor recommends pinning the mini roller to the rock, so in this situation a few pre-installed pins might be necessary if the roller needs to be relocated as water levels drop.

With either of these two portable systems, the slope of the shore shouldn't exceed an angle greater than what you are willing to manually drag a boat up. Beyond that, you will need something with a winch (more on the various winch-assisted systems later).

Launching Dollies

Although still muscle powered, a launching dolly can greatly reduce the burden of boat removal by introducing wheels into the formula. (Rolling friction is less than sliding friction; see Friction on the Waterfront, chapter 14). Aside from the many possible homebrew solutions, several easy-rolling, hand-operated launching dollies and lightweight canoe caddies are commercially available — not roadworthy, but certainly worthy of hauling out

The launching dolly is basically a light-duty, hand-operated boat trailer.

sailing dinghies, canoes, rowboats, and the like. To use a launching dolly or caddy, the slope into the water should be minimal and the launching surface smooth rock or hard packed, and the operator should not be adverse to a little manual labor. Sure beats dragging the boat across the beach by hand, though.

Roller Ramps

Another option for boats up to about 18 feet long is the roller ramp (not to be confused with the roller-dock ramp). This is essentially a stationary boat trailer complete with winch but without wheels. But unlike boat trailers or portable skid tracks and the like, roller ramps are designed for full-time seasonal storage — firmly attached to the shoreline and ready to serve. The boat is eased up to the ramp, hooked to the winch (hand or electrically operated), and then hauled up over a series of rollers — not unlike those on a top-of-the-line boat trailer, only normally more of them. In concept it's similar to the roller ramp the local grocery-store checkout used to have, except that there's less chance of getting the wrong groceries.

A good roller ramp will have wobbly rollers — rollers that automatically adjust to variances in hull shape as the boat traverses the ramp. All rollers should have bushings, and stainless-steel axles are a

What a Drag

When dry-docking a diminutive dinghy (or other similar-sized craft), and the shoreline is not suited to launching dollies and such, the customary practice is to drag the boat up onto the dock. Unfortunately, this isn't good for the boat or dock, or the back of the person doing the dragging. What is needed is a suitable rolling surface at dock's edge over which to slide the boat (reducing friction reduces effort). The following are two clever homebrew solutions, the inventiveness not mine.

The simplest roller consists of a ¾- to 1-inch-diameter steel rod, about a foot or two long, its length determined by the possible contact area of the boat. The rod is covered with a sleeve of PVC or PE piping ¼ inch larger in diameter than the rod, similar in concept to a rung on a portable skid track. Two blocks of scrap wood, drilled partway through to accept the ends of the rod, hold the rod an inch or so above and beyond the upper edge of the dock. The wooden blocks are cut L-shaped to fit around a dock's 90-degree edge and are screwed down to the dock's platform, the plastic-covered roller rod held between. Rounding the edges of the wooden brackets will lessen the odds of scraping the boat bottom. The boat rolls up and across the covered rod when pulled onto the dock.

Almost as simple a solution is recycled skateboard wheel-and-axle assemblies, called *trucks.* Mount the trucks at dock's edge, preferably on angled wedges so the wheels conform to the shape of the bow of your prized boat. Because skateboard wheels can scuff the surfaces they

contact, wrapping the wheels in a homemade padded sleeve can help preserve your boat's bottom. The boat is simply pulled up and across the wheels onto the dock.

welcome bonus. To help center the craft and cope with initial load, the first sets should be double rollers.

If your waterfront is located in the more northern climes of North America, move the ramp to higher ground for winter storage to prevent damage from ice.

Boat Lifts, Marine Railways, and Davits

This trio of dry-docking systems can each serve a broad range of vessels, from small watercraft to megaboats and all floating things in between. Because boat lifts and marine railways have much in common, and are the most popular of dry-docking choices, we will begin with an overview of those two systems.

Shoreline conditions and purchaser preferences usually influence the decision between boat lifts and marine railways. Lifts and railways can be handyman designed and built, assembled from a manufactured kit, or installed by the factory or dock builder. If your boat is over 20 feet long and/or worth more than you can afford to gamble, you would be wise to stick with the expertise of established manufacturers and at least start with a manufactured kit. (The most basic manufactured lift or railway system, installed yourself, will set you back about as much as a first-class boat trailer.)

A negative side to boat lifts and marine railways — and davits, for that matter — is their appearance. All three tend to pop into your view like a tacky billboard on the horizon. Furthermore, the bottom of a dry-docked boat blocking the view can be downright ugly — right up there with recycled car tires stapled to the side of the dock. Because marine railways can sometimes cart a boat out of the line of vision, perhaps right into a land-based boathouse, the railway route has the potential to be less obtrusive. But whichever dry method you opt for, use some discretion and taste in locating these boat savers on your shoreline.

Sometimes a canvas canopy can help hide a dry-docked boat. These quasi-boathouses — often optional extras from the manufacturers — are also an economical way to get your boat out of the sun, wind, and rain.

The roller ramp works well for dry docking small craft up to about 18 feet, such as sailing dinghies and personal watercraft.

The best materials for boat lifts and marine railways are steel and aluminum, the latter weighing about half as much as the former. Weight could be important if you remove your dry dock for the winter. Other things to look for common to most dry-docking systems include stainless-steel cables and bushings at all pivot points and pulleys. Without bushings, parts that rub together will eventually wear and/or enlarge bolt and axle housings and/or seize. When pulleys stop turning, that lovely stainless cable you paid for will soon shred. By the way, stainless cables not only resist corrosion but, because of their lay, are also more flexible than standard steel versions, which means less resistance, which in turn means less effort required to move things. And anything that reduces effort has got my vote. Speaking of which, big bolts — such as ¾ inch — are less likely to cross-thread and easier to install than smaller ones if working under water when visibility and oxygen are both in low supply.

And although it may seem obvious, lifts, railways, and davits are designed to move boats, not people.

Need a Lift, Sailor?

A boat lift is essentially an "elevator" that lifts up a boat in a cradle or sling, typically to just above the waterline. (A possible exception to this height rule is the wooden boat — some owners prefer to keep the bottom of the boat in touch with water to prevent the hull from drying out.) Depending on make and model of both lift and boat, most boat lifts will handle fluctuations in water levels ranging from 2 to 4 feet before the lift has to be relocated (again, check with the manufacturer).

One advantage of a boat lift over a marine railway is that no valuable shore space is taken up by track. Also, boat lifts can be installed where the shoreline is too steep to accommodate a marine railway.

Boat lifts come in a variety of configurations, yet all will squeeze into one of three general categories: the stand-alone lift, the supported lift, and the overhead lift.

Stand-alone lift

The stand-alone lift rests on submerged lands. This restricts its use to a depth of about 6 to 8 feet of water. It also rules it out for deep mud. The

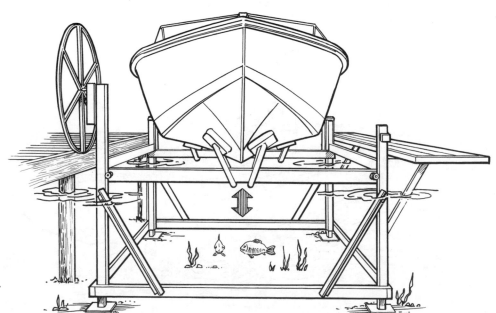

The stand-alone lift needs firm submerged lands to rest on, limiting it to 6 to 8 feet of water. Note the "walk-around" platform opposite the dock side.

lift's framework surrounds a cradle or sling. Usually the lift is placed next to a dock to allow easy access to the boat. An exception to this convenient arrangement is sometimes found in shallow-water situations, such as along the north shore of Lake Erie where you can walk out for miles (or so it seems). Here, I have seen stand-alone boat lifts a hundred feet out from shore, the boat hoisted high above the water to avoid the waves. The boat owner hikes out through the shallow water to the boat.

Where lifts have open water on at least one side, manufacturers such as Nyman Marine offer optional "walk-arounds." These are basically platforms, typically about 2 feet wide by 12 feet long, that attach to the lift, providing a place to stand while boarding or servicing the boat.

One stand-alone lift known as the Leisure Boat Lift differs substantially from the others in that, instead of the customary four-poster framework, it makes use of a single, large, rectangular column. Not only is it visually less obtrusive than conventional lifts, but because of its design and bulk (1,400 pounds) it's better suited to fending off nature's nasty hissy fits.

To compensate for unlevel land, look for stand-alone lifts with adjustable legs.

Supported lift

The supported lift is worth considering if your water depth is greater than 6 to 8 feet, or there's toe-sucking deep mud lurking under the water. Similar in concept to the stand-alone version, the supported lift runs parallel to, and is secured to, a bulkhead, dock, or cliff instead of resting on submerged lands. There is no maximum water depth for these lifts. Some supported lifts retain a surrounding framework similar to the stand-alone lift, but most are open on at least one unsupported side. Some versions are angled back toward the shore or dock at about 45 degrees to distribute the boat's weight over a greater area. These are capable of carrying a heavier load with less strain. Smaller versions of this type of lift work well for dry-docking personal watercraft like Sea-Doos. An interesting variation on the supported lift is one manufactured by Ace Boat Hoist. It uses driven piles for its legs, a good solution to dry docking where the submerged land is too soft to support a stand-alone lift.

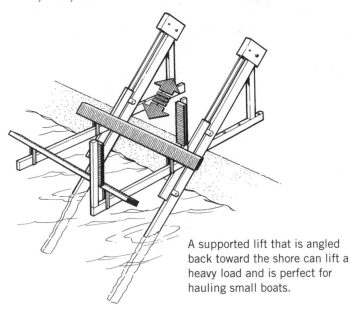

A supported lift that is angled back toward the shore can lift a heavy load and is perfect for hauling small boats.

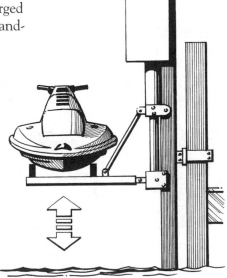

Because a supported lift relies on an adjacent bulkhead, dock, or similar bit of bulk — rather than submerged lands — for support, it can be used in deep water.

The manner in which a boat sits in a cradle or sling is similar for most lifts and railways. With a cradle, the boat rests on a wood or steel bunk — often carpet covered to protect the boat's hull. The bunk should be adjustable to accommodate your boat's particular hull shape and have adjustable arms to hold the vertical guide poles (see below). A nice feature to look for is a bow stop or motor stop, a cushioned bumper that prevents your boat from drifting too far forward when docking. If various hull configurations need to be hoisted (one at a time, please, folks), a sling can be used in place of a cradle; however, the cradle gives better support for the hull during longer periods of parking and seasonal storage. Whatever your choice, no sling, cradle, or dolly should obstruct access to a boat parked next to the dock.

Although the source of power can be either muscle or motor, a conventional boat lift hoists its load using one of two basic systems: the cantilever (or scissor) lift and the vertical lift. The *cantilever lift* has a parallelogram-shaped cradle that changes from a very squat shape to a rectangular shape as it is raised. The closer the cradle gets to the rectangular shape, the easier the lifting process becomes. A *vertical lift* hoists straight up, or at least at a constant angle, the effort to raise your craft unchanging. Vertical lifts take up less shoreline space than cantilever lifts, generally lift higher, and are usually the only choice for large, heavy craft. Cantilever lifts are the best choice for shallow water, operating in water depths as little as 4 to 6 inches plus the draft of the boat. And you can angle a cantilever lift from front to back, putting the stern end 2 to 3 inches lower into soft submerged lands, making the entrance even lower. A vertical lift, however, must be kept level in order to work. Cantilever lifts are often easier to raise (noticeable only if using a manually operated winch) and, because the vertical cousins are more complex, cantilever versions sometimes occupy the lower end of a manufacturer's price range (but not always).

Driving lessons

Piloting your boat onto a submerged cradle, sling, or dolly is a breeze — even if the breeze is stiff. Steer between the four guide poles, secure the stern to the two poles at the rear, step out onto the dock, and winch your boat out of the water. Pull out the transom plugs and the job's done. The bow tends to be self-centering. Because high waves can toss your boat around before it's free of the water, guide poles should be flexible enough to absorb a bit of boat bashing.

When a boat is to be dry-docked for more than a day, there is less strain on the hull and dry-docking system if the boat's weight is distributed equally fore and aft. Try to get the boat's balancing point rather than its midpoint centered (outboards are usually parked farther forward than inboards, for instance).

To launch the old dory, simply reverse the procedure, lowering the cradle, sling, or dolly into the water until the boat floats, the breaking of champagne bottles over bow being optional.

When a boat is parked, the front of the cradle, sling, or dolly must be 6 to 12 inches higher than the rear to allow water to drain. And don't forget to remove those transom plugs. The weight of an uncovered boat filling up during a heavy rain storm can collapse a lift or davit, or damage a marine railway.

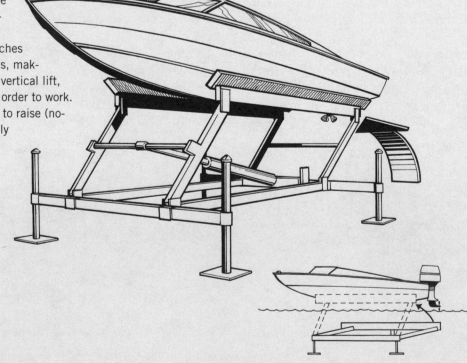

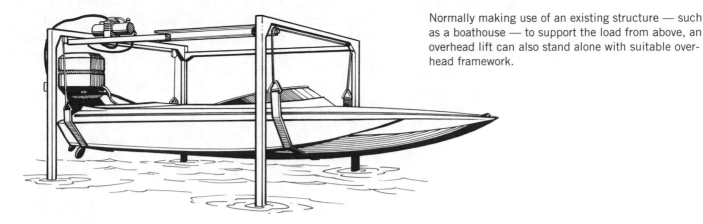

Normally making use of an existing structure — such as a boathouse — to support the load from above, an overhead lift can also stand alone with suitable overhead framework.

Overhead lift

The overhead lift is usually supported by an existing overhead structure like the rafters of a boathouse. A winch hoists up a sling, or sometimes a cradle and framework.

On the Right Track

A marine railway consists of a dolly riding on a track, the cradle or sling that holds the boat now supported by the dolly carting the boat out of water. A marine railway can be adapted to fluctuating water levels by extending the tracks out over submerged lands far enough to allow water access to the dolly even at the lowest water levels.

U-store-it

A decided advantage of the marine railway is its adaptability to a year-round storage facility. At the end of the season, winch the boat onto the railway's dolly, secure the dolly in place, then get the boat ready for winter. (You may also have to store parts of the railway; see Dry-Dock Maintenance.) For boat owners accustomed to the cost of storing their floating loved ones at a marina, a marine railway could soon pay for itself. And where conditions or laws prevent building a boathouse in the water, a marine railway makes it possible to get

larger boats into a land-based boathouse. Marine railways also can be adapted to small floatplanes.

When winter conditions demand that floating docks or pipe docks be removed, a marine railway can take much of the drudgery out of both removal and replacement. Just winch the dock sections up the railway onto safe ground after the boat is in place.

A marine railway may not be the best choice if you've got an abrupt drop-off at water's edge or a steep cliff on your shoreline.

Dealing with the big banks

How steep an incline can a marine railway handle? Although some of the more experienced builders have installed rails over slopes approaching 40 degrees — about an 8-foot rise for every 10 feet of horizontal run — that's rare. In most cases, you're pushing the limits of the system at about half that rise (4 in 10).

Another point to consider is that the steeper the incline, the deeper the water needs to be at the point of entry so that the cradle doesn't bottom out before the boat floats. Steep banks and sharp drop-offs up to about 6 feet can be tamed with reinforced sections of rail and support legs, or by constructing a ramp, or altering the uplands to create a more graduated incline (see Once I

Built a Railway). But generally any bank over 12 feet high limits your dry-docking choices to a boat lift, or possibly a davit.

An expensive exception to this rule (cash always finds the exceptions) is the parallel cradle marine railway. As with the supported lift, the cradle in this case runs parallel to the shore (which can be a rise up to 70 degrees), the cradle sitting perpendicular on the dolly and traveling sideways up the railway, still pulled by cable, the angle of the boat remaining level.

Once I Built a Railway

The boat lift — because of its complicated construction — is not an easy device for workbench wizards to design and fabricate. This doesn't stop all committed tinkerers, though it probably should stop more. Better to buy a factory-built unit and modify it to suit your needs than to tackle the whole design and build process yourself.

The marine railway is better suited to home-handyperson solutions. However, as boat size and weight increase, the latitude for experimental flops decreases. Folks with boats that are larger and heavier than a basic 20-foot runabout should stick with a manufactured kit but install it themselves. I've spoken with manufacturers who claim that 70 percent of the marine railways they sell are customer installed.

Whichever way you decide to go dry, many of the following construction and installation tips will apply. And whether boat lift, marine railway, or even davit, all can entail alterations to the shoreline. So before you (or your contractor) proceed, have the project okayed by the various levels of government that claim a legal interest in such matters.

The larger the wheels, the easier the dolly will roll, 6 inches being about the minimum diameter. All wheels should have bearings or bushings, and be equipped with grease fittings (which should get serviced regularly).

Parts such as the dolly can be bolted together, but joints in individual sections of rail are best welded. However, sections of rail also can be joined by heavy-duty

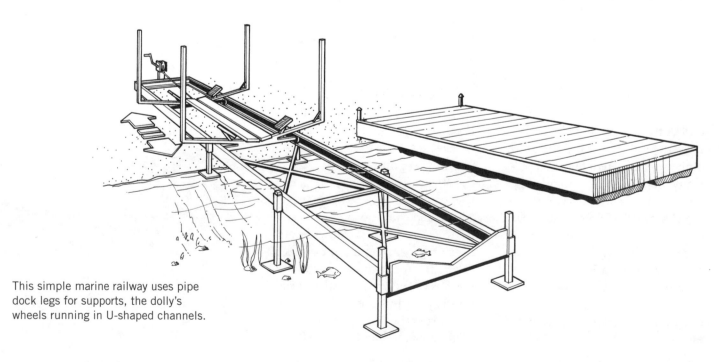

This simple marine railway uses pipe dock legs for supports, the dolly's wheels running in U-shaped channels.

bolts run through brackets below each rail, the bolts then acting as a hinge, allowing the sections to pivot. In planning your railway, place these hinged points at any pronounced changes in elevation (such as where it enters a boathouse), being careful that the change in angle doesn't bottom out the dolly as it rolls along the rails.

To keep the rails an equal distance apart, weld in crossers at least every 3½ feet and at section joints. Triangulated bracing between the rails will increase the railway's strength. The track need not be pinned to the shore unless there is a steep incline or you have a very heavy boat (generally over 6,000 pounds), in which case you should probably defer to an experienced professional.

On the level

Once the location is chosen, level the site as best you can within the permissible guidelines of local regulations. Be careful not to create a route for downpour runoff that could in turn erode the bed or shoreline. For lighter boats, it's not essential for the track to be perfectly level from side to side, but the closer it is to level, the easier time the dolly will have of it. Lengthwise, the track must be on a continuous slope into the water, relying on gravity to launch the boat. This may require propping up the shore end of the track with blocks, wooden cribs, or pipe-dock legs — the best choice for raising and leveling a marine railway (assuming you choose legs and brackets strong enough for the task). Weld the pipe-leg brackets to the rails. And don't forget that the boat needs to be higher at the bow when parked to allow for draining.

The track must extend far enough into the water so that the boat can float above the dolly during landing or launching, even at low water. Include a stop at the bottom of the rail to prevent the dolly from leaving the track when it reaches the end of the line. If the track is laid in deep sand or mud, rest it on solid concrete slabs (such as patio stones), or ties of 4 x 4 fir. Sharp drop-offs may require cribs, sawhorselike metal stands, or similar triangulated structures (such as cross-bracing if you're using pipe legs for support). Supports must be stable and capable of carrying the load of the boat and dolly in foul weather. Weight is only a concern if you have to remove the railway each fall and reinstall it in the spring.

Hello, dolly

When a boat is steered onto a marine railway dolly and tied in place, there is a tendency for waves to lift the boat and derail the train. The bigger the boat, the more buoyancy (and exposure to wind), the more likelihood of a train wreck. So, unlike regular choo-choos, the rolling stock of the marine railway must be secured to the track. Most manufacturers favor either an L-shaped safety hook attached to the axle, the small section of the L fitting snug under the rail lip, or enclosing the wheels top and bottom in parallel lengths of 90-degree-angled metal, forming a variation of a sideways U. Consensus among installers is that the latter allows slightly more latitude when straying from a level railway bed.

A potential problem with L-shaped hooks is that occasionally the hooks seize on the axle ends of the wheels and then jam on the rails. Usually this is a result of the railway's owner not greasing the hook's pivot point as per manufacturer's recommendations. Typically, the neglectful owner then bends the hook back to free the dolly, which in turn means that the dolly is no longer secured to the track. This is a wreck in waiting. So grease the hooks regularly at the axles with a water-resistant grease.

And while shopping for dollies, keep in mind that if your boat is designed as a planing hull (such as with most ski boats), weight will be biased more toward the stern. To help compensate for this shift in load, some marine railway manufacturers are installing dual wheels at the rear of the dolly.

The best place for the winch is attached to the upper end of the track, which keeps the forces contained within the railway. For the same reason, the winch should always pull the dolly, not the boat. Pulling the boat is like hooking a locomotive up to the passengers instead of the passenger car.

Those with small boats (a utility boat or runabout less than 14 feet long) need not spend big bucks in order to have a marine railway that works. As with all do-it-yourself projects, time, toil, and ingenuity are the currency exchanged here. The following is a brief sampling of the homegrown projects I am aware of. Undoubtedly, there are many more.

Beachfront ingenuity

One nifty arrangement for very light utility boats uses a dolly bolted together from wood 2 x 4s and a metal channel riding on recycled plastic lawn-mower wheels. The rails are shallow upright U-channels wide enough to hold the wheels. The rope attached to the dolly is fed through a clothesline pulley at the top and then to a hand-operated winch mounted at waist height for easy operation.

The winch is secured to a stout tree. Simple and workable for small, lightweight craft.

A cottager with a small sailing dinghy used a length of manufactured composite-wood joist (a kind of wooden I-beam that is increasingly common in home construction), laid on its side on the shore. Nonswiveling casters, in pairs, were attached to the beam about every foot or so. The beam was in two sections, hinged to allow the lower section to tilt down into the water. A block and tackle was used to winch up the boat, but a basic boat-trailer winch would also work. Unfortunately, this composite I-beam is designed for indoor use only, not to be left in water or even exposed to weather for that matter, so frequent and liberal coats of a high-quality, oil- or epoxy-based paint would be necessary to keep the beam from swelling, breaking up, and rotting.

A home-baked marine railway built for slightly bigger boats used rails of round tubing from discarded scaffolding, the lengths welded together. The dolly was a modified boat trailer, its tires removed from the wheels and an additional axle bolted to the trailer tongue, the wheels again without tires. The inside curvature of the four naked wheels wrapped around the top of the tubular rails. A boat winch mounted at the end of the rail pulled the dolly (née boat trailer) and boat up the track.

Although in this example the owner could not get down to the dock with his car to pull the boat and trailer out for end-of-season storage, there is no reason why this could not be done in a more accessible situation. The front axle would have to be detached

and the rear wheels swapped for
ones with tires, and then presto,
railway dolly becomes boat trailer.
The beauty of the latter solution
lies in the cost benefits of using the
trailer and flexibility of storing the
boat well above spring flood or ice
breakup. This railway showed no
means of hinging the rail sections
together to allow for variations in
inclination, or any means to keep
the dolly on track in high waves,
which leaves something for the
next user to solve.

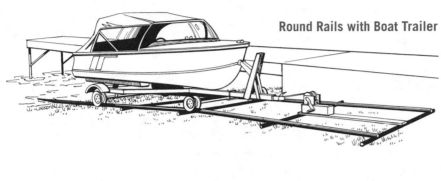

Round Rails with Boat Trailer

Boat owners have developed many creative ways of launching their vessels. These three examples are all variations on the marine railway.

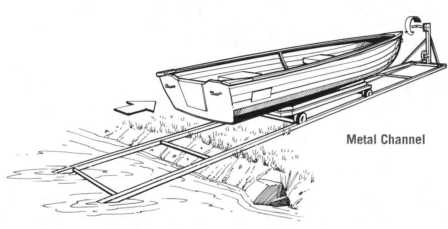

Metal Channel

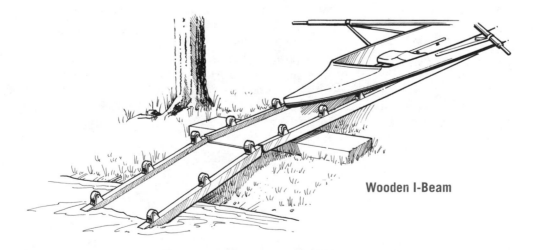

Wooden I-Beam

The task all dry-docking systems have in common is to raise the boat out of the water. For systems that make use of machinery — such as boat lifts, marine railways, and davits — that task is performed by a winch.

Technically, a winch is simply a drum that winds up a rope, cable, or chain to hoist up the load (our boat in this case). On its own, a winch offers no mechanical advantage (see Popular Mechanics, chapter 14), but the method we use to turn that drum can provide leverage. The mechanical advantage of the winch-lever combo depends on the length of the winch's handle (the radius if the handle is a wheel) and/or the amount of gear (or pulley) reduction between the applied force (you, the kids, or a motor) and the winch. As mechanical advantage increases (with a longer arm on the handle of a hand-operated winch, for instance), it becomes easier to raise the boat's weight. Unfortunately, as the workload decreases, the time it takes to do that work increases. Nothing comes for free.

Steeper inclines and heavier boats put more strain on the winch. As the load increases, so must the strength and mechanical advantage of the winch. Castings, nuts and bolts, thickness of cables, size of motor, etc., must all be upgraded.

Starting in the bargain basement of winches, we find the ubiquitous basic hand-operated boat winch. It's simple and economical, typically incorporating an antireverse cog to prevent the cable from unwinding if you lose your grip on the handle. When the cog is released the boat lowers, almost instantly. While this isn't usually a problem when a boat trailer is sitting in the water, it can lead to some unpleasant surprises for dry-docking systems that rely on gravity to return the boat to water. Even if a faster-than-intended launch does no harm to the boat, the twirling winch handle can break an arm. This type of winch is not recommended for dry-docking anything but small, lightweight watercraft on marine railways located along gentle slopes.

One large step up from the bargain basement are hand-operated winches incorporating a brake mechanism that allows you to lower your aquatic loved one gently back into the water. Even farther removed from the bargain basement (in both technology and cost) are worm gear winches. Worm gear winches are considered the most reliable and easiest to operate. They're smooth, gentle, and never unwind on their own accord. But neither are they inexpensive.

If your boat weighs more than 4,000 pounds, or the incline of the railway is steep, you'll probably want an electric winch for the increased speed if not the reduced effort. If walking over to the winch to push a button is still too much work, you can get a remote control for your motor (such as the RMC unit from Davit Master, or similar devices from other suppliers). A remotely controlled motor also allows you to walk next to the boat and help guide it as it enters or exits the water. This can be a big advantage for single-person dry-docking in rough water.

Winches come in a variety of sizes and load ratings. Consult the manufacturer, supplier, or local dock builder for size recommendations for your application. As a final note on winches, although stainless-steel cables cost more initially, they last substantially longer than steel or galvanized cables, and are not as prone to fraying.

Raised without a winch

A few manufacturers (Nyman Marine Corporation, for instance) offer boat lifts incorporating a water-based hydraulic system instead of a winch for raising and lowering the cradle. Pressurized water, either from city tap water or an on-site pump, is forced into a hydraulic cylinder (sometimes more than one cylinder), pushing the arm of the hydraulic cylinder out. This in turn raises the cradle. When the water is let out, the arm slides back into the cylinder and the cradle lowers. The action is smooth but slow, no cables or chains are used, and if you have pressurized water at your waterfront you can avoid the potential hazards of electricity near the water. However, a typical hydraulic system does use about 6 U.S. gallons of water (5 Imperial gallons/23 liters) for every foot the hoist is lifted, which is a lot of chlorinated city water to dump into the open water at your shoreline every time you want the boat lowered. If the system you are considering can accommodate clean fresh water, and your shoreline fronts clean fresh water, the hydraulic lift can be an interesting but expensive alternative to the winch. But the water used in the lift must be very clean, salt-free, and contain no algae. The water surrounding the lift must be free of zebra mussels (which can attack and destroy the seals on the hydraulic cylinders). Also, should the lift need to be stored for winter, draining all water out of the system to prevent damage from freeze-up can be difficult.

Davits

A davit is a small boom crane used to raise and lower a boat. A single davit works well for smaller boats such as personal watercraft, but for larger craft davits are normally employed in pairs, one each at the bow and stern.

In a typical setup, a sling is attached to the boat and the davit swung out over the boat and hooked onto the sling. Using a muscle- or electrically powered winch, davits hoist the craft straight up out of the water and hold it suspended in the air until someone wants to go for a spin. Then the boat is winched back into the water.

With a bit of boat acrobatics, davits can sometimes swing a boat up onto a seawall or dock for winter storage. Davits are well suited to installation along canals where the water is deep and docks and piers don't project much beyond the shoreline. Some paired davits are rated for over 8,000 pounds, making them good for boats up to approximately 28 feet.

Depending on design, davits can be base mounted (onto the platform of a breakwall or heavy-duty dock, for instance) or side mounted (onto piles, the sides of a bulkhead, or a cliff). Davit manufacturers can advise you on the best design for your waterfront, and your boat's manufacturer can tell you how best to attach the sling.

Davits are an expensive way to dry-dock, but certainly worth considering.

Sizing Up Your Dry Dock

History has shown that folks are rarely satisfied with the boat they own, typically lusting for larger craft. Unfortunately, that new and bigger boat usually requires upgrading the dry dock too. One dock builder I know sold three marine railways over a span of a mere 8 weeks to a gentleman of means new to waterfront residency. The last was the largest the dock builder made, just to be on the safe side. But as a reward for being such a good customer, the gentleman's final railway did end up on the cover of the dock builder's brochure. Whether lift or railway, the dock builder now strongly suggests that people install a unit one size larger

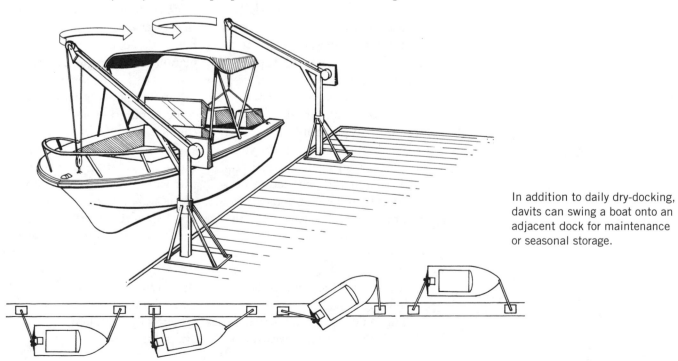

In addition to daily dry-docking, davits can swing a boat onto an adjacent dock for maintenance or seasonal storage.

than required, even if harboring only the teeniest of notions of captaining bigger vessels in the future. It's a tip that could save you both money and aggravation, although you might miss out on the fame of being cover customer of the year for some company's brochure.

Boat Trailers

While I spoke disparagingly of boat trailers at the outset as a reasonable alternative for dry-docking a boat, they're tough to beat for getting the boat in and out of the water if you only need to do it once in a while. Consider a trailer if you can safely leave the boat moored beside the dock between launchings, if speedy removal isn't important, and if the task isn't a daily routine.

Dry-Dock Maintenance

Mechanized dry-docking systems tend to be high-maintenance items. Regularly, an owner should check cables for signs of rust and broken strands. Some models may require that cables, pulleys, and winches be periodically lubricated. If a dolly doesn't appear to be rolling as well as it did when new, chances are good the wheels haven't been greased recently (use a water-resistant grease). At least once a season, check all nuts and bolts for tightness, in particular those securing cable clamps. And if the structure is made of steel, an occasional coat of paint will help deter rust.

Folks with a high tolerance for risk may choose to leave boat lifts in the water year-round if ice conditions and spring breakup are not severe. But never leave a boat in a lift if the water is subject to freezing.

The same caveats apply to marine railways. If ice or nasty weather is a concern at your waterfront, detach the sections of track that connect the land sections to underwater sections, and any underwater sections that could be harmed by ice and waves. Store those sections on land.

One innovative solution to the hassles of winter storage and spring launch for railways and lifts is to sandwich them between two lift pipe docks (see chapter 6). What you get is a good dock on either side of the boat for easy access and loading, and at the end of the season the boat lift or railway rises up out of the water with the lift dock like a massive drawbridge. Come spring, it simply lowers back down into the water again, ready for boats and deck chairs. I guess you could call it a dry dock for the dry dock. The same manufacturer also offers a lift marine railway without the attached docks but, as previously discussed, lifts and railways can be pretty ugly, even before you decide to raise the whole shebang up into the air for a better view.

While on the subject of maintenance, check manufacturers' warranties before you buy to ensure that your application is covered. For instance, it's not unusual for a manufacturer to offer different warranties for the same product depending on whether it is installed in fresh or salt water. Read the fine print.

There's no arguing the convenience of mooring your boat in the water; it only gets less convenient and more expensive than a dry dock if the boat is damaged by the forces of nature or the wakes of other boaters. Somewhere, from mooring lines to railway lines, there is a solution to your particular parking problems, a solution dictated by boat, boater, budget, and nature.

section 6

Repairing and Upgrading

Nothing, including diamonds, is forever, especially the wood on your dock, it seems. All the materials of the world — whether appearing naturally in our environment or of human invention — are subject to wear, decay, and abuse from various nature- or humanity-sponsored mischief. In this section, we will talk about how wear and tear can affect your dock, pointing out the most probable trouble spots and likely damage, and how and when to repair it. And we'll discuss when repairing a dilapidated dock just doesn't make sense. Sometimes it's better to sign a check and have a new dock installed.

Upgrading existing docks is a subject that dances between closely related partners — repairs and new construction. So if you're keen to bring that family heirloom up to current standards of safety and convenience of use, you'll need to read this section plus the appropriate chapters that pertain to your dock and the updates you have planned for it.

Note: For additional information on correct dock construction, see the appropriate chapter for the type of dock being repaired, chapter 9 for construction tips, and chapter 18 for plans.

dare to repair

Tour any of North America's waterfronts and there they are — docks that soak the ends of your sneakers as they dip into the water; docks that tremor every time a wake washes toward shore; docks that are pulling apart at the joints; docks without enough room or buoyancy to hold two people, let alone the lawn chairs. There's no shortage of docks that need attention.

One surefire fix is to scrap the wretched wharf and build a new dock to the standards of an expert dock builder. But holy-shamoly, that can be a major expenditure. While I've never known anyone to regret the cost, it may not be necessary. Sometimes the dock can be rehabilitated.

The first step is to determine whether it's worth it. This requires an honest appraisal of your dock's structural soundness. As we'll see, design faults often can be rectified, but if your dock is falling apart, the easiest and most economical solution may be to trade in your wallet for a new dock.

A major problem for many do-it-yourselfers is cheapness. What's the first thing they tell you about? How well the project was built? Nope.

They proudly list how much money they saved with each circumvention of some proven standard of construction. Unfortunately if you skimp on the essentials the dock will soon will be groaning for repairs even if it isn't a design disaster. This is not to say that we do-it-yourselfers should abandon our tradition of frugality, we just need to temper it with a little reality.

Do-it-yourselfers love nails — low cost, available in a huge variety of shapes and sizes, and as easy to install as hitting your thumb with a hammer. But nails are a poor choice for docks. As explained in chapter 8, professional dock builders use a variety of brackets and reinforcers collectively known as dock hardware. The good news is that you can often retro-fit dock hardware, giving the dock a new lease on life.

Whether building new or upgrading, good hardware is the best investment you can make in a do-it-yourself dock. If money's tight, put new hardware on an old dock to make it work for a few more years, then reuse the hardware later to build the grand dock of your dreams.

Sound construction techniques are the best defense against dock disasters, but even then, nature refuses to recognize the concept of permanence.

Floater Faults

The weakest point on a floating dock is the corners, where wind and wave tend to twist and distort the dock into a parallelogram. The problem with many is that the headers (the outer end boards) are simply nailed to the stringers (the outer side boards) with no additional bracing. A 4 x 4 block bolted vertically inside each corner will greatly improve the strength. Often, you can slip these blocks in from the bottom of an existing dock, then drill for the bolts from the sides. If your dock already has corner blocks that are nailed in place, get out the drill and bolt the blocks in tight.

A much better solution — in fact the only one if a durable dock is your goal — is to add metal corner brackets, bolted in place. Most varieties can be fitted to existing docks, even to docks with 4 x 4 blocks already occupying the corners. Remove the 4 x 4s and put proper corners in it. Depending on the design of the dock, it may be a little more complicated than that, but as long as the wood in the corners has not begun to rot, it's usually not a major task.

Born to Dance

While on the subject of hardware, a common weakness with floating docks is the use of hinges rather than connectors to join the sections (see Hinges and Connectors, chapter 8). And the smaller the sections, the more likely they are to dance. Great Northern Docks markets connectors that are perhaps the easiest to retro-fit to an existing dock. Another cheap solution that sometimes works — depending on the design of the hinge — is to unbolt the hinge and re-install it

sideways (see chapter 8 for more on this and other cheater connectors). This quells most of the up-and-down dance and adds little to sideways sway but is seldom as strong as a dedicated connector.

Economic Stability

With floating docks, size counts. It's simply a matter of leverage. The lower, longer, wider, and heavier the dock, the less it's going to take any notice of visitors or nature's hissy-fits. Narrow, short lightweights bounce and jostle and tip at the slightest provocation (which is why the kids like them). Fortunately, you don't always have to scrap an anorexic floater and start from scratch to stabilize it. The secret is to marry the existing dock (assuming that it's structurally sound) to at least part of that formula, especially the long and wide of it.

How? You could convert a narrow existing section into a ramp or walkway leading out to a new and bigger platform, making an L- or T-shape. Just adding more narrow sections out in a straight line only lengthens the problem, it doesn't solve it.

A bad trip

T-shapes and L-shapes act like stabilizing pontoons while often providing a sheltered parking spot to moor the boat (see chapter 2). However, when adding new sections to old, do-it-yourselfers often trip up when it comes to differences in freeboard (the distance between the surface of the water and the top of the dock's decking).

Let's suppose the existing dock is framed in 2 x 6s and you decide to incorporate it as a floating walkway leading out to a much bigger, new section framed in sturdier 2 x 10s, thus making a T-shaped dock.

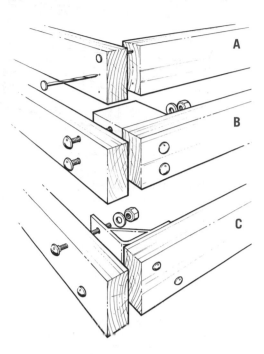

Corners are a floating dock's weakest point — nailed together (A), they will soon fall apart. Bolting corners together with a reinforcing block helps (B). But by far the best remedy is to use metal corner brackets, bolted in place (C).

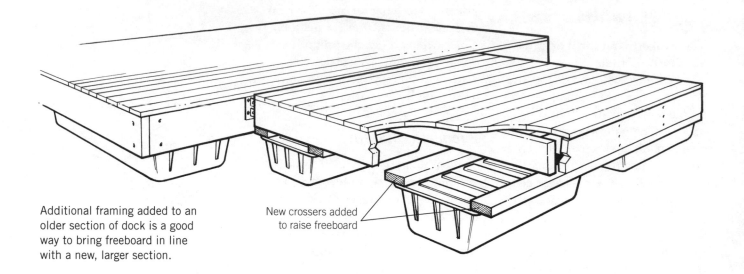

Additional framing added to an older section of dock is a good way to bring freeboard in line with a new, larger section.

New crossers added to raise freeboard

Where the two sections meet, any difference in freeboard — about 4 inches in this case — will show up as a step. Actually, steps less than 5 inches usually don't get noticed, which is why people trip over them.

To match the freeboard of the old section to the new, add additional framing to the bottom of the existing dock — between existing framing and floats — so that its decking is raised up until it's even with the decking of the new section. A bit of work, yes, but such a rebuild does more than eliminate differences in freeboard (and therefore steps between sections) — the added framing also increases the strength of the old section.

While this fix seems to run counter to the "keep it low" golden rule of float-dock construction, in this case the narrow section is but a small part of the total, and it's the total we're concerned with.

Float Notes

If a big floater is unstable, usually something's amiss with the location,

quantity, and/or quality of the dock's flotation.

Proper location isn't merely a matter of keeping the floats under the dock, although that's certainly a good start. Relocating the flotation closer to the headers and stringers may reward you with a big improvement in stability for a potentially small investment in time and money (see Flotation Location, chapter 3).

If your dock is sitting excessively low in the water (perhaps with a freeboard of less than 12 inches) and still wobbles, there may not be sufficient buoyancy. The solution is to add more flotation.

Location and quantity of flotation also play a role in the ramp dip, that quaint curtsy a dock does every time someone traipses down the ramp. A portion of the weight of both the ramp and the traipsers rests on the hinges where the dock and ramp meet. Do-it-yourselfers rarely take this weight into consideration. So an extra dose of flotation is just what the dock called for. If the additional flotation won't fit between the existing floats, additional flotation can sometimes be stacked below the existing floats, assuming the water is deep enough to accommodate the added depth. Another possible location is under the end of the ramp (many dock builders place flotation here as a matter of course). The ramp then no longer relies on the dock for buoyancy.

A different slant

A loss of buoyancy could also cause the dock to become unstable. Such losses rarely happen evenly, which explains why docks occasionally list. Loss of buoyancy is caused by a deterioration of the flotation, either through the flotation absorbing water and/or by damage to the float itself.

Air-filled flotation devices can leak. When this happens, the results are usually dramatic enough that no one needs to tell you that the dock has acquired a peculiar angle. When foam and foam-filled floats become waterlogged, the process is slower and more subtle.

Foam comes in several flavors (see chapter 3). If your dock is supported by white EPS foam billets, proceed no farther — you've found your problem. Only blue Styrofoam BB foam billets should be considered for dock flotation — other variants of EPS are fragile and take on water too readily.

You may be able to replace deteriorated foam with either Styrofoam BB or foam-filled dedicated plastic float drums. One advantage float drums have over foam billets is that in many cases damaged units can be repaired (see Patching Plastic). Float drums are, however, more expensive than foam billets.

Leg transplant

Folks with a small, single-section, floating dock bobbing about in shallow water, and no desire to make the dock bigger, have another potential cure for the wobbles. Sometimes you can turn a floating dock into a pipe dock by adding pipe-dock hardware, legs, and base plates to the sides.

But do not attempt the reverse. Adding floats to a pipe dock that's only 4 feet wide doesn't work — the dock's not wide enough, and in most cases pipe docks are not heavy enough to serve as floaters.

Sea Legs

Unlike floating docks, pipe docks aren't much for dancing, although some are mad keen on doing the sway. Others will spend all summer developing a slouch that mimics the list of a floating dock. In either case, the cause often can be traced to the legs.

Do-it-yourself pipe docks usually sport solid wooden frames, which is okay because wood is easy to work with and still relatively inexpensive. But don't use wood for legs. Wood tends to rot quickly when used as dock legs. Replacing wood legs with galvanized pipe solves that problem, particularly when used with the appropriate brackets.

Brace Yourself

Pipe-leg brackets come in two basic varieties — those that mount on the outside of the frame and those that mount on the inside. Outside versions are much easier to retro-fit — just bolt them on — but tend to bruise boats and swimmers. Choosing pipe-leg brackets that mount inside the frame solves that problem, but these are more difficult to retro-fit.

Constant stress eventually causes bolt holes to wear, regardless of leg type. Therefore all wooden pipe docks, no matter what depth the water, should have leg braces (see chapter 4 for your choice on braces). Depending on design, some braces can be an easy add-on for existing docks.

Crippled Cribs

The only time you can repair a crib is when it has been constructed with a good solid floor. Unfortunately, the primary fault of crib docks is that the floors don't get built properly, if built at all. So as waves and ice pound the crib, it lifts, the rocks slowly tumble out through the bottom, and the crib topples over. At that point, it's too late for repairs.

If that's your situation maybe you should consider yourself lucky; repairing cribs is serious labor. To protect fish habitats, several jurisdictions insist that all the existing rocks in a broken crib be removed, *not* tossed out into the water, and that rocks to fill the new crib not be taken from under the water, only from the shore above the high-water mark or from the pile you removed from the existing crib. So at a minimum you're going to need a barge

to pile the rocks on, several good backs, and maybe a chiropractor who makes house calls.

If the crib sits straight and has been constructed according to accepted good practice — with a sturdy floor — and is suffering only from rot at the waterline, it's worth saving. The steel corner rods usually will have to be cut at the top (the nut typically rusted solid in place on the threaded rod), and the rotten sections of timber removed. In most cases the rot ends about a foot below low water. When replacing those upper timbers, you will notice that the threaded rod (if it needed cutting) is now too short to hold the whole shebang together.

Custom Rods

One solution is to recess the nut into the upper timber. However, this creates a swell place for water to pool and rot to begin anew. A better solution, but more work, is to add a bit of new rod to the old using a rod joiner — basically a very tall nut, typically about 1 inch high. But first the existing rods must be cut again — to about ½ inch above the timbers located at least two timbers

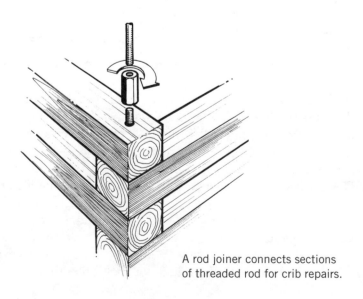

A rod joiner connects sections of threaded rod for crib repairs.

down from the top. Place a large washer around the rod, screw on the joiner tight enough to clamp the lower crib together (which should leave about ½ inch of the joiner unused), then screw another piece of short rod into its top, the length of the additional rod determined by the height of the upper timber plus about ¾ to 1 inch. Add the upper timbers and bolt them down. You will have to enlarge the bolt hole in the bottom of the upper timbers to accommodate the joiner, but since the hole points downward it's unlikely to provide a very good home for rot. And, in case you might want to do this again, grease the rods where nuts and joiners contact the threads (using water-resistant grease), increasing your chances of being able to make future repairs without cutting the rods.

If the rod has rusted beyond use, then it's time to drill new holes and put new rods in. This requires a long drill. And then you have to go diving to install the bottom washer and plate with a nut on it.

If just the thought of holding your breath in deep water long enough to secure a few washers and nuts in place leaves you gasping for air, breathe easy — there's another option. Take the threaded rod to a machine shop and have a 10-inch lag bolt welded onto the end of it. Then drill down to just into the bottom timber and screw the modified rod in. It's not as strong as a rod held by nuts at both ends, but it will work for most repairs.

Leaning Crib of Pisa

When a crib begins to lean, you can convert it into a tourist attraction or rebuild, or call in a contractor who prefers to put money into machinery than into chiropractors.

An experienced marine contractor may be able to drive steel piles down through the crib, right through the rocks into submerged lands, then build a new structure on top. The existing crib is simply left where it is to rot away at its leisure. In many cases, this is the least expensive and least environmentally disruptive option. What you end up with is a permanent pile dock, the piles surrounded and protected by a cribbed rock pile, which some dock builders contend is even stronger than a concrete pier.

And if, for whatever reason, a new crib must be built, some contractors construct the crib on the deck of a barge, fill it up with rocks while still on deck, pick it up with a crane, and lower it into place. Which just goes to prove that no matter how well equipped a do-it-yourselfer thinks his or her workshop is, there's always somebody who will put it to shame.

Patching Plastic

One of the advantages of the HDPE plastic drum float (or HDPE pipe) is that it's easily repaired if punctured — molten PE bonds to itself just like metal does when welding.

Stick It

A relatively painless way to make these repairs is with PE repair sticks specifically designed to fit into a standard hot-glue gun, a tool that is even easier to use than a mucilage bottle. To my knowledge, the only manufacturer of such sticks is Follansbee Dock Systems, a West Virginia dock builder that also manufactures a wide variety of quality dock floats and hardware. The sticks will work on anything made of polyethylene. A package of four sticks costs about what a couple of glossy boating magazines will set you back, but the sticks are designed to save you money instead of coaxing you to spend more.

Another product that works is P-Tex sticks, also PE. P-Tex is used to repair the bases of downhill and cross-country skis. Although they look like they might fit, the sticks are too small to work in a standard hot-glue gun and will ruin the gun. Try it yourself if you doubt me. So whether repairing dock floats or skis, the technique is essentially the same: You light the tip of the P-Tex stick with a match or lighter and dribble the molten plastic down into the crack in the float. The difficulty is in maintaining a blue flame (orange or yellow flames create too much carbon, which interferes with the bond). The solution is to hold the flaming end of the stick about ¼ inch above the crack to be repaired. Besides helping to maintain that blue flame, this also heats the area of the crack for a better bond. And it's a good idea to V-groove the crack before you begin (a utility knife will work) to encourage the molten plastic to run into the crack. (Keep water on hand in case the flame gets bigger than desired.) It's a bit messy but if you're quick, the molten mass can be shaped with a clean, flat-bladed screwdriver. Fortunately, a blemished finish normally doesn't affect the strength of the repair. P-Tex sticks are available from many ski shops, which might make them hard to find in the summer when you need them for repairs on dock floats.

Weld It

A method I've used many times to repair a wide variety of broken plastic things, from the shredder on our Cuisinart to my granddaughter's toys, is to weld the plastic back together (just like metal, remember). For this you need a soldering gun and preferably a piece of similar plastic to serve as welding rod (cut into sticks works best). For PE dock floats, P-Tex makes a good rod, or if you've got any extra PE water-intake line kicking about it will work equally well. Using the soldering gun (best equipped with a wide tip), carefully heat up both sides of the puncture while melting the welding rod into the crack, smoothing it out as you follow along the crack. Let it cool and you're ready to float again.

Melt It

Regardless of the technique you use, be careful not to melt away the plastic around the crack, making a big hole out of a small one. Also, older plastic is more brittle and therefore more difficult to repair. If you need to build up an area (such as when you gouged the float while dragging the dock out for winter), do it in layers rather than attempting to pile the stuff on in one go. Even a shattered section can be repaired as long as you have all the pieces, although replacement chunks could be fabricated out of old PE water line or other abandoned PE products. Make sure all the water is drained out of the float drum before beginning. With foam-filled drums, the longer the damaged float has been taking on water, the more difficult it will be to drain. If severely waterlogged, it's likely the float will have to be replaced. And since all of these methods produce copious fumes, work only in an open area with a good breeze.

Foam It

If the foam inside the float has been damaged or gouged out you can replace it with foam kits, available through most marine outlets. The kits are pricey and usually make more foam than you'll need for simple repairs. (Each makes about 5 cubic feet of foam, which is enough to fill over half the average float.) Instead, use a can of urethane foam insulation "available at fine hardware stores everywhere." For small repairs, it's much less money and a little less messy.

Rotten Repairs

(For information on preventing decay, see chapter 7.)

Anywhere wood meets wood, metal, or dock floats you can expect rot. Fortunately, if caught in time, it can often be repaired. For instance, if only a few decking boards are gone, these can be replaced and the framing saved. If the decking has surface cracks and splinters, you could try a new coat of stain, which sometimes "sticks" the splinters down to the decking; but if that doesn't work, you've wasted your time and stain on decking that will still have to be replaced to solve the problem.

Cutting Corners

If only the corners of a floating dock or pipe dock suffer from decay, you may be able to remove the corner brackets, header, and one or two decking boards, then get out the saw and cut the stringer and any underside structural stuff back past the rot. Then install a new header, the old corner brackets, and reattach any underside structure you had to cut in the process. Although shorter by maybe 6 inches, the dock

is now ready for a few more years of service. Make sure you use dock connectors when joining the sections back together — the shortened section is more likely to rock and roll without them.

If an individual stringer or header has rotted, typically where it meets the decking, you may be able to sandwich it between new planks. You'll need to scrape away as much of the existing rot as possible to prevent it from infecting the new wood. If the entire frame has rotted you may be able to reuse the decking and hardware.

When Accessories Abandon Ship

Cleats, rings, and dock ladders normally pull out of decking for one or more of three reasons: the fasteners weren't up to the task of holding them in place, the holes around the fasteners are worn, or the wood is rotten.

Nails or screws won't hold a stressed-out cleat, ring, or ladder in place. And as the nails and screws wiggle their way out, water can seep in, the rot-causing microorganisms arriving quicker than a neighbor can sniff out a barbecue. Obviously, the use of galvanized bolts and nuts, with big washers on the underside of the decking, will noticably slow the onset of wood wear and rot.

Dock epoxy

Because wood is soft, cleats, dock rings, and even dock ladders will eventually cause wear around the bolt holes. The difference between wear and rot is that wear can be repaired while rot must be removed. If the bolt holes are dry and solid around their circumference, it's possible to stuff the holes with epoxy repair putty (such as Gitrot, Smith's

Fill-It, or Supermend), redrill the holes, and re-install the hardware. Don't be tempted to repair enlarged holes with the old glue-and-toothpicks trick for filling small screw holes in doorjambs — the hole in this case is too big.

Epoxies consist of two components, which have to be mixed together in exact proportions in order to work as the manufacturer intended. Temperature also can play a role in the effectiveness of the product. Adhere to the manufacturer's instructions to avoid compromising the strength of the repair, or ending up with a big gooey mess filling the bolt hole. Also, when properly mixed there is a limited amount of working time before the epoxy hardens. And often a sealer must be applied to the wood before installing the epoxy. The other catch to know about before you begin slapping gobs of epoxy filler around your dock is that each brand of filler dries its own color, none of which is likely to match the color of your dock. You may want to restrict the use of such fillers to areas that remain out of sight.

For holes made larger by rot, the diseased wood can sometimes be repaired with an epoxy putty, but it's often easier to replace the rotted section, particularly if you want the cleat or whatever to have a firm hold. An even easier solution is to relocate the offending device to an area of good wood and hope that by exposing the old holes to air, ventilation will put a halt to the rot. After the old holes have dried out you can scrape them clean and fill them, perhaps with an epoxy putty. However, don't attempt to redrill them and re-install dock accessories in these filled holes — the mending material is only as secure as the wood that it's attached to, which in this case is rotten. Not even your best Boy Scout knots will secure a boat to a dock if the cleats or rings pull out.

section 7

Plans and Sources

So far, you have learned how to analyze your waterfront and your needs, choose an appropriate dock, choose the materials to build your dock, use the materials to their best advantage, secure your dock in place once built, make your dock boat and people friendly, and even repair your dock when it eventually begins to show signs of wear. Now we actually build your dock.

Chapter 18 offers plans to build one section each of various pipe docks, floating docks, and a crib, plus a typical ramp, mounting board, and landing platform. Build one section, mix and match, or multiply and modify to suit, drawing on all the information you have learned to date. It's your dock and your solution.

Sources reveals where to find manufacturers, materials, and services should local sources be unable to provide you with what you need to realize your solution.

The final section, How to Use and Enjoy Your Dock, is not included in this book. It's the one you write. I suspect it will require long hours of research, perhaps while seated in a dockside deck chair, a cool drink on it's arm, the waves lapping underneath, your eyelids closed to gather deep thoughts. At least until the kids dive off the end of the dock and interrupt your thoughts with a splash of cold reality. Hum . . . Maybe an extra section, tacked on the end to form an L, would make more room for relaxed ruminating. Where's that graph paper?

dock plans

The designs that follow are all for economical, versatile, rectangular sections. Each section can work on its own or be joined to other sections and likely to a ramp to make a complete dock. Sections can be combined into an infinite variety of longer rectangles, T-shapes, and L-shapes by adding more rectangles. Before ordering your material or starting construction, consult the gull's-eye view of your waterfront you made in chapter 2 showing the configuration of your proposed dock. Note where each section begins and ends, including the ramp, and where hinges, connectors, and filler boards are required.

If you are not a professional builder or drafting expert, the dock plans on the following pages need some explanation. Look at the sample plan below, and read the captions. It will only take you a few minutes, and it may very well save you a great deal of confusion down the road.

Plan

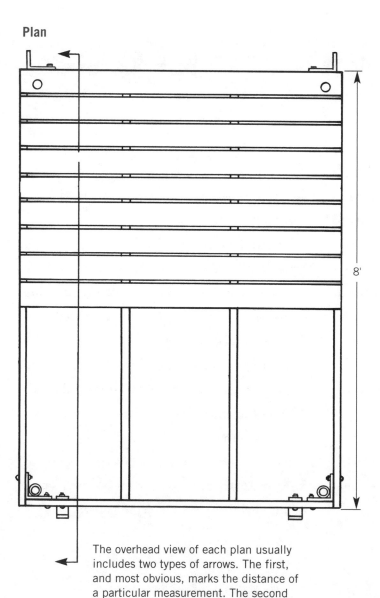

8'

The overhead view of each plan usually includes two types of arrows. The first, and most obvious, marks the distance of a particular measurement. The second type of arrow designates on the master plan a section that is also depicted in a separate, detailed, side-view illustration.

Side Elevation, Section

The side-view illustration shows the dock plan from a different angle. It's as if someone sawed the dock open, allowing you to take a look inside.

Eight Important Notes Regarding Bills of Materials

1. The quantities listed assume that all materials actually wind up in the dock. But because life is not perfect, extra material may have to be ordered if some pieces are not up to snuff (such as the inevitable "bad" piece of wood decking).

2. To help understand where each piece goes, lengths of dimensional lumber 4 feet or more long are shown as separate pieces but may be combined (for instance, one 12-footer for two 6-footers) for ease of ordering.

3. Each bill of materials applies only to the section illustrated and the style of hardware shown on it. If you use a different style of hardware, or build a different-sized section, use the material list as a guide, altering it to suit your new plans while adhering to the rules of good dock design discussed in the preceding chapters.

4. A full set of dock hardware is shown on each design (and listed in the bill of materials). However, since some hardware (such as hinges and connectors) is shared by two joining sections, you will need to delete a set for each join. Consult the gull's-eye view of your entire dock and adjust each sample bill of materials to compile a list of total hardware requirements.

5. Filler boards between ramps and floating-dock sections should be used only if water-level fluctuation is not severe enough to cause the edge of the unattached side of the board to rise above the decking, resulting in a swell place to trip an unsuspecting dock user. As with hinges and connectors, count the number of filler boards (one per join) on the gull's-eye view of your entire dock (remembering that each section will still need its own filler board support).

6. See The Fastener Debate, chapter 8, before deciding between screws and nails — or just use deck screws. All dock hardware is hot-dip galvanized, as are all bolts.

7. Floating docks will need appropriate anchors and sufficient ⅜- to ½-inch galvanized chain to secure the dock to the anchors (see chapter 12).

8. Dock bumpers, cleats, dock ladders, and other accessories are not included in the plans or materials lists. Add them to your shopping list as required.

Before Lifting Hammer and Saw

The plans in this chapter are based on good, widely used dock-building practices but cannot take into consideration the variability of local regulations (see chapter 1), sites and situations (see chapter 2), the quality of construction materials, personal skills, or the unpredictable forces of nature. Therefore neither the author nor the publisher assumes any responsibility for the suitability of any of these designs for your site, your skills, or those of anyone who assists you. If you have any doubts regarding either the dock or its builders, consult a professional dock builder for advice.

Wood-Frame Pipe Dock (Basic)

Bill of Materials for 6' x 8' Section

Material	Quantity	Length/Size
Wood		
Stringers	4	2 x 6, 8'
Headers	2	2 x 6, 6'
Decking	17	5⁄4 x 6, 6'
Hardware		
Inside pipe-leg bracket/ combination corner bracket	4	
Legs with feet	4	length as required
Dock hinges for dock-to-ramp connection	4	
Leg braces	1 set (minimum)	
Fasteners		
Carriage bolts with washers and nuts (or machine bolts with extra washers for the bolt-head end)	12	2½" x ½"
Carriage bolts with washers and nuts (or machine bolts with extra washers for the bolt-head end)	4	3" x ½"
#8 deck-screws or galvanized nails	200	2½"

Adjustments to bill of materials if adding additional dock section:

At water end of dock:
Pipe-dock connectors (as shown in illustration) or dock hinges — 2
Add 4 bolts, 2½" x ½", for pipe-dock connectors [or replace the required number of 2½" bolts (4 in this example) at the water end with 3" bolts of the appropriate type to accommodate attaching dock hinges]

At shore end of new section:
Replace the pipe-leg brackets with standard corner brackets (each section sharing support with the previous section's end legs)

Cutaway Perspective

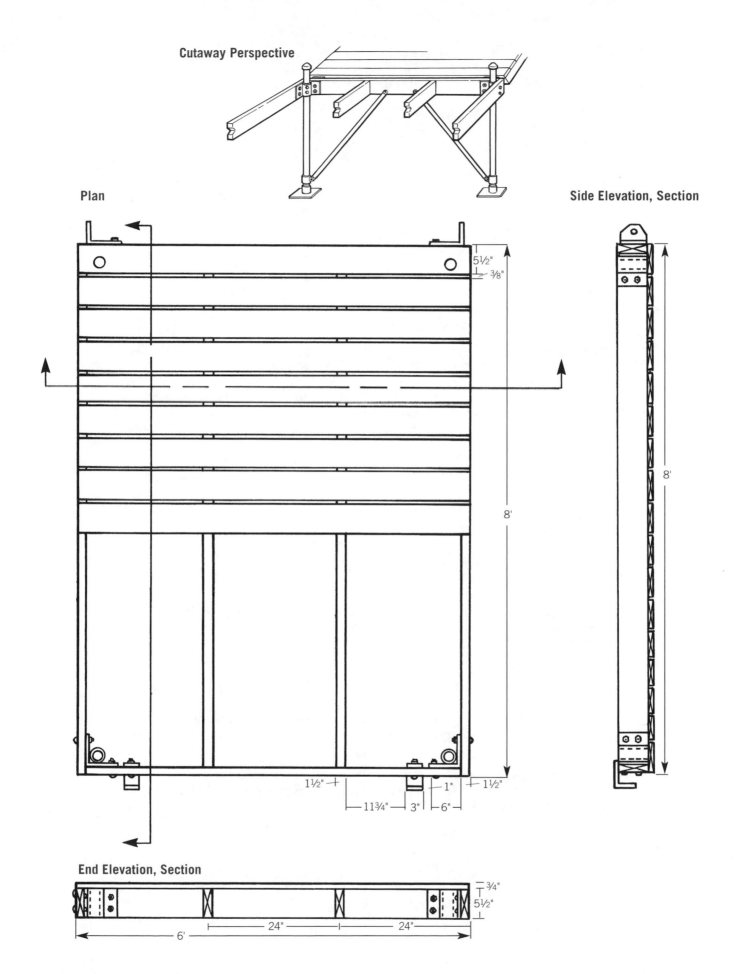

Plan

5½"
⅜"

8'

1½"
11¾" 3" 6"
1" 1½"

Side Elevation, Section

8'

End Elevation, Section

¾"
5½"

24" 24"
6'

Wood-Frame Pipe Dock
with Removable Decking Panels

Bill of Materials for 6' x 8' Section		
Material	**Quantity**	**Length/Size**
Wood		
Outside stringers	2	2 x 8, 8'
Headers	2	2 x 8, 6'
Center stringers	2	2 x 6, 8'
Decking	16	2 x 6, 6'
Filler board	1	2 x 6, 6'
Crossers	1	2 x 4, 6'
Panel runners	4	2 x 4, 8'
Decking and filler board supports (splice leftovers for one end decking support)	3	2 x 2, 8'
Hardware		
Inside pipe-leg bracket/combination corner bracket	4	
Legs with feet	4	length as required
Dock hinges for dock-to-ramp connection	2	
Leg braces	1 set (minimum)	
Fasteners		
Carriage bolts with washers and nuts (or machine bolts with extra washers for the bolt-head end)	12	2½" x ½"
Carriage bolts with washers and nuts (or machine bolts with extra washers for the bolt-head end)	4	3" x ½"
#8 deck screws or galvanized nails	250	2½"

Adjustments to bill of materials if adding additional dock section:

At water end of dock:
Pipe-dock connectors (as shown in illustration)   2
     or dock hinges
Additional filler board (2 x 6 x 6') and required support (2 x 4 or ripped, scrap 2 x 6, now 2 x 3)
Add 4 bolts, 2½" x ½", for pipe-dock connectors [or replace the required number of 2½" bolts (4 in this example) at the water end with 3" bolts of the appropriate type to accommodate attaching dock hinges]

At shore end of new section:
Replace the pipe-leg brackets with standard corner brackets (each section sharing support with the previous section's end legs)

**Perspective
(without decking)**

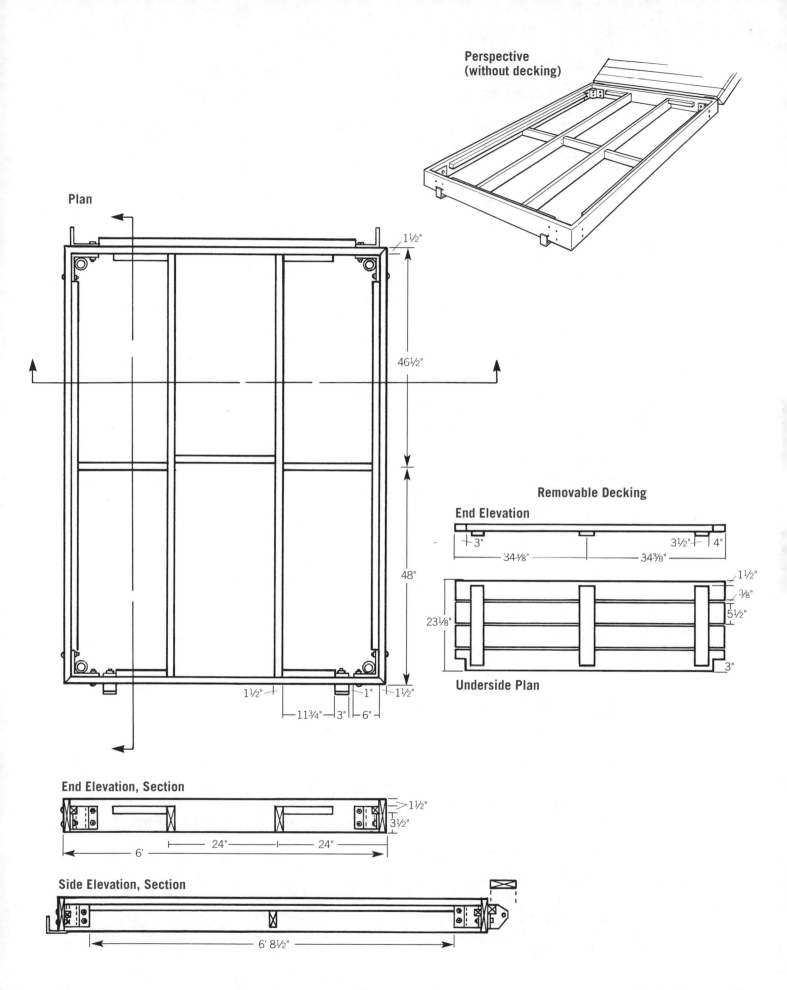

Plan

1½"

46½"

48"

1½"

1½" ┤├ 1" ┤├ 1½"

├─11¾"─┤├3"┤├─6"─┤

Removable Decking

End Elevation

├ 3" ┤   3½" ┤├ 4"

├──── 34⅜" ────┤├──── 34⅜" ────┤

1½"
⅜"
5½"

23⅛"

3"

Underside Plan

End Elevation, Section

1½"
3½"

├──── 24" ────┤├──── 24" ────┤

├──────── 6' ────────┤

Side Elevation, Section

├──────────────── 6' 8½" ────────────────┤

Wood-Frame Floating Dock
with Dedicated Plastic Float Drums

Bill of Materials for 6' x 20' Section

Material	Quantity	Length/Size
Wood		
Skirt stringers (optional)	2	2 x 10, 20'
Skirt headers (optional)	2	2 x 10, 6'
Inner stringers	4	2 x 8, 20'
Inner headers	2	2 x 8, 6'
Decking and crossers	48	2 x 6, 6'
Filler board	1	2 x 6, 6'
Flotation		
Foam-filled plastic float drums	6	24" x 48" x 20"
Hardware		
Corner brackets with slot for anchor chains	4	5"
Dock joist hangers or corner brackets	4	5"
Dock hinges for dock-to-ramp connection	2	
Fasteners		
Carriage bolts with washers and nuts (or machine bolts with extra washers for the bolt-head end)	8	4½" x ½"
Carriage bolts with washers and nuts (or machine bolts with extra washers for the bolt-head end)	16	4" x ½"
Carriage bolts with washers and nuts (or machine bolts with extra washers for the bolt-head end)	8	2½" x ½"
Carriage bolts with washers and nuts or lag bolts (depending on float manufacturer's recommendations, but carriage bolts are the preferred choice)	24	3" x ½"
#8 deck screws or galvanized nails	500	2½"

Adjustments to bill of materials if adding additional dock section:

At water end of dock:

Dock connectors   2

Additional filler board (2 x 6 x 6') and required support (2 x 4 or ripped, scrap 2 x 6, now 2 x 3)

Substitute the required number of 4" bolts (8 in this example) at the water end for 4½" bolts of the appropriate type to accommodate attaching dock connectors

Note: The offset of the drum float at the land end is designed to help cope with the leverage a ramp exerts on the dock. If building an additional section, place the inner float in line with the two outer floats (same pattern as opposite end of dock) and subtract one crosser from the bill of materials.

Further Notes: Due to variances in design, you may have to alter crosser spacing and some of the other measurements to accommodate different styles of hardware and floats than those illustrated. To save costs, the 2" x 10" skirt can be eliminated without noticeably affecting the strength of the dock — it just won't look as nice.

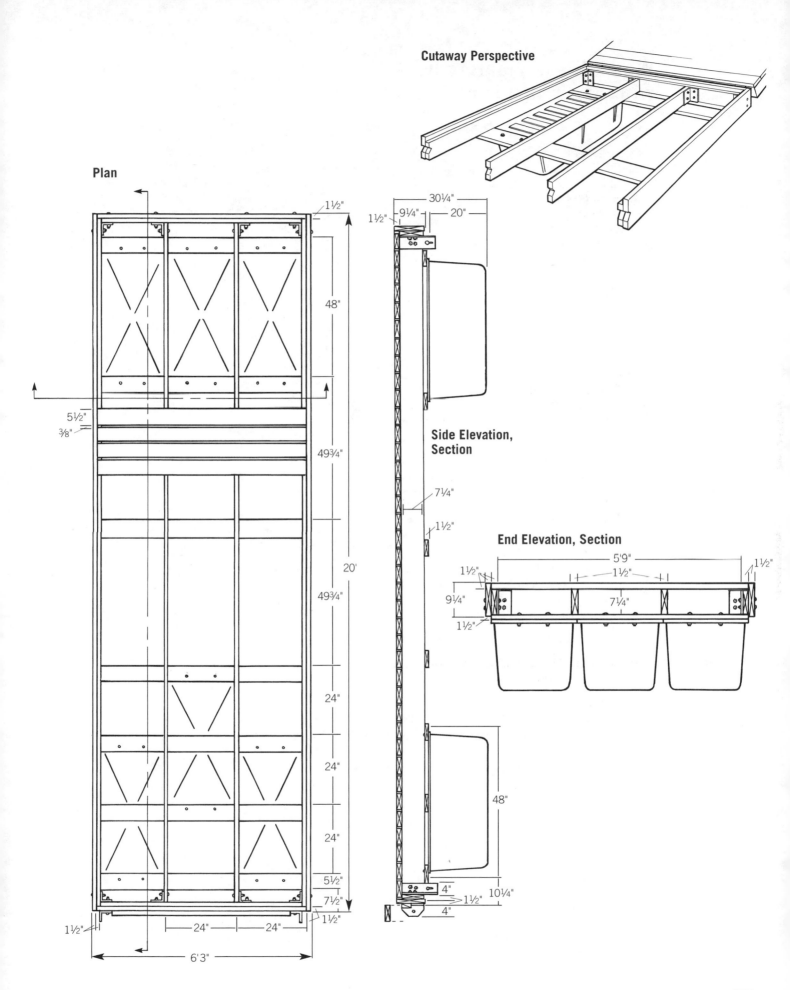

Cutaway Perspective

Plan

1½"

48"

5½"
⅜"

49¾"

20'

49¾"

24"

24"

24"

5½"

7½"

1½"

1½"

24"

24"

1½"

6'3"

30¼"

1½" 9¼" 20"

Side Elevation, Section

7¼"

1½"

4"

1½"

4"

10¼"

End Elevation, Section

1½"

5'9"

1½"

1½"

9¼"

7¼"

1½"

48"

Wood-Frame Floating Dock
with Styrofoam Flotation Billets (Basic)

Bill of Materials for 6' x 20' Section		
Material	**Quantity**	**Length/Size**
Wood (upper level)		
Stringers	4	2 x 4, 20'
Headers and crossers	12	2 x 4, 6'
Vertical supports joining levels	2	2 x 4, 8'
Decking	40	5/4 x 6, 6'
Wood (lower level)		
Stringers	4	2 x 8, 20'
Headers	2	2 x 8, 6'
Crossers	10	2 x 4, 6'
Skids	2	2 x 4, 18'
Flotation		
Dow Styrofoam BB flotation billets	4½	7" x 20" x 8'
6-mil black PE sheeting	200 sq'	
Galvanized hardware cloth (or sand screen)	200 sq'	
Hardware		
Corner brackets with slot for anchor chains	4	9"
Dock hinges for dock-to-ramp connection	2	
Fasteners		
Carriage bolts with washers and nuts (or machine bolts with extra washers for the bolt-head end)	40	2½" x ½"
Carriage bolts with washers and nuts (or machine bolts with extra washers for the bolt-head end)	8	3" x ½"
#8 deck screws or galvanized nails	700	2½"

Adjustments to bill of materials if adding additional dock section:

At water end of dock:
Dock connectors   2
Substitute the required number of 2½" bolts (8 in this example) at the water end for 3" bolts of the appropriate type to accommodate attaching dock connectors

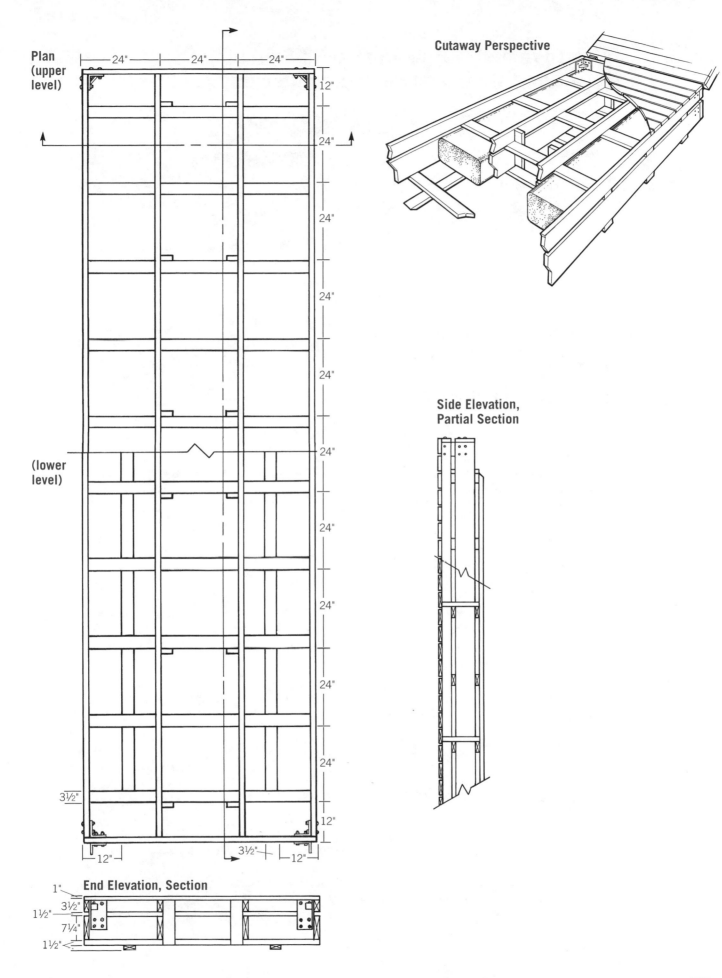

**Plan
(upper
level)**

24" 24" 24"

12"

24"

24"

24"

24"

24"

**(lower
level)**

24"

24"

24"

24"

24"

3½"

12"

3½"

12"

12"

Cutaway Perspective

**Side Elevation,
Partial Section**

End Elevation, Section

1"

3½"

1½"

7¼"

1½"

Wood-Frame Floating Dock with Styrofoam Flotation Billets and Permenent Decking (Deluxe)

Bill of Materials for 6' x 20' Section		
Material	**Quantity**	**Length/Size**
Wood (upper level)		
Outside stringers	2	2 x 8, 20'
Headers	2	2 x 8, 6'
Center stringers	2	2 x 6, 20'
Vertical supports joining levels	2	2 x 6, 8'
Decking	41	2 x 6, 6'
Filler board	1	2 x 6, 6'
Decking supports and longitudinal braces	2	2 x 4, 20'
Crossers	10	2 x 4, 6'
Cedar shims	20	¼" to ½"
Wood (lower level)		
Stringers	4	2 x 8, 20'
Headers	2	2 x 8, 6'
Crossers	10	2 x 4, 6'
Skids	2	2 x 4, 20'
Spacers	1	2 x 4, 4'
Flotation		
Dow Styrofoam BB flotation billets	4½	7" x 20" x 8'
6-mil black PE sheeting	200 sq'	
Galvanized hardware cloth (or sand screen)	200 sq'	
Hardware		
Corner brackets with slot for anchor chains	4	5"
Corner brackets with brackets to support inspection ports	8	5"
Joining plates	4	
Dock hinges for dock-to-ramp connection	2	
Fasteners		
Carriage bolts with washers and nuts (or machine bolts with extra washers for the bolt-head end)	56	2½" x ½"
Carriage bolts with washers and nuts (or machine bolts with extra washers for the bolt-head end)	8	3" x ½"
#8 deck screws or galvanized nails	1,000	2½"

Adjustments to bill of materials if adding additional dock section:

At water end of dock:

Dock connectors   2

Additional filler board (2 x 6 x 6') and required support (2 x 4 or ripped, scrap 2 x 6, now 2 x 3)

Substitute the required number of 2½" bolts (8 in this example) at the water end for 3" bolts of the appropriate type to accommodate attaching dock connectors

Cutaway Perspective

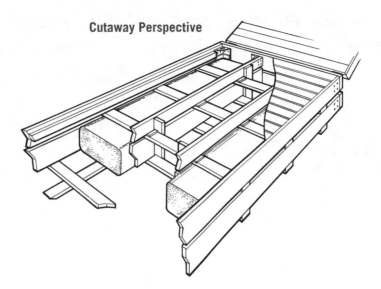

Plan (upper level without decking)

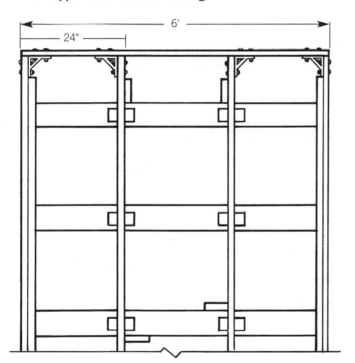

6'

24"

End Elevation, Section

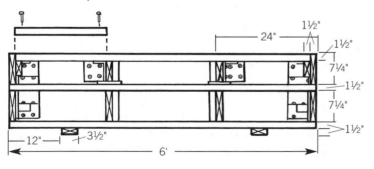

24"

1½"

1½"

7¼"

1½"

7¼"

1½"

12"

3½"

6'

Plan (lower level)

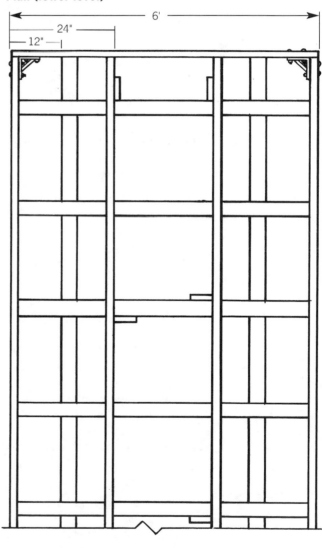

6'

24"

12"

Wood-Frame Floating Dock with Styrofoam Flotation Billets and Removable Decking Panels (Deluxe)

Bill of Materials for 6' x 20' Section

Material	Quantity	Length/Size
Wood (upper level)		
Outside stringers	2	2 x 8, 20'
Headers	2	2 x 8, 6'
Center stringer	1	2 x 6, 20'
Vertical supports joining levels	2	2 x 6, 8'
Decking	41	2 x 6, 6'
Filler board	1	2 x 6, 6'
Decking supports and longitudinal braces	4	2 x 4, 20'
Crossers	10	2 x 4, 6'
Panel runners	8	2 x 4, 8'
Cedar shims	10	¼" to ½"
Wood (lower level)		
Stringers	4	2 x 8, 20'
Headers	2	2 x 8, 6'
Crossers	10	2 x 4, 6'
Skids	2	2 x 4, 20'
Spacers	1	2 x 4, 4'
Flotation		
Dow Styrofoam BB flotation billets	4½	7" x 20" x 8'
6-mil black PE sheeting	200 sq'	
Galvanized hardware cloth (or sand screen)	200 sq'	
Hardware		
Dock joist hangers or corner brackets	6	5"
Corner brackets with slot for anchor chains	4	9"
Corner brackets	4	5"
Dock hinges for dock-to-ramp connection	2	
Fasteners		
Carriage bolts with washers and nuts (or machine bolts with extra washers for the bolt-head end)	56	2½" x ½"
Carriage bolts with washers and nuts (or machine bolts with extra washers for the bolt-head end)	8	3" x ½"
#8 deck screws or galvanized nails	1,000	2½"

Adjustments to bill of materials if adding additional dock section:

At water end of dock:

Dock connectors — 2

Additional filler board (2 x 6 x 6') and required support (2 x 4 or ripped, scrap 2 x 6, now 2 x 3)

Substitute the required number of 2½" bolts (8 in this example) at the water end for 3" bolts of the appropriate type to accommodate attaching dock connectors

Cutaway Perspective

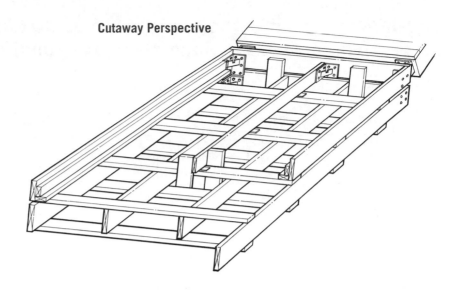

Plan (lower level)

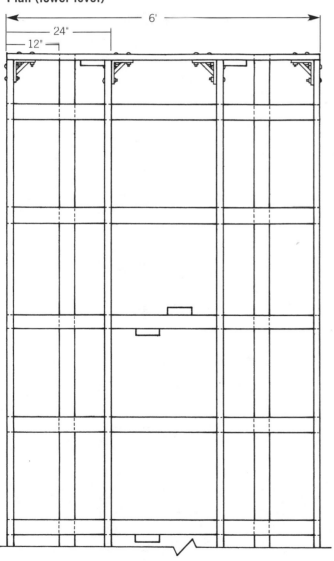

End Elevation, Section

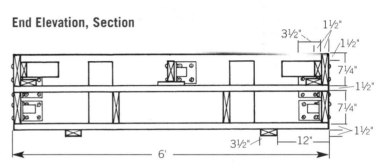

plan continued on next page

Wood-Frame Floating Dock with Styrofoam Flotation Billets and Removable Decking Panels (Deluxe) *continued*

Plan

Side Elevation, Section

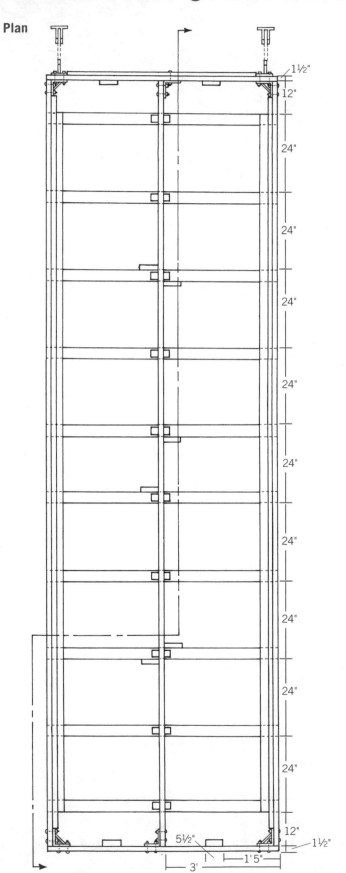

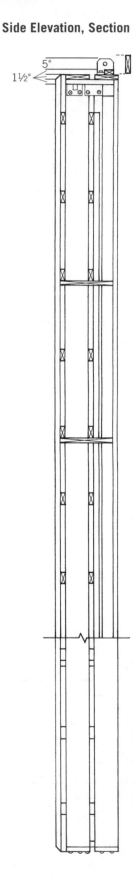

Styrofoam Billet Placement

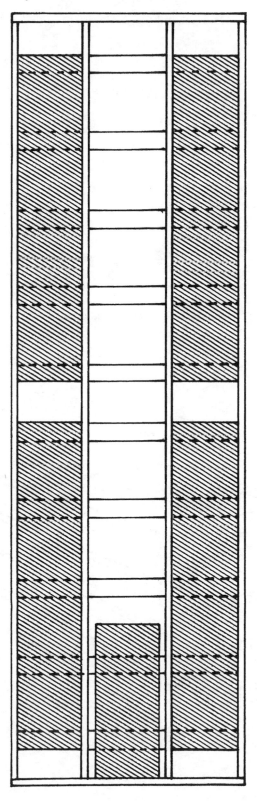

Wood Crib

Bill of Materials for Crib 5½' x 5½' x 5' High		
Material	**Quantity**	**Length/Size**
Wood		
Douglas fir for crib frame	23	6 x 6, 6'
Upper stringers	2	6 x 6, length as required
Cedar decking	as required	2 x 6, 6'
Rock		
Rocks, taken from above the high water mark	enough to fill crib	at least 6" diameter
Hardware		
Hot-dip galvanized threaded rod with nuts and washers	4	¾"–1", length (5'–3" length as required for crib illustrated)
Fasteners		
Hot-dip galvanized spikes	10	10"

Note: A subframe for the decking is often constructed above the crib using similar techniques and materials as required for a ramp or pipe dock.

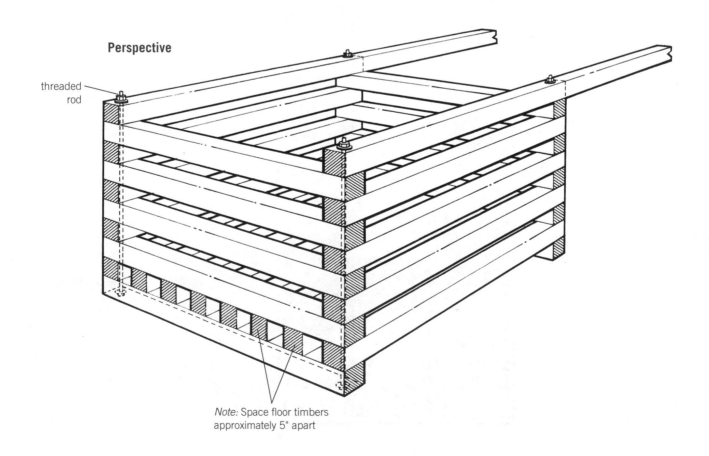

Perspective

threaded rod

Note: Space floor timbers approximately 5" apart

Mounting Board (Basic)

Bill of Materials for Board 6' Wide		
Material	**Quantity**	**Length/Size**
Wood		
Double header	2	2 x 6, 6'
Support for filler board	2	2 x 2, 4'
		or
	1	2 x 2, 5'
Hardware		
Pipe-leg brackets	2	
Legs (feet optional)	2	length as required
Dock hinges for board-to-ramp connection	2	
Fasteners		
Carriage bolts with washers and nuts (or machine bolts with extra washers for the bolt-head end)	8	4½" x ½"
#8 deck screws or galvanized nails	20	2½"

Plan

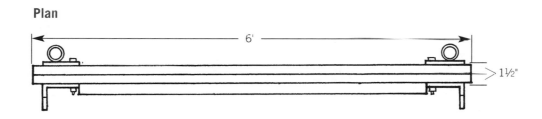

Dockside Elevation

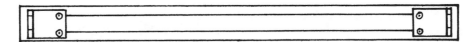

Wood-Frame Ramp (Fancy) with Herringbone Decking

Bill of Materials for 6' x 10' Section

Material	Quantity	Length/Size
Wood		
Outer stringers	2	2 x 8, 10'
Headers	2	2 x 8, 6'
Inner stringers	2	2 x 6, 10'
Decking	24	2 x 6, 6'
Filler board	1	2 x 6, 6'
Crossers	2	2 x 4, 12'
Side decking supports	2	2 x 2, 10'
End decking supports, angled corner decking supports	2	2 x 2, 8'
Hardware		
Corner brackets	4	
Dock hinges	4	
Fasteners		
Carriage bolts with washers and nuts (or machine bolts with extra washers for the bolt-head end)	8	2½" x ½"
Carriage bolts with washers and nuts (or machine bolts with extra washers for the bolt-head end)	8	3" x ½"
#8 deck screws or galvanized nails	400	2½"

Plan

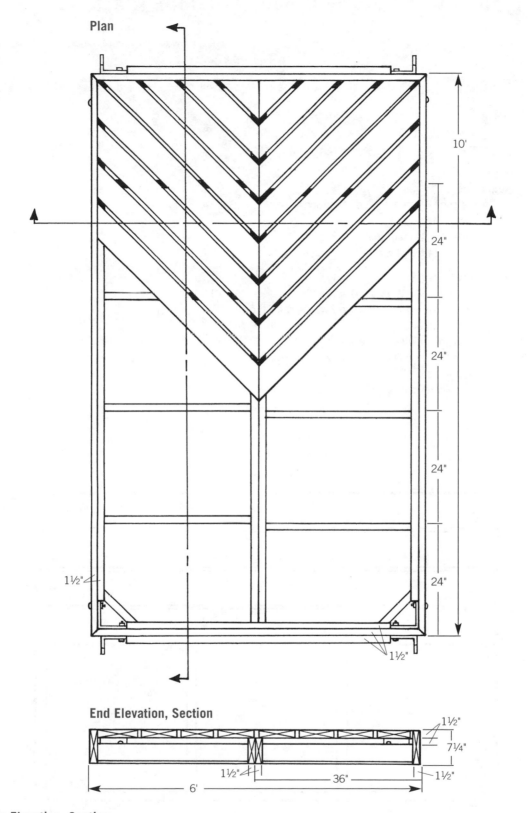

End Elevation, Section

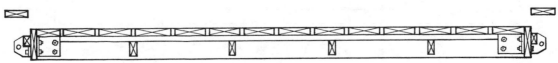

Side Elevation, Section

Typical Wood-Frame Landing Platform (Basic)

Bill of Materials for 6' x 4' Section

Material	Quantity	Length/Size
Wood		
Stringers	2	2 x 6, 8'
Headers	2	2 x 6, 6'
Decking	8	$\frac{5}{4}$ x 6, 6'
Hardware		
Inside pipe-leg bracket/combination corner bracket	4	
Legs (feet optional, length as required)	4	
Dock hinges for platform-to-ramp connection	2	
Fasteners		
Carriage bolts with washers and nuts (or machine bolts with extra washers for the bolt-head end)	12	$2\frac{1}{2}$" x $\frac{1}{2}$"
Carriage bolts with washers and nuts (or machine bolts with extra washers for the bolt-head end)	4	3" x $\frac{1}{2}$"
#8 deck screws or galvanized nails	150	$2\frac{1}{2}$"

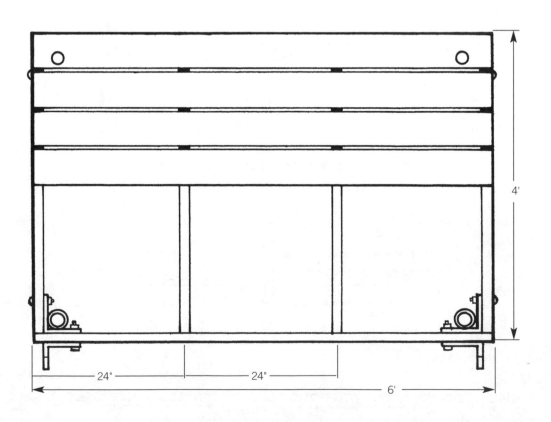

Sources

Note: Products listed are suppliers' principal dock-related products.

Dock Builders & Dock-Building Supplies

Bauhaus Docks
R.R. 2
Kilworthy, ON P0E 1G0
705-689-2545
888-74-DOCKS (743-6257)
fax: 705-689-8985
e-mail: info@bauhaus.ca
website: http://www.bauhaus.ca
Everything dealing with docks, boathouses, and dry docking

Bellingham Marine Industries
P.O. Box 8
1001 C Street
Bellingham, WA 98225
360-676-2800
fax: 360-734-2417
e-mail: bmi@bellingham-marine
Concrete floating docks

Composite Wood Specialties
PO Box 356
Orillia, ON L3V 6J6
705-325-8090
fax: 705-325-7864
e-mail: cwsca@bconnex.net
website: http://www.bconnex.
   net/~cwsca
Bauhaus Composite Decking System

Docks and Decks Unlimited
1332 Pioneer Road
Sudbury, ON P3G 1A6
705-523-2169
fax: 705-523-0651
e-mail: rgainer@sby.auracom.com
Docks and Re-Tire Dock Anchor

Docks and Lifts Unlimited
(Highway 11 West, Keewatin)
P.O. Box 2670
Kenora, ON P9N 3X8
807-547-4444
fax: 807-547-4000
Docks and lifts

Docks by Muskoka Leisure
R.R. 2
Kilworthy, ON P0E 1G0
705-689-5646
fax: 705-689-5646
e-mail: docks@bconnex.net
website: http://www.bconnex.net/~
   docks/
Floating docks, pipe docks, and hardware

Double O Marine Products
100 North Harbour Road West
P.O. Box 175
Goderich, ON N7A 3Z2
519-524-1986
fax: 519-524-2301
e-mail: maitmar@hurontel.on.ca
website: http://www.maitland
   marina.on.ca
Big O floating docks

Dow Chemicals
Canada
2150 Winston Park Drive
Unit 12
Oakville, ON L6H 5V1
800-268-4840
(for literature only: 800-395-1143)
fax: 905-829-4320

Dow Chemicals
United States
P.O. Box 1206
Midland, MI 48641-1206
517-636-3100
800-441-4369
fax: 517-832-1465
e-mail: aarmbruster@dow.com
website: http://www.styrofoam.com
Styrofoam BB flotation billets

Fendock
335 Roosevelt Avenue
Ottawa, ON K2A 1Z2
613-722-6581
888-FEN-DOCK (Canada only)
fax: 613-722-3168
website: http://home.on.rogers.
   wave.ca/fendock
   Lightweight aluminum pipe docks

Follansbee Dock Systems
State Street
P.O. Box 640
Follansbee, WV 26037
304-527-4500 / 800-223-3444
fax: 304-527-4507
website: http://foldocks.lbcorp.com
Docks and hardware of all types, great variety of drum floats, glue-gun repair sticks for PE

Great Northern Docks
Route 302
P.O. Box 1615
Naples, ME 04055
207-693-3770 / 800-423-4042
fax: 207-693-3111
Docks and hardware of all types, Drag-On Floats

Houston Marine Systems
(Highway 35, Coboconk)
R.R. 1
Kirkfield, ON K0M 2B0
705-454-2045 / 888-467-3625
Floating docks, pipe docks, and hardware

Jibb's Floats
Site 2, Box A-5
Sesekinika, ON P0K 1S0
705-642-3548
fax: 705-642-3548
e-mail: envirobuoy@
   dockfloatation.com
website: http://www.
   dockfloatation.com
Floating docks, Enviro-Buoy Dock Float

Karol Bolts & Fasteners
P.O. Box 182
Lawrence, NY 11559
800-527-6526/516-599-6218
e-mail: info@karolbolts.com
website: http://www.karolbolts.com

Naylor Systems
R.R. 2
Cameron, ON K0M 1G0
705-359-1386
800-663-4281 (Ontario only)
fax: 705-359-1455
e-mail: naylor.systems@
   sympatico.ca
Aluminum pipe docks, roller ramps, and all types of dry docking

Seaco Marine Dock Systems
866-A King Edward Street
Winnipeg, MB P3H 0P7
204-783-4450 / 800-665-2008
fax: 204-744-9571
e-mail: seaco@seacomarine.com
website: http://www.seacomarine.
   com
Enviro Float Drums, floating dock kits

Technomarine
598 Leclerc
Repentigny, QC J6A 2E5
540-585-6114 / 800-667-3625
fax: 540-585-6840
e-mail: info@technomarine.ca
website: http://www.
   technomarine.ca
Docks and float drums

Techstar Plastics
15400 Old Simcoe Rd.
Port Perry, ON L9L 1L8
905-985-8479 / 800-263-7943
(Toronto 439-6111)
fax: 905-985-0265
e-mail: sales@techstarplastics.com
Techstar dock floats and floating docks

Dock Accessories
(See also Dock Builders)

Bear Industries
R.R. 1, Box 19
Kleinburg, ON L0J 1C0
905-893-0481 / 800-479-2327
fax: 905-893-3321
e-mail: wakewatchers@
   lindsaycomp.on.ca
website: http://www.lindsaycomp.
   on.ca/wakewatchers/index.htm
Wake Watchers tension mooring system

Dock Edge + Inc.
35 Citron Court
Concord, ON L4K 2S7
905-738-8884
fax: 905-738-8295
e-mail: dockedge@aracnet.net
Dock bumpers, mooring whips, and cleats

Douglas R. Hughes and Associates
111 Esna Park Drive, Unit 9
Markam, ON L3R 1H2
905-477-8326
fax: 905-479-0990
e-mail: 55bf5b@ibmmail.com
Moor-Aid mooring whip

Mooring Products
1590 N Federal Highway
Pompano Beach, FL 33062
954-942-0200
fax: 954-942-0204
website: http://www.mypid.com/
   mooring/
Mooring whips, dock bumpers, boat lifts, and davits

Pelican Rope Works
4001 Carriage Drive
Santa Ana, CA 92704
714-545-0116 / 800-624-1116
fax: 714-545-7673
website: http://www.pelicanrope.
   thomasregister.com/olc/
   pelicanrope/
Quality ropes

Dry Docking
(See also Dock Builders)

Ace Boat Hoist
2211 S. Tamiami Trail
Venice, Florida 34293
941-493-8100 / 800-826-3573
fax: 941-493-7857
Boat lifts and davits

Davit Master
5560 Ulmerton Road
Clearwater, Florida 34620
813-573-4414 / 800-878-5560
fax: 813-572-0590
e-mail: davitmastr@aol.com
website: http://www.davitmaster.
   com
Boat lifts and davits

Marine Cradle Shop
66 Bullock Drive, Unit 4
Markam, ON L3P 3P2
905-294-3507
fax: 905-294-3507
Launching dollies

Seitech Marine Products
52 Maritime Drive
P.O. Box 514
Porstmouth, RI 02871-0514
401-683-6898
fax: 401-683-6897
e-mail: sei52@aol.com
website: http://www.seitech.com
Launching dollies

Sierra Manufacturing
16715 NE 79th Street
Redmond, WA 98052
425-391-1101 / 888-GO-NYMAN
  (888-4666-9626)
fax: 425-885-7167
e-mail: sierramfg@sierraind.com
website: http://www.gonyman.com
*Nyman Marine boat lifts, including
hydraulically operated lifts*

Whitehall Reproductions
450A Swift Street
Box 1141, Station E
Victoria, BC V8W 2T6
250-384-6574
800-663-7481 (except Alaska,
  Hawaii)
fax: 250-384-6506
e-mail: whitehall@whitehallrow.
  com
website: http://www.whitehallrow.
  com
Beach Hauler portable skid tracks

Decking

Composite Wood Specialties
R.R. 2
Kilworthy, ON P0E 1G0
705-689-6090
fax: 705-689-8985
e-mail: cwsca@bconnex.net
Bauhaus Composite Decking System

MacMillan Bloedel
925 West Georgia Street
Vancouver, BC V6C 3L2
604-661-8000 / 800-432-MBBM
  (800-432-6226)
fax: 604-661-8535
e-mail: jk.kearns@mbltd.com
website: http://www.mbcedar.com
Cedar

Nicholson & Cates
(Canadian distributor)
905-335-3366
800-263-6223 (Ontario only)
fax: 905-335-2328
e-mail: niccates@worldchat.com
Trex wood-polymer composite

Royal Crown Ltd.
State Road 15N, P.O. Box 360
Milford, IN 46542-0360
219-658-9442
fax: 219-658-3147
Brock Dock PVC

Trex Company
20 South Cameron Street
Winchester, VA 22601
540-678-4070
800-BUY-TREX (list of North
  American retailers)
fax: 540-678-1820
website: http://www.trex.com
Trex wood-polymer composite

Miscellaneous

BCS Inc.
(Canadian distributor)
861 Morton Line, RR 1
Cavan, ON L0A 1C0
705-944-5556
800-516-6663 (Canada only)
Fill-It, Clear Penetrating Epoxy Sealer

Boatlife (Life Industries Corp.)
2081 Bridgeview Drive North
Charleston, SC 29405
803-566-1225
fax: 803-566-1275
e-mail: boatlifes@aol.com
Git-Rot

Smith & Company
5100 Channel Avenue
Richmond, CA 94804
415-237-6842
800-234-0330 (U.S. only)
e-mail: smi3th@netcom.com

Titan Corp.
5629 208th Street Southwest
Lynnwood, WA 98036
206-775-2582
Supermend epoxy

Recommended Further Reading and How-To Books

Chapman's Nautical Guides: Knots, Brian Toss, Hearst Marine Books, New York, NY. ISBN 0688094155. Everything you need to know about tying rope for boats.

Chapman's Piloting: Seamanship and Small Boating Handbook, E. Maloney and C. Chapman, Hearst Marine Books, New York, NY. ISBN 0688148924. Best book there is on boating (includes knots), but not cheap.

Skip's Tips: Painter's Handbook, R.A. (Skip) Lennox, ICI Paints, 8200 Keele St., Concord, ON L4K 2A5. ISBN 1895292662. Because it's published by a paint manufacturer, obviously the author doesn't suggest leaving cedar to naturally grey. However, it's still a great little (and cheap) book full of helpful painting advice.

Cottage Life Magazine, 54 St. Patrick St., Toronto, ON. Although its primary focus is on Ontario-based cottages, this glossy magazine has some excellent articles of interest to anyone owning, and using, waterfront property. Published six times a year.

Cottage Water Systems, Max Burns, Cottage Life Books, Toronto, ON. ISBN 096969220X. Yes, it's written by me and therefore this review is subject to some prejudice, but I still feel this is the best book you can buy if your home is not serviced by municipal sewers and water, as is the case for many waterfront properties. Covers water and where to find it (even when everything is frozen), pumps, water quality and purification, and septic systems and septic alternatives.

New Complete Do-it-yourself Manual, Reader's Digest Association, Inc., Pleasantville, NY. ISBN 0895773783. A little weak on detail (a natural byproduct of attempting to cover everything), but an excellent introduction to almost any task you might want to tackle at home. Good sections on tools and fasteners and the proper way to use both.

Stonework: Techniques and Projects, Charles McRaven, Storey Publishing, Pownal, VT. ISBN 0882669761. Build walkways down to the dock, retaining walls at water's edge — all sorts of nifty stone projects. Stone looks great, is priced right, and, assuming nature doesn't decide to undo everything in the proverbial "storm of the century," will last forever. This book does a nice job of making working with stone seem easy, with plenty of neat examples to get your imagination going, if not your muscles.

Glossary

Accretion: The process by which submerged lands or uplands move along a shoreline and accumulate in one spot.

Aggregation: In the context of shorelines and dock building, essentially the same as accretion.

Applied force: The force used to move an object. You apply the force; the object moves. For instance, that force could be you pushing down on a lever or pulling on a rope to move a dock. Or perhaps it could be the force applied to a tall glass in order to bring a cool drink to your lips.

Breakwater: An offshore structure designed to provide shelter from waves. It can be floating, freestanding, or linked to and extending from shore.

Bulkhead: A wall built parallel to the shoreline, usually near or at the high-water mark, to mitigate wave and current erosion of the uplands, and often used as a retaining wall to keep uplands from becoming submerged lands.

Corner braces: The angled braces generally found adding strength to where the main dock section has sections perpendicularly attached to it, such as with finger docks, or the arms of a U- or L-shaped dock. The braces are usually covered with decking to provide increased dock space and better traffic flow. Not to be confused with corner brackets, which securely bolt the corners of a dock's frame together.

Cottage: Also known as a camp, chalet, cabin — the variation often regionally based. Traditionally, a North American vacation home, but could also be a full-time residence either located in "cottage country" or one architecturally similar. When at the cottage, one is "cottaging."

Crosscut: A cut across the grain, which in most cases means cutting at an angle to the width of the board, rather than along its length (*see* rip).

Crosser: Any structural member of a dock's frame running parallel to the headers but within the perimeter of the frame. Crossers are also known as cross-braces.

Decking: Also called planking or deck boards, this is what forms the dock's upper horizontal surface, usually made from wood, but it could also be plastic, a wood-and-plastic composite, steel, or concrete.

Decking runner: The longitudinal boards that hold a removable decking panel together.

Dimensional stock: Square-edged, dressed lumber, sold in standard sizes, theoretically measured in rough-sawn condition before planing takes place, which accounts for you being shortchanged whenever you purchase a piece (a 2 x 4 measuring only 1½ inches by 3½ inches, and so on).

Dimpler: An attachment for a variable-speed electric drill that converts it into mediocre screw gun. Limited longevity but cheap.

Draft: The depth of water an object, such as a boat or floating dock, needs in order to float.

Give: The flex in a material, such as a piece of wood's willingness to bend.

Header: The end structural member of a dock's frame.

High-water mark: Also known as "ordinary high-water mark," or by initials only (HWM). The highest point on land to which an adjacent body of water traditionally rises, usually determined by careful examination of vegetation, soil erosion, and water marks. This differs from high water, which usually means the daily or seasonal point of high water, a point typically lower that the high-water mark. In many jurisdictions, the high-water mark is the legal marker used to determine where permits are required before work on the shoreline (such a dock installation) can begin. In some cases, work is permitted anywhere above the mark, at others there can be a substantial setback from that mark, and in a few areas it doesn't matter. Check with local authorities rather than risk fines and/or time in the pokey. (*See also* Low-water mark.)

Littoral drift: Sand, mud, and natural debris that waves and currents move along parallel to the shoreline.

Lot-line setback: The amount of space, usually specified by local law, an object must be set back from the edge of a piece of property and/or a structure on an adjacent lot.

Low-water mark: Also known as "ordinary low-water mark," or by initials only (LWM). The lowest point of land to which a body of water traditionally recedes. In other words, the opposite end to the high-water mark.

PWC: Personal watercraft, small boats such as Jet Skis and Sea-Doos powered by impeller-driven jetted water. Noisy and generally not well liked except by those who own them.

Pressure-treated wood: Wood that has been immersed in a pesticide while in a pressurized chamber. The pesticide of choice for this process is CCA (copper chromated arsenate), which leaves a light green finish on the wood. However, other toxins have been used. By pressurizing, the preservatives are forced deeper into the pores of the wood than is the case for staining or soaking. Unfortunately, quality control has always been a problem in this industry, some companies rushing the wood through the treatment process to get it to market as quickly as possible. This invariably yields minimal penetration, which in turn means minimal protection. Bargain pressure-treated wood is often little better than standard lumber. (*See also* S-DRY and S-GRN.)

Reset: The process of tapping piles back into submerged lands with a pile driver. Piles tend to rise out of submerged lands, either nudged by ice or all on their own.

Rip: To cut lengthwise in the direction of the grain (*see* Crosscut).

S-DRY: Wood that is kiln-dried. More costly than wood left to dry at its own leisure (*see* S-GRN) but typically much straighter, less prone to warping, and better at holding paints, stains, and preservatives.

S-GRN: Wood cut and sold without any artificial drying process. Typically wet with sap, so not capable of holding a paint, stain, or preservative well. Less money than kiln-dried wood (*see* S-DRY).

Seiche: A not particularly well-understood phenomenon where the level of an enclosed body of water (such as a lake or bay) randomly oscillates from shore to shore. As the water level drops on one side of a lake — sometimes by as much as a few meters in a few hours — the opposite side rises correspondingly, the water then flowing back and forth between shores until the energy is spent.

Site evaluation: A status report on the existing waterfront, and an inventory and activity list of present uses (and/or a wish list of proposed uses).

Skirt: An additional, cosmetic, outer layer of wood that encloses the frame.

Slip: A water-based parking spot for a boat, typically enclosed on three sides.

Stanchion: An outer pipe through which a pipe dock's leg slides, the leg held vertically in place with cinch bolts.

Stringer: A longitudinal structural member of a dock's frame.

Submerged lands: All land lying under a body of water, such as the land under a pond, river, lake, or ocean.

Sway cables: Cables that give lateral support to a raised lift dock in order to prevent the dock from swaying in high winds. Typically installed at about a 30- to 45-degree angle to the dock, one per side, the cables run back to shore or a crib or bulkhead. Turnbuckles are used to keep the cables taut.

Uplands: All land lying above the high-water mark.

UV stabilizer: A chemical added to a manufactured material, such as carbon black to polyethylene, to slow the process of UV or photo-degradation. Basically, a plastic's or paint's answer to sunscreen.

Index

Page references in *italics* indicate illustrations; page references in **bold** indicate charts.

Other Storey Titles You Will Enjoy

Rustic Retreats: A Build-It-Yourself Guide, by David and Jeanie Stiles. Illustrated, step-by-step instructions for more than twenty low-cost, sturdy, beautiful outdoor structures. Projects include a water gazebo, sauna hut, triangular tree house, log cabin, and yurt. Also contains sections on basic building techniques, essential tools, joints and joining methods, and safety concerns. 160 pages. Paperback. ISBN 1-58017-035-8.

Landscaping Makes Cents: A Homeowner's Guide to Adding Value and Beauty to Your Propery, by Frederick C. Campbell and Richard L. Dubé. Add substantial investment value and beauty to a home with this guide to landscape design. Explains how to create a landscape plan, determine a budget, choose a contractor, and achieve substantial financial return on a limited budget. Includes tips for the beginning landscaper and handy checklists and charts to ensure the successful completion of any project. 176 pages. Paperback. ISBN 0-88266-948-6.

Waterscaping: Plants and Ideas for Natural and Created Water Gardens, by Judy Glattstein. Packed with information on moist and wet spot gardening, installing pools, container water gardens, and border treatments. 192 pages. Paperback. ISBN 0-88266-606-1.

Building with Stone, by Charles McRaven. An introduction to the art and craft of creating stone structures, including finding stone, tools to use, and step-by-step instructions for projects such as walls, buttresses, fireplaces, a barbecue pit, a stone dam, and even a home or barn. Also includes instruction on proper restoration techniques for stonen structures. 192 pages. Paperback. ISBN 0-88266-550-2.

Building Stone Walls, by John Vivian. A step-by-step guide to building both freestanding and retaining walls. Includes equipment requirements, instructions for creating wall foundations, coping with drainage problems, and hints for incorporating gates, fences, and stiles. 112 pages. Paperback. ISBN 0-88266-074-8.

Step-by-Step Outdoor Stonework, edited by Mike Lawrence. Over twenty easy-to-build projects for your patio and garden, including walls, arches, bird baths, sun dials, and fountains. Includes information on estimating costs, selecting tools and materials, and preparing the site. 96 pages. Paperback. ISBN 0-88266-891-9.

Stonescaping: A Guide to Using Stone in Your Garden, by Jan Whitner. A thorough guide to incorporating stone into many garden features, including paths, steps, walls, ponds, and rock gardens. More than 20 designs are included. 176 pages. Paperback. ISBN 0-88266-755-6.

Stonework: Techniques and Projects, by Charles McRaven. This complete guide includes fully illustrated, step-by-step instructions for 22 projects, including walls, porches, pools, seats, waterfalls, and even a bridge. Advice on gathering and handling stone and hiring stonemasons is also included. 192 pages. Paperback. ISBN 0-88266-976-1.

These and other books from Storey Publishing are available wherever quality books are sold, or by calling 1-800-441-5700. Visit us at www.storey.com.